# Lecture Notes in Computer Science  13854

Founding Editors

Gerhard Goos

Juris Hartmanis

The series Lecture Notes in Computer Science (LNCS), including its subseries Lecture Notes in Artificial Intelligence (LNAI) and Lecture Notes in Bioinformatics (LNBI), has established itself as a medium for the publication of new developments in computer science and information technology research, teaching, and education.

LNCS enjoys close cooperation with the computer science R & D community, the series counts many renowned academics among its volume editors and paper authors, and collaborates with prestigious societies. Its mission is to serve this international community by providing an invaluable service, mainly focused on the publication of conference and workshop proceedings and postproceedings. LNCS commenced publication in 1973.

Shaoying Liu · Zhenhua Duan · Ai Liu
Editors

# Structured Object-Oriented Formal Language and Method

11th International Workshop, SOFL+MSVL 2022
Madrid, Spain, October 24, 2022
Revised Selected Papers

*Editors*
Shaoying Liu
Hiroshima University
Hiroshima, Japan

Zhenhua Duan
Xidian University
Xi'an, China

Ai Liu
Hiroshima University
Hiroshima, Japan

ISSN 0302-9743                 ISSN 1611-3349 (electronic)
Lecture Notes in Computer Science
ISBN 978-3-031-29475-4         ISBN 978-3-031-29476-1 (eBook)
https://doi.org/10.1007/978-3-031-29476-1

This Springer imprint is published by the registered company Springer Nature Switzerland AG
The registered company address is: Gewerbestrasse 11, 6330 Cham, Switzerland

# Preface

Formal engineering methods aim to take advantage of formal methods to improve the effectiveness and efficiency of conventional software engineering technologies used in practice. As a specific formal engineering method, the Structured Object-Oriented Formal Language (SOFL) and the related SOFL method have demonstrated how this goal can be achieved by providing a comprehensible specification language, functional scenario-based modeling, verification, and validation techniques, and efficient tool support through appropriate integrations of formal techniques and software engineering techniques. Meanwhile, the Modeling, Simulation and Verification Language (MSVL) offers a parallel programming language and a supporting toolkit MSV that enable us to model, simulate, and verify systems rigorously. In spite of the progress we have made in these two different but related approaches, challenges still remain for further research in order to fulfill our ultimate goals.

Following the success of the previous SOFL+MSVL workshops, the 11th international workshop on SOFL+MSVL 2022 was jointly organized online by Shaoying Liu's research group at Hiroshima University, Japan and Zhenhua Duan's research group at Xidian University, China as a satellite event of ICFEM 2022 organized in Madrid, Spain during October 24–27, 2022. The aim of the workshop was to bring together industrial, academic, and government experts and practitioners of SOFL, MSVL, or other formal engineering methods to communicate and to exchange ideas. The workshop attracted 26 submissions on Model Checking, Markov Decision Processes, Model Analysis, Formal Specification, Verification, Testing, Algorithms, and Tool Implementation. Each submission was carefully reviewed by the program committee based on its technical quality, relevance, significance, and clarity. As the result, 12 papers were accepted for publication in the workshop proceedings and the acceptance rate is approximately 46%.

We would like to thank the ICFEM 2022 organizers for their support for the organization of the workshop and all the PC members for their great efforts and cooperation in reviewing and selecting the submitted papers. We would also like to thank the keynote speaker Prof. Shin Nakajima for his inspiring talk and all the participants for attending the presentation sessions and actively joining the discussions at the workshop. Finally, our gratitude goes to the editors of Springer for their continuous support in the publication of the workshop proceedings.

October 2022

Shaoying Liu
Zhenhua Duan
Ai Liu

# Organization

## Program Chairs

| | |
|---|---|
| Shaoying Liu | Hiroshima University, Japan |
| Zhenhua Duan | Xidian University, China |
| Ai Liu | Hiroshima University, Japan |

## Program Committee

| | |
|---|---|
| Yuting Chen | Shanghai Jiao Tong University, China |
| Busalire Emeka | Hosei University, Japan |
| Kazuhiro Ogata | JAIST, Japan |
| Xinfeng Shu | Xi'an University of Posts and Telecommunications, China |
| Rong Wang | Galileo Co. Ltd., Japan |
| Xi Wang | Shanghai University, China |
| Xiaobing Wang | Xidian University, China |
| Bin Yu | Xidian University, China |
| Zhen You | Jiangxi Normal University, China |

# Risks Management Around Machine Learning Software (Keynote Speech)

Shin Nakajima

**Abstract.** As widely recognized, quality issues of machine learning software become a major concern, because such software systems are embedded in social infrastructure, which motivates research activities to apply Software Engineering practices to the machine learning software development. In early days, the test oracle problem was addressed in view of testing baseline functionalities such as model accuracy or model robustness; metamorphic testing with carefully generated fuzz is found useful. Later, the ethical aspects, fairness and privacy, are considered mandatory, and the quality assurance activities put focus more on data modeling with posteriori testing of fairness or privacy. Those quality characteristics are more or less inconsistent and thus need a thorough study of the trade-off between them. To work on the issues, a multi-layered quality model is introduced together with both technical and non-technical ways for the quality management. All these mitigate risks that machine learning software may bring about. Moreover, machine learning software is subject to laws or regulations, which may incur risks affecting the machine learning innovation. The risk management of machine learning software must consider all these aspects, from the baseline functionalities to the ethical and lawful aspects. This talk sketches recent activities on the quality assurance of machine learning software, primarily viewed from the AIQM (Artificial Intelligence Quality Management), a joint industry-academia-government project in Japan, and some of the legal issues with regard to European GDPR and AI-ACT, or domestic IPR in Japan.

# Contents

## Algorithms and Verification

# Model Checking and Markov Decision Process

# Formal Derivation and Verification of Critical Path Algorithm for Directed Acyclic Graph

Zhen You[1,2], Xinwu Yi[1,2,3]($\boxtimes$), Jinyun Xue[1,2], Hongwen Hu[1,2,3], Jiewen Huang[4], and Zhuo Cheng[1,2]

[1] State International S&T Cooperation Base of Networked Supporting Software, Jiangxi Normal University, Nanchang 330022, China
mandalore@jxnu.edu.cn
[2] Provincial Key Lab of High-Performance Computing, Jiangxi Normal University, Nanchang 330022, China
[3] Computer Information Engineering School, Jiangxi Normal University, Nanchang 330022, China
[4] Jiangxi Provincial Education Examination Authority, Nanchang 330008, China

**Abstract.** Graph structure is widely used in network design, path planning, relational processing, electronic circuit design, and power grid tide management. However, the complexity and variety of relationships between different data objects create difficulties in the derivation of graph algorithms, the correctness of algorithms cannot be easily guaranteed in some complex problems. In this paper, we formally derive the loop invariant of critical path by using the new definition and new strategies of loop invariant in PAR method. Furthermore, the Apla abstraction algorithm program is designed, and the executable code is generated by the PAR platform. Finally, the correctness of the algorithm is proved by using the Dijkstra's weakest precondition method. The critical path is a typical dynamic programming problem. The recursive relation of the critical path can be automatically detected when the loop invariant is derived by using the PAR method, and the reliability of the Apla algorithm program is ensured by using the formal verification technique. The formal derivation and verification of the critical path algorithm in this paper can be extended to solve other dynamic programming type problems.

**Keywords:** Critical path · DAG · Dynamic programming · PAR method · Dijkstra's weakest precondition method

## 1 Introduction

Directed Acyclic Graph (DAG) is a kind of important and traditional nonlinear data structure in graph theory. DAG can be used to describe the construction process of a project, and DAG critical path algorithm can estimate the minimum time necessary to complete the project. When a DAG is used in a computer to describe the construction process of a project, the minimum time necessary to complete the project is equal to the length of the critical path from the source to the sink in the DAG. Here the path length is the sum of the durations of the activities on the path, the sum of the weights on each

S. Liu et al. (Eds.): SOFL+MSVL 2022, LNCS 13854, pp. 3–11, 2023.
https://doi.org/10.1007/978-3-031-29476-1_1

directed edge. The path with the critical path length is called the critical path. Estimating the minimum time necessary for the completion of the entire project is actually a requirement for the critical path in the activity on edge network.

The development of graph algorithms can be implemented by either non-formal or formal methods. It has been proven that the correctness of an algorithmic program can be logically guaranteed by a formal derivation or formal verification of the program using mathematical methods [1]. The solution of critical path problems usually uses dynamic programming algorithms, and the most creative step of dynamic programming is to find recursive relation. Non-formal methods such as partition method, greedy method, dynamic programming method, backtracking method, branch-and-bound method can solve many practical problems, but they do not have effective methods and techniques to guarantee its effectiveness and correctness. Article [2] finds recursive relational equations using dynamic programming, but does not use formal methods for derivation and verification to guarantee the correctness of the algorithm. The book [3] represents computational derivation steps for the largest sub-paragraph sum problem in terms of program statutes, highlighting the typical steps involved in program derivation sessions. Kourie [3] devised a style of program development based on constructive correctness that combines the Guarded Command Language of Dijkstra and Morgan's refined evolutionary rules.

In this paper, we use the PAR method to formally derive the loop invariant of critical path algorithm based on the recurrence relation of the problem solution sequence, and then we design an abstract Apla algorithm program and formally verify it by using Dijkstra's weakest precondition method. Finally, the verified Apla algorithm program can be automatically transformed into executable code in PAR platform. This complete process of formal derivation and verification achieves the reliability of graph structure algorithms, the derived loop invariant can be quickly found to the recursive relation of the dynamic programming problem, and the generation of concrete executable programs from the abstract Apla program can improve the efficiency of the algorithm.

## 2   PAR Method and PAR Platform

PAR method was proposed by Prof. Xue in 1997 [4], and it was basically a unified and systematic method called Partition and Recur for developing efficient and correct algorithmic programs. The PAR method is guided by program correctness proofs and predicate calculus theory such as predicate logic, Floyd's inductive assertion method, Dijkstra's weakest predicate and Hoare's axiomatic semantics, and makes full use of data abstraction and functional abstraction method to provide formal and automated support for the algorithm design of software development. The approach covers several known algorithm design techniques, including dynamic programming, greedy method, enumeration, divide and conquer method.

PAR method defines two support languages: Radl (algorithm and statute description language) and Apla (abstract programming language). PAR method and PAR platform include new definition of loop invariant its two development strategies and generator such as Apla2C++ Generator, Apla2Java Generator, Apla2C# Generator.

Apla modeling language is based-object abstract programming language, and it fully supports abstract data types, which also defines common data types as predefined data types. Apla abstract program could be translated some executable code, such as Java, C++ by using some generator tools of PAR Platform.

Until now, our research group have already successfully applied PAR method and PAR platform to solve lots of problem, including unified recurrence relations expression for three kinds of binary tree traversal [5], distributed virtual reality [6], information system [7].

In the following sections of the paper, we develop loop invariant [8] and derivate and proof algorithm based on Dijkstra's weakest precondition method [9, 10] and our loop invariant development strategies of the PAR method [11]. Meanwhile, the abstract programming language Apla [8] will be applied to write directed acyclic graph critical path programs, all of them could be translated into executable C++ or Java program.

# 3 Formal Derivation of Critical Path Algorithm

This section is the main work of our paper. In this section, we formally derived and verified the algorithmic program of DAG's critical path.

## 3.1 Describing Formal Specification

W is the weight matrix of the graph, where unreachable means -1; L[i][j] records the critical path from i to j that passes through some vertices in "1, 2,...,m". The start vertex of graph is labeled 1, the end vertex is labeled n, and the remaining vertices are labeled 2,3,...n-1. Introduce three variables i, j and m to represent the vertices inside the graph. There are the pre and post assertions described by algebraic.

$$PRE - condition\, Q : (''i, j : 1 \leq i \leq n \wedge 1 \leq j \leq n : L[i][j] = W[i][j]) \wedge k = 1 \quad (1)$$

$$POST - condition\, R : L[1][n] = (MAX\, m : 1 \leq m \leq n : L[1][m] + L[m][n] \quad (2)$$

## 3.2 Dividing the Problem

For all nodes i and j, the subproblem with problem size k records the critical path from i to j that passes through some vertices in "1,2,...,k". The original problem of size k is decomposed into subproblems of size k-1, then into subproblems of size k-2, and the above steps are repeated until the subproblem of size 1.

## 3.3 Constructing Recursive Relation

Define the function F(k) to represent all the critical paths from i to j in the record graph that pass through some vertices in "1,2,...,k".

$$F(k) = (''i, j : 1 \leq i \leq n \wedge 1 \leq j \leq n : L[i][j] = (MAX\, m : 1 \leq m \leq k : L[i][m] + L[m][j])) \quad (3)$$

$$F(k - 1) = (''i, j : 1 \leq i \leq n \wedge 1 \leq j \leq n : L[i][j] = (MAX\, m : 1 \leq m \leq k - 1 : L[i][m] + L[m][j])) \quad (4)$$

Initial state:

$$F(1) = (''i, j : 1 \leq i \leq n \wedge 1 \leq j \leq n : L[i][j] = W[i][j]) \tag{5}$$

The above of expression $L[i][j] = W[i][j]$ describe that the critical path from i to j that does not pass through any node is equal to $W[i][j]$.

Terminal state:

$$F(n) = (''i, j : 1 \leq i \leq n \wedge 1 \leq j \leq n : L[i][j] = (MAX\ m : 1 \leq m \leq k : L[i][m] + L[m][j])) \tag{6}$$

The terminal expression describe that all the critical paths from i to j pass through some vertices in "1,2,...,n".

Based on the relationship (3) and relationship (4), we derive the recursive relation as follow.

$$F(k) = \max(F(k-1),\ L[i][k] + L[k][j]) \tag{7}$$

### 3.4  Writing Radl Algorithm

Radl (Recurrence-base algorithm design language) is a custom generic statute and algorithm description language. Its main function is to describe the statute of the problem, transformation rules and description for the algorithm, consisting of two parts: algorithm statute language and algorithm description language. According to the recursive relation, we divide recursive relation the algorithm as follows.

```
Radl algorithm
ALGORITHM: critical_path
{|[var i, j, k:integer]|Q∧R }
BEGIN:  k=1++1; i=1++1; j=1++1;
          (∀i,j: 1≤i≤n∧1≤j≤n:L[i][j]=MAX(m, 1≤m≤k: L[i][m]+L[m][j]) )
TERMINATION:k=n
RECUR: F(k)= max( F(k-1), L[i][k]+L[k][j])
END
```

### 3.5  Developing Apla Program

The Apla programming language of PAR is an abstract programming language with a generalization mechanism that enables algorithmic program formal development of algorithmic programs. Based on the formal derivation above, we use Apla to design an algorithm for critical path.

**Apla Program Code**

```
program Critical_Path;
const n=8; var i,j,k:integer; W, L:array[0..n,array[0..n,integer]];
begin
   writeln("Input adjacency matrix values");
   i:=1;
   do i≤n→j:=1; do j≤n →read(W[i][j]);L[i][j]:=W[i][j]; j:=j+1; od;
        i:=i+1;
   od; k:=1;
   do k≤n → i:=1;
           do i≤n→j:=1;
                do j≤n →if (L[i][j]<L[i][k]+L[k][j])→
                          L[i][j]:=L[i][k]+L[k][j]; fi; j:=j+1;
                od; i:=i+1;
           od; k:=k+1;
   od;
   writeln("Critical path length:",L[1][n]);
end.
```

# 4   Formal Verification of Critical Path Algorithm

PAR can derive the loop invariant with the help of the new definition of the cycle invariant and two new strategies. High-efficiency and correctness are two features of algorithmic program.

## 4.1   Developing Loop Invariants

A loop invariant is generally considered to be "a predicate that is true before and after each execution of the loop". The development of loop invariants is a key technique for formal program derivation and correctness proofs, and is one of the most creative efforts in the field of algorithmic programming. The PAR approach proposes a new definition of loop invariants and new strategies for developing loop invariants [11].

**Definition 4.1** [ for the loop invariant]
Given loop DO and its set A of all loop variables. An assertion which reflects variation law of each element of A, and is invariably true before and after each iteration is called invariant loop DO.

**Strategy 4.1** [ for the existing algorithmic program]
Based on the Verification Conditions of Loop Program Correctness, investigate the pre-condition $Q(A)$ of the loop and assertion $R(Y)$ AND $R(X)$ AND $R(Z)$ AND NOT $B$ on the termination, analyze background knowledge, mathematical properties of the problem to be solved by the program and the properties of the program itself, describe the variation laws of all loop variables by induction reasoning. The laws are needed loop invariants.

**Strategy 4.2** [ for not developed algorithmic program]
Investigate the pre and post condition as well as the mathematical properties of the problem, use the design techniques of efficient algorithm to determine general strategy of solving the problem (in most cases, to determine the recurrence relation of problem-solving sequence) and all needed variables, describe the variation laws of each variable.

The laws are needs loop invariants; if the number of the sub-solutions in the recurrence relation is more than 1, one sequence variable which will be used as a stack or a set variable must be added and content of the sequence is defined recursively.

Based on the above strategy, we can easily derive the loop invariant $\rho$ and boundary function $\tau$.

$$\{\; \rho: \quad (\forall m:1{\leq}m{\leq}k: F(m)=\max(\; F(m-1),\; L[i][m]+L[m][j]))\}$$
$$\{\; \tau: n-k+1 \;\}$$

## 4.2  Verifying Correctness of the Loop Statements in the Apla Program

Because there is *do* statement in the program, in order to prove **{Q}do{R}** is right, five theorems' expressions of Dijkstra's weakest precondition to prove loop statement should be verified.

**Theorem-WP1:** $Q \Rightarrow \rho$;
**Theorem-WP2:** $\rho \wedge C \Rightarrow WP("S", \rho)$;
**Theorem-WP3:** $\rho \wedge \neg Guard \Rightarrow R$;
**Theorem-WP4:** $\rho \wedge Guard \Rightarrow \tau>0$;
**Theorem-WP5:** $\rho \wedge Ci \Rightarrow WP\,(\text{"}\tau 1:=\tau;S\text{"}\,,\tau<\tau 1)$;

(1)  **Proving Theorem-WP1**

$Q \Rightarrow \rho$
$\equiv((\forall i,j:\; 1{\leq}i{\leq}n \wedge 1{\leq}j{\leq}n:L[i][j]=W[i][j])\; \wedge k=1) \Rightarrow (\forall m:1{\leq}m{\leq}k:\; F(m)=\max(\; F(m-1),$
$L[i][m]+L[m][j]))$
$\equiv((\forall i,j:\; 1{\leq}i{\leq}n \wedge 1{\leq}j{\leq}n:L[i][j]=W[i][j])\; \wedge k=1) \Rightarrow (\forall m:1{\leq}m{\leq}1:\; F(m)=\max(\; F(m-1),$
$L[i][m]+L[m][j]))$
$\equiv((\forall i,j:\; 1{\leq}i{\leq}n \wedge 1{\leq}j{\leq}n:L[i][j]=W[i][j]) \wedge k=1) \Rightarrow F(1)=\max(\; F(0),\; L[i][0]+L[0][j]))$
$\equiv((\forall i,j:\; 1{\leq}i{\leq}n \wedge 1{\leq}j{\leq}n:L[i][j]=W[i][j]) \wedge k=1) \Rightarrow F(1)= (\forall i,j:\; 1{\leq}i{\leq}n \wedge 1{\leq}j{\leq}n:\; W[i][j]\;)$
$\equiv\text{true}$

## (2) Proving Theorem-WP2

$\rho \wedge C \Rightarrow$ WP("S",   $\rho$)

$\equiv((\forall m:1\leq m\leq k:$ F(m)=max( F(m-1), L[i][m]+L[m][j])) $\wedge$ k $\leq$ n ) => WP("do-do-if; k:=k+1;", ($\forall m:1\leq m\leq k:$ F(m)=max( F(m-1), L[i][m]+L[m][j])))

$\equiv((\forall m:1\leq m\leq k:$ F(m)=max( F(m-1), L[i][m]+L[m][j])) $\wedge$ k $\leq$ n) => WP("k:=k+1;", ($\forall m:1\leq m\leq k:$ F(m)=max( F(m-1), L[i][m]+L[m][j]))) $\wedge(\forall i, j : 1\leq i\leq n \wedge 1\leq j\leq n:$ (L[i][j] <L[i][k]+L[k][j] $\wedge$ L[i][j]=max(L[i][j], L[i][k]+L[k][j]) )

$\equiv((\forall m:1\leq m\leq k:$ F(m)=max( F(m-1), L[i][m]+L[m][j])) $\wedge$ k$\leq$ n) => ($\forall m:1\leq m\leq k+1:$ F(m)=max( F(m-1), L[i][m]+L[m][j]))) $\wedge(\forall i,j: 1\leq i\leq n \wedge 1\leq j\leq n:$ (L[i][j]<L[i][k+1]+ L[k+1][j] $\wedge$ L[i][j]=max(L[i][j], L[i][k+1]+L[k+1][j]) )

$\equiv((\forall m:1\leq m\leq k:$ F(m)=max( F(m-1), L[i][m]+L[m][j])) $\wedge$ k$\leq$ n) => ($\forall m:1\leq m\leq k:$ F(m) =max( F(m-1), L[i][m]+L[m][j])) $\wedge$ (F(k+1)=max( F(k), L[i][k+1]+L[k+1][j])) $\wedge$ ($\forall i,j: 1\leq i\leq n \wedge 1\leq j\leq n:$ (L[i][j]<L[i][k+1]+L[k+1][j] $\wedge$ L[i][j]=max(L[i][j], L[i][k+1]+ L[k+1][j]) )

$\equiv((\forall m:1\leq m\leq k:$ F(m)=max( F(m-1), L[i][m]+L[m][j])) $\wedge$ k$\leq$n) => (F(k+1)=max( F(k) , L[i][k+1]+L[k+1][j])) $\wedge(\forall i,j: 1\leq i\leq n \wedge 1\leq j\leq n:$ (L[i][j]<L[i][k+1]+L[k+1][j] $\wedge$ L[i][j] =max(L[i][j], L[i][k+1]+L[k+1][j]) )

$\equiv$true

## (3) Proving Theorem-WP3

$\rho \wedge_\neg C \Rightarrow R$

$\equiv((\forall m:1\leq m\leq k:$ F(m)=max( F(m-1), L[i][m]+L[m][j])) $\wedge$ k>n) => L[1][n]=( MAX m: 1\leq m\leq n: L[1][m]+L[m][n])

$\equiv((\forall m:1\leq m\leq k:$ F(m)=max( F(m-1), L[i][m]+L[m][j])) $\wedge$ k>n) $\wedge$ F(n)=max( F(n-1), L[ i][n]+L[n][j])) => L[1][n]=( MAX m: 1\leq m\leq n: L[1][m]+L[m][n])

$\equiv((\forall m:1\leq m\leq k:$ F(m)=max( F(m-1), L[i][m]+L[m][j])) $\wedge$ k>n) $\wedge$ ( $\forall i,j: 1\leq i\leq n \wedge 1\leq j\leq n$ : L[i][j]=MAX(m, 1\leq m\leq n: L[i][m]+L[m][j])) => L[1][n]=( MAX m: 1\leq m\leq n: L[1][m] +L[m][n])

$\equiv((\forall m:1\leq m\leq k:$ F(m)=max( F(m-1), L[i][m]+L[m][j])) $\wedge$ k>n) $\wedge$ ( $\forall i,j: 1\leq i\leq n \wedge 1\leq j\leq n:$ L[i][j]=MAX(m, 1\leq m\leq k: L[i][m]+L[m][j])) $\wedge$ L[1][n]= MAX(m, 1\leq m\leq n: L[1][m]+L [m][n]) => L[1][n]=( MAX m: 1\leq m\leq n: L[1][m]+L[m][n])

$\equiv$true

## (4) Proving Theorem-WP4

$\rho \wedge C \Rightarrow \tau>0$

$\equiv((\forall m:1\leq m\leq k:$ F(m)=max( F(m-1), L[i][m]+L[m][j])) $\wedge$ k$\leq$n ) => n-k+1>0

$\equiv$true

(5)  **Proving Theorem-WP5**

$\rho \wedge C \Rightarrow WP("\tau_1: =\tau; S" \tau<\tau_1)$

$\equiv ((\forall m:1\leq m\leq k: F(m)=max(F(m-1), L[i][m]+L[m][j])) \wedge k>n) \Rightarrow WP("\tau_1: =\tau;$
if;k:=k+1" $\tau<\tau_1)$

$\equiv ((\forall m:1\leq m\leq k: F(m)=max( F(m-1), L[i][m]+L[m][j])) \wedge k>n) \Rightarrow WP("do\text{-}do\text{-}$
if;k:=k+1" $\tau<n\text{-}k+1)$

$\equiv ((\forall m:1\leq m\leq k: F(m)=max( F(m-1), L[i][m]+L[m][j])) \wedge k>n) \Rightarrow WP("k:=k+1" \tau<n\text{-}$
k+1)

$\equiv ((\forall m:1\leq m\leq k: F(m)=max( F(m-1), L[i][m]+L[m][j])) \wedge k>n) \Rightarrow n\text{-}k<n\text{-}k+1$

$\equiv ((\forall m:1\leq m\leq k: F(m)=max( F(m-1), L[i][m]+L[m][j])) \wedge k>n) \Rightarrow true$

$\equiv true$

# 5  Conclusion and Future Work

The dynamic programming method is a common algorithm design technique for solving optimization problems. The solution of the critical path problem satisfies the optimality principle, so it can be solved by the dynamic programming method, but the dynamic programming solution relies on the programmer's creative mind, and the PAR method solves the process with the idea of formal derivation and verification. The article [12] represent an approach for the transformational development of efficient imperative network algorithms is presented which is based on Möller's algebra of formal languages. It contains a very flexible methodology that contemplates the description of a rather general derivation method. However, it does not have a unified formal method for derivation to improve efficiency, and there is no verification of the algorithm to guarantee its correctness. Kourie's program development [3] starts with formal statutes of the problem and gradually refining the statutes into code. The difficulty of its derivation process is that the derivation of these algorithms is based on loop invariants whose loop invariants are obtained by speculation at the beginning of the derivation. However, the development of loop invariants is a difficult aspect of loop programs [13].

The main purpose of this paper is to derive and verify the algorithm for the critical path of DAG by using PAR method and Dijkstra's weakest precondition method. It is evidenced that developing a loop invariant by using our PAR Method has the advantages of improving the efficiency and reliability of critical path algorithm. This paper is a typical useful application of PAR in solving dynamic programming. The PAR method can also be extended to solve other dynamic programming problems such as matrix concatenation problem, longest common subsequence problem, knapsack problem, optimal binary search tree problems. In the near future, the Isabelle Theorem Prover can be used to assist the verification and reduce the workload of manual proofs.

**Acknowledgement.** This work was funded by Projects of Jiangxi Provincial Nature Science Foundation (Grant No.20212BAB202018), Provincial Virtual Simulation Experiment Education Project of Jiangxi Education Department (Grant No.2020–2-0048) and the Science and Technology Research Project of Jiangxi Province Educational Department (Grant No. GJJ210333).

# References

1. Michael, J.B., Dinolt, G.W., Drusinsky, D.: Open questions in formal methods. Computer **53**(5), 81–84 (2020)
2. Malde, K., Giegerich, R.: Calculating PSSM probabilities with lazy dynamic programming. J. Funct. Program. **16**(1), 75–81 (2006)
3. Derrick, G. Bruce, W.: The Correctness-by-Construction Approach to Programming. Springer, Berlin, Heidelberg (2012)
4. Xue, J.: A unified approach for developing efficient algorithm of programs. J. Comput. Sci. Technol. **12**(4), 314–329 (1997)
5. You, Z., Xue, J., Zuo, Z.: Unified formal derivation and automatic verification of three binary-tree traversal non-recursive algorithms. Cluster Comput. **19**(4), 2145–2156 (2016)
6. Zhen, Y., et al.: A multiplayer virtual intelligent system based on distributed virtual reality. Int. J. Pattern Recogn. Artif. Intell. **35**(14), 2159050, 1–21 (2021)
7. Xue, J., Cheng, Z., Yang, Q.: Methodology and platform of IS code generation. In: ICBDM 2020: 2020 International Conference on Big Data in Management, pp. 49–57 (2020)
8. Jinyun, X.: PAR method: abstract programming language apla. Technical report. Key Laboratory of high performance computing technology. Jiangxi Normal University (in Chinese) (2001)
9. Dijkstra, E.W.: A Discipline of Programming. Prentice-Hall, Englewood Cliffs (1976)
10. Dijkstra, E.W., Scholten, C.S.: Predicate Calculus and Program Semantics. Springer, New York (1989)
11. Jinyun, X.: Two new strategies for developing loop invariants and their applications. J. Comput. Sci. Technol. **8**(2), 147–154 (1993). (in Chinese)
12. Durán, J.E.: Transformational derivation of greedy network algorithms from descriptive specifications. In: Boiten, E.A., Möller, B. (eds.) Mathematics of Program Construction. MPC 2002. Lecture Notes in Computer Science, vol. 2386, pp. 40–67. Springer, Berlin, Heidelberg (2002). https://doi.org/10.1007/3-540-45442-X_5
13. Si, X. Dai, H., Raghothaman, M.: Learning loop invariants for program verification. Neural Inf. Process. Syst. (2018)
14. Fowler, M., Kraemer, E., Sitaraman, M.: Tool-aided loop invariant development: insights into student conceptions and difficulties. In: ITiCSE 2021: 26th ACM Conference on Innovation and Technology in Computer Science Education, pp. 387–393. ACM (2021)

# An Approach of Transforming Non-Markovian Reward to Markovian Reward

Ruixuan Miao[1], Xu Lu[1(✉)], and Jin Cui[2]

[1] Institute of Computing Theory and Technology and State Key Laboratory of Integrated Services Networks, Xidian University, Xi'an, People's Republic of China
xlu@xidian.edu.cn
[2] School of Computer Science, Xi'an Shiyou University, Xi'an, People's Republic of China

**Abstract.** In many decision-making problems, a rational reward function is required, which can correctly guide agents to make ideal operations. For example, an intelligent robot needs to check its power before sweeping. This kind of reward functions involves historical states, rather than a single current state. It is referred to as non-Markovian reward. However, state-of-the-art MDP (Markov Decision Process) planners only support Markovian reward. In this paper, we present an approach to transform non-Markovian reward expressed in $LTL_f$ (Linear Temporal Logic over Finite Traces) into Markovian reward. $LTL_f$ is converted into an automaton which is compiled to standard MDP model. Then the reward function of the model is further optimized through reward shaping in order to speed up planning. The reshaped reward function can be exploited by MDP planners to guide search and produce good training results. Finally, experiments with augmented International Probabilistic Planning Competition (IPPC) domain demonstrates the effectiveness and feasibility of our approach, especially the reshaped reward function can significantly improve the performance of planners.

**Keywords:** Non-Markovian Reward · Reward Shaping · MDP · Temporal Logic

## 1 Introduction

Markov Decision Process (MDP) is now widely accepted as the preferred model for decision-theoretic planning problems. In MDP, agents typically receive positive and negative rewards based on their current state. For example, an intelligent robot needs to check its power before sweeping whenever receiving a sweeping command. The rewards of a decision process depend on the sequence of states rather than the current state is called Non-Markovian Reward Decision Process (NMRDP). An NMRDP can be specified by many kinds of formal languages such as temporal logics. Linear Temporal Logic (*LTL*) over infinite traces is originally proposed in Computer Science and used

This research is supported by National Natural Science Foundation of China (61806158); China Postdoctoral Science Foundation (2019T120881, 2018M643585); Fundamental Research Funds for the Central Universities (XJS220304); Special scientific Research Project of Education Department of Shaanxi Province (21JK0844)

S. Liu et al. (Eds.): SOFL+MSVL 2022, LNCS 13854, pp. 12–29, 2023.
https://doi.org/10.1007/978-3-031-29476-1_2

in formal verification. As a variant of *LTL*, *LTL* over Finite Traces ($LTL_f$) is a formal language which is more attractive in AI scenarios focusing on finite behaviors, such as planning, plan constraints and user preferences [1]. Here we use $LTL_f$ to specify non-Markovian rewards. Moreover, $LTL_f$ formulas can be transformed to corresponding Deterministic Finite Automata (DFA) theoretically.

In MDP, the goal is to find the best solution to maximize the rewards. RDDL (Relational Dynamic Diagram Language) is designed to compactly support the representation of a wide range of relational MDP and efficient simulation of these problems [2]. It is well suited to design domains of MDP that are probabilistically complex. Current state-of-the-art MDP planners are based on heuristic search and variants of the upper confidence bounds applied to trees (UCT) algorithm [2]. However, these planners struggle with non-Markovian reward since they only support traditional Markov property. Non-Markovian rewards do not provide sufficient guidance for these planners, thus causing relatively myopic lookahead. Back to the example of sweeping robot, traditional probabilistic planning systems can generate good-quality solutions to MDP described by RDDL [2]. However, they cannot make sure a solution conforming to the correct order of actions sweeping and checking its power.

Previous work proposes Truncated Linear Temporal Logic (TLTL) as a specification language to specify complex rules the robot should follow. The work also proposes a RL approach to learn tasks expressed as TLTL formulae that generates a reward function towards fulfilling that specification. The proposed RL approach is demonstrated in a toast-placing task learned by a Baxter robot [3]. Reward Machine is a type of finite state machine that supports the specification of reward functions while exposing reward function structure to the learner and supporting decomposition. Recent study proposes Q-Learning for Reward Machines (QRM), which appropriately decomposes the Reward Machine and uses off-policy Q-learning to simultaneously learn sub-policies for the different components. QRM can exploit a Reward Machine's internal structure to decompose the problem and improve sample efficiency. In that study, experiments in three domains demonstrate that QRM can be effectively applied in both discrete and continuous environments and can find optimal policies in cases [4].

Our concern in the paper is to specify and effectively exploit non-Markovian rewards in MDP. Our contribution is: we propose a novel approach to transform non-Markovian rewards specified by $LTL_f$ to Markovian rewards, and the former is converted into DFA in advance. Moreover, we use reward shaping techniques based on DFA in order to improve the efficiency of reinforcement learning. We demonstrate the feasibility of the approach by providing empirical evaluations on the International Probabilistic Planning Competition (IPPC) benchmark domains.

The remainder of the paper is organized as follows: we introduce the mathematical definitions used in this paper in Sect. 2. In Sect. 3, we present an approach of transforming non-Markovian rewards to Markovian rewards. In Sect. 4 we provide experimental results with detailed analysis to show the feasibility of our approach. Finally, Sect. 5 concludes with remarks about future work.

## 2  Background

### 2.1  Linear Temporal Logic Over Finite Traces

*LTL* Is a compelling language which provides an intuitive but accurate representation for expressing temporal properties over infinite sequences of states [11]. $LTL_f$ is a variant of *LTL* and concentrates on expressing temporal properties over finite sequence of states. Let *Prop* be the set of propositions. An $LTL_f$ formula $\varphi$ is defined as follows:

$$\varphi := True|False|p|\neg\varphi|\varphi_1 \wedge \varphi_2|O\varphi|\varphi_1 U \varphi_2$$

where $p \in Prop$ is an atomic proposition, $O$ (next) and $U$ (until) are temporal operators. $LTL_f$ is extended with the modality *final* to specify properties that hold in the final state of the trace. Other propositional and temporal operators are derived on the basis. For example, $\Diamond$ (eventually), $\Box$ (always), R (release) and • (weak-next) defined by:

$$\Diamond\varphi \equiv TU\varphi$$

$$\Box\varphi \equiv \neg\varphi\Diamond\neg\varphi$$

$$\varphi_1 R\varphi_2 \equiv \neg(\neg\varphi_1 U \neg\varphi_2)$$

$$\bullet\varphi \equiv final \vee O\varphi$$

$LTL_f$ are interpreted over finite traces of propositional states, $\sigma = s_1...s_n$, where each $s_i$ is a set of propositions that are true in $s_i$. We say that $\sigma$ satisfies $LTL_f$ formula $\varphi$, denoted $\sigma \models \varphi$, when $\sigma, 0 \models \varphi$, where:

$\sigma, i \models True$, every state satisfies *True*.

$\sigma, i \models False$, every state falsifies *False*.

$\sigma, i \models p$, for each $p \in Prop$ iff $s_i \models p$.

$\sigma, i \models \neg\varphi$ iff $\sigma, i \models \varphi$ does not hold.

$\sigma, i \models \varphi_1 \wedge \varphi_2$ iff $\sigma, i \models \varphi_1$ and $\sigma, i \models \varphi_2$.

$\sigma, i \models O\varphi$ iff $i < n$ and $\sigma, (i + 1) \models \varphi$.

$\sigma, i \models \varphi_1 U\varphi_2$ iff there exists a $i \leq j \leq n$ such that $\sigma, j \models \varphi_2$, and $\sigma, k \models \varphi_1$, for each $i \leq k \leq j$.

We explain the meaning of the basic temporal operators below.

① $O\varphi$ says that $\varphi$ holds at the next instant.

② $\varphi_1 U\varphi_2$ says that at some future instant $\varphi_1$ will hold and until that instant $\varphi_2$ holds.

③ $\Diamond\varphi$ says that $\varphi$ will eventually hold before the last instant.

④ $\Box\varphi$ says that from the current instant till the last instant $\varphi$ will always hold.

⑤ $\bullet\varphi$ says that $\varphi$ need to hold in the next instant if such next instant exists.

⑥ $\varphi_1 R\varphi_2$ says that $\varphi_2$ must be true until and including the instant where $\varphi_1$ first becomes true; if $\varphi_1$ never becomes true, $\varphi_2$ must remain true.

## 2.2 Markov Decision Process

MDP is a classical mathematical description of sequential decision problems. It is widely used in applications where an autonomous agent is influencing its surrounding environment through actions [5].

An MDP is a tuple $M = < S, A, P, R, T, \gamma, s_0 >$, where $S$ is a finite set of states; $A$ is a finite set of actions; $P(s, a, s')$ is the probability of reaching $s'$ from the state $s$ by applying the action $a$; $R : S \times A \times S \rightarrow \mathbb{R}$ is a reward function; $T \in \mathbb{N}$ is the horizon; $\gamma \in (0, 1]$ is the discount factor; $s_0 \in S$ is the initial state. The state transitions of an MDP satisfy the Markov property which is defined as follows:

$$\text{Prob}[s_{t+1}|s_t] = \text{Prob}[s_{t+1}|s_1 \ldots s_t]$$

where $s_t \in S$ is a state at instant $t$. This definition means that the next state depends only on the current state.

A stationary policy for an MDP is a function $\pi : S \rightarrow A$, where $\pi(s) \in A$ is the action to be executed in state $s$. The value of the policy in state $s$ at instant $t$, noted $V_\pi(s)$, is the sum of the expected future rewards over the horizon $T - t$, discounted by how far into the future they occur:

$$V_\pi(s) = E[\sum_{i=t}^{T-1} \gamma^t R(s_t, \pi(s_t), s_{t+1})|s_t = s]$$

In MDP, the value of a policy $\pi$ is the value $V_\pi(s_0)$, and the larger this value, the better the policy [6]. An optimal policy for an MDP over horizon $T$ with initial state $s_0$ satisfies $\pi_* = argmax_\pi V_\pi(s_0)$.

The purpose of solving MDP is to choose the optimal policy $\pi$ that will maximize the sum of rewards. There are many MDP planners which can generate good-quality solutions such as mGPT [7], PILOT [8], PROST [9] and A2C-Plan [10]. Among these, PROST is one of the most famous MDP planners, which is a Monte-Carlo sampling algorithm based on UCT and heuristic search. PROST can compute which action to take in the current state, execute that action and update the current state according to the outcome. The input language of Prost is RDDL.

## 2.3 Deterministic Finite Automata

In the theory of computation, a branch of theoretical computer science, DFA is a finite-state machine that accepts or rejects a given string of symbols, by running through a state sequence uniquely determined by the string [12]. Upon inputting a symbol, a DFA jumps deterministically from one state to another by transition.

**Definition:** A DFA is a tuple $A_\varphi = < Q, \Sigma, \delta, q_0, F >$, where $Q$ is a finite set of states; $\Sigma$ is a finite set of input alphabet; $\delta : Q \times \Sigma \rightarrow Q$ is a transition function; $q_0 \in Q$ is an initial state of DFA; and $F \subseteq Q$ is a set of accepting states of DFA. Let $\sigma = s_1 s_2 ... s_n$ be a string over the alphabet $\Sigma$. The automaton $A_\varphi$ accepts the string $\sigma$ if a sequence of states $q_0 q_1 ... q_n$ exists in $Q$ with the following conditions:

1. $q_{i+1} = \delta(q_i, s_{i+1}), for\, i = 0, 1, ..., n - 1$
2. $q_n \in F$

In words, the automaton $A_\varphi$ starts at the initial state $q_0$. The first condition says that given each character of string $\sigma$, $A_\varphi$ will transform from state to state according to the transition function $\delta$. The second condition says that the last input of the string $\sigma$ causes the automaton to halt in one of the accepting states. Otherwise, the automaton $A_\varphi$ rejects the string $\sigma$.

## 3  Transforming NMRDP to MDP

### 3.1  Non-Markovian Reward

Compared with Markov reward, the only difference of non-Markovian reward is that the reward function of non-Markovian reward is determined by a series of historical states. Therefore, we define NMRDP to generalize the MDP model by allowing reward functions to describe the history of visited states [13].

**Definition:** An NMRDP is a tuple $M =< S, A, P, R, T, \gamma, s_0 >$, where $S, A, P, T, \gamma$ and $s_0$ are the same as MDP. The only difference is that the reward function of NMRDP is $R : S^* \rightarrow \mathbb{R}$, where $S^*$ is a sequence of states. The function says that non-Markovian reward (which is a real number) is determined by a sequence of states.

In this paper, we use a group of pairs $R = \{(\varphi_i : r_i)|1 \leq i \leq n\}$ to describe the reward function of NMRDP, where each $\varphi_i$ is an $LTL_f$ formula and each $r_i \in \mathbb{R}$, resulting in Temporally-Extended Reward Function (TERF) [14].

**Example 1:** We will show a TERF as an example. Suppose that there is a robot who needs to check whether the electricity is sufficient before sweeping the floor. The corresponding TERF is defined as $(\varphi : r)$. We can define the reward $r$ as 100 and such task can be expressed by $LTL_f$ formula:

$$\varphi = (\Diamond sweep) \wedge (\neg sweep\ U\ check\_electricity)$$

The key idea of the approach is to transform NMRDP $M$ with TERF $R = \{(\varphi_i : r_i)|1 \leq i \leq n\}$ to MDP $M'$ based on DFA. The approach comprises three steps.
  **Step1.** Transform Each $\varphi_i$ of TERF into a DFA $A_\varphi$.
  **Step2.** Construct an MDP $M'$ from NMRDP $M$ and the DFA $A_\varphi$.
  **Step3.** Optimize the reward function of MDP $M'$.
In what follows, we elaborate on each step using the example of sweeping robot.

## 3.2 Transforming each $\varphi_i$ of TERF into a DFA

In step 1, we transform each tuple $(\varphi : r)$ in TERF into a tuple $(A_\varphi : r)$, where $A_\varphi$ is a DFA corresponding to $LTL_f$ formula $\varphi$. The approach can also work for rewards specified by other dialects of *LTL* with finite semantic models, where there is a corresponding automata representation. For example, PLTL can be transformed to NBA (that can be determined to a DFA) [15].

**Example 2:** As                                                                                     defined
in Example 1, TERF is $(\varphi = (\Diamond sweep) \wedge (\neg sweep \ U \ check\_electricity) : 100)$. We can construct a DFA for $\varphi$, which is shown as follows:

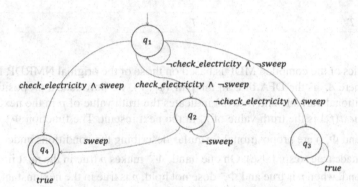

**Fig. 1.** DFA for $\varphi$

Automata states are represented by nodes, and transitions are represented by arcs in the figure. The double-ringed node indicates the accepting state. From Fig. 1, we can see that state $q_4$ is an accepting state. Moreover, once state $q_3$ holds there is no chance to transfer to state $q_4$, hence state $q_3$ is an error state. If the final state of a sequence of states is state $q_4$, then $\varphi$ is satisfied.

## 3.3 Constructing an MDP from TERF and DFA

In step 2, we construct an MDP by augmenting extra propositions with respect to DFA, making it possible for the reward functions to become Markovian. In the compiled MDP, each state in DFA corresponds to an extra proposition, which reflects the changes of the states of DFA. We should note that there are two groups of propositions in the generated MDP, the propositions generated by the automata states and the original propositions of NMRDP. The other thing we need to do is to compile the reward function into an MDP model. Table 1 contains technical details of the compilation.

**Table 1.** Details of the Compilation

|  | Original NMRDP | Compiled MDP |
|---|---|---|
| Initial state | $s_0$ | $s_0' =$ <br> $s_0 \cup \bigcup_{(\varphi:r)\in R}\{f_{q_0} \mid q_0 \text{ is the initial state of } DFA\}$ |
| Successor state axioms | $next(p) \leftrightarrow (\Phi_p^+) \vee (p \wedge \neg\Phi_p^-)$ | $next(p) \leftrightarrow (\Phi_p^+) \vee (p \wedge \neg\Phi_p^-)$ <br> $next(f_q) \leftrightarrow (\Phi_{f_q}^+) \vee (f_q \wedge \neg\Phi_{f_q}^-)$ |
| Reward function | $R = \{(\varphi_i : r_i)\}_{i=1...n}$ | $R' = \sum_{(\varphi:r)\in R}\sum_{q\in A_\varphi \wedge q \text{ is accepting state}} r_i \tau_{f_q}$ |
| Discount factor | $\gamma$ | $\gamma$ |
| Horizon | $T$ | $T$ |

Dynamics of the compiled MDP is based on those of the original NMRDP. For each $q \in A_\varphi$, where $A_\varphi$ is the DFA of $\varphi$ in the pair $(\varphi : r)$, we introduce a proposition $f_q$. $p$ is a propositional variable and $next(p)$ indicates the truth value of $p$ in the next instant. Likewise, $next(f_q)$ is the truth value of $f_q$ in the next instant. The function $\Phi_p^+$ and $\Phi_{f_q}^+$ (resp. $\Phi_p^-$ and $\Phi_{f_q}^-$) are propositional formulas describing the conditions under which $p$ and $f_q$ are made true (resp. false). On one hand, $\Phi_p^+$ makes $p$ true in the next instant. On the other hand, when $p$ is true and $\Phi_p^-$ dose not hold, $p$ is true in the next instant. Finally in the definition of $R'$, which is the reward function of MDP, $\tau_{f_q}$ is the indicator function which evaluates to 1 when $f_q$ is true, and 0 otherwise.

In the compiled MDP, the execution of actions simulates the stochastic transition model in NMRDP to update the proposition $p$. Meanwhile the propositions representing the states of DFAs are updated to simulate the transitions of each automaton $A_\varphi$. Then the agent collects rewards upon satisfaction of each $LTL_f$ formula $\varphi$ in the compiled MDP (agent gets rewards when reaching any accepting state of automaton $A_\varphi$). The discount and the horizon remain the same as NMRDP. In each step, the original propositions have the same changes in NMRDP and MDP.

**Example 3:** We construct an MDP $M'$ from the DFA shown in Example 2. There are four introduced propositions $\{f_{q_1}, f_{q_2}, f_{q_3}, f_{q_4}\}$ corresponding to the four nodes ( $f_{q_1}$ is in the initial state). The successor state axioms for the four propositions are defined as follows:

$$next(f_{q_1}) \leftrightarrow (f_{q_1} \wedge \neg check\_electricity \wedge \neg sweep)$$

$$next(f_{q_2}) \leftrightarrow (f_{q_1} \wedge check\_electricity \wedge \neg sweep) \vee (f_{q_2} \wedge \neg sweep)$$

$$next(f_{q_3}) \leftrightarrow (f_{q_1} \wedge sweep \wedge \neg check\_electricity) \vee f_{q_3}$$

$$next(f_{q_4}) \leftrightarrow (f_{q_1} \wedge check\_electricity \wedge sweep) \vee (f_{q_2} \wedge sweep) \vee f_{q_4}$$

We can simply define the reward function as $R = 100\tau_{f_{q_4}}$. In this example, the solution of the agent is to check the power before sweeping the floor, so the state transition order of DFA should be $q_1 \rightarrow \cdots \rightarrow q_1 \rightarrow q_2 \rightarrow \cdots \rightarrow q_2 \rightarrow q_4$ or $q_1 \rightarrow \cdots \rightarrow q_1 \rightarrow q_4$.

### 3.4 Optimizing the Reward Function of MDP

When the size of the DFA is large, the corresponding compiled MDP model is also large. Therefore, it is difficult for an MDP planner to solve that model. Reward shaping is a common technique in MDP which aims to improve searching by transforming the reward function [11]. The transformed reward functions have the form: $R'(s, a, s') = R(s, a, s') + F(s, a, s')$, where $R$ is the original reward function and $F$ is the shaping reward function. The intuition behind reward shaping is that by increasing (resp. Decreasing) the rewards in states that lead to other high-value (resp. Low-value) states, MDP planners can generate good-quality solutions.

We can guide agents by defining reshaping functions in order to increase the effectiveness of search and the quality of solutions. Nevertheless, some arbitrary shaping reward functions that can take some "bugs" may mislead the agent into learning suboptimal policies. For example, if there is a sequence of states $s_1...s_n$ that can make the agent travel through them in a cycle ($s_1 \rightarrow s_2 \rightarrow \cdots \rightarrow s_n$), and gain positive rewards from the sum of shaping reward functions ($F(s_1, a_1, s_2) + F(s_2, a_2, s_3) + \cdots + F(s_{n-1}, a_{n-1}, s_n) + F(s_n, a_n, s_1)) > 0$, the agent may "distracted" from the optimal policy and repeatedly go round the circle. In what follows, we introduce a shaping reward function:

$$F(s, a, s') = \gamma\rho(s') - \rho(s)$$

where $\rho : S \rightarrow \mathbb{R}$ is the potential function of state $s$; $\gamma$ is the discount factor of MDP; $s$ is a state of MDP; $s'$ is the next state of $s$ after applying $a$; $a$ is an action of MDP.

If $F(s, a, s')$ is chosen from a restricted class of potential-based shaping reward functions defined as $F(s, a, s') = \gamma\rho(s') - \rho(s)$, then this guarantees preservation of optimal and near-optimal policies [16]. The reason why the preservation of near-optimality is desirable since it provides guarantees for suboptimal solutions obtained by state-of-the-art heuristic search approximate approaches.

For the structure of the compiled MDP, we can exploit the propositions corresponding to DFA to design shaping reward functions. Concretely, the potential function $\rho(s)$ is decomposed to the sum of potential functions $\beta : Prop \rightarrow \mathbb{R}$ of $f_q$ (which holds in $s$). Then $\rho(s)$ has the form as follows:

$$\rho(s) = \sum_{f_q \in s,, q \in Q} \beta(f_q)$$

Because two consecutive states are used in the shaping reward function $F(s, a, s')$, we need to record the values of the automata propositions in the previous instant. Accordingly, we augment the compiled MDP with additional propositions $prev\_f_q$ for each $f_q$.

The value of $prev\_f_q$ is updated with respect to the successor state axioms:

$$next(prev\_f_q) \leftrightarrow f_q$$

Therefore, the shaping reward function can be instantiated into the following form:

$$F\left(s, a, s'\right) = \gamma \sum\nolimits_{f_q \in s, q \in Q} \beta(f_q) - \sum\nolimits_{prev\_f_q \in s, q \in Q} \beta\left(prev\_f_q\right)$$

**Example 4:** In the example of the sweeping robot, the potential function $\beta$ serves positive rewards when $f_{q2}$ or $f_{q4}$ hold and serves negative reward when $f_{q3}$ holds. We can optimize the reward function by assigning potentials $\beta(f_{q1}) = 0, \beta(f_{q2}) = 50, \beta(f_{q3}) = -50,$ $\beta(f_{q4}) = 100$. The closer to the accepting state, the higher the potential value. We can get the reward function after reward shaping:

$$R' = 100\tau_{f_{q4}} + \gamma(50\tau_{f_{q2}} - 50\tau_{f_{q3}} + 100\tau_{f_{q4}}) - (50\tau_{prev\_f_{q2}} - 50\tau_{prev\_f_{q3}} + 100\tau_{prev\_f_{q4}})$$

## 4 Empirical Evaluation

In this section, we show the feasibility of the approach through experiments over MDP problems from IPPC. We replace the Markovian rewards by TERFs and use different configurations of PROST as the MDP planner including IPPC 2011, IPPC 2014 and UCTSTAR. Experiments are conducted on a laptop running Ubuntu 20.04 (virtual machine) on an Intel(R) Core (TM) i7-8570H CPU 2.20GHZ and 8GB of RAM. The upper bound of used memory for PROST is 250Mb. We set the number of training trials to 30.

The literature [11] also provides an approach to achieve non-Markovian rewards by embedding it into MDP model. It transforms the non-Markovian rewards to corresponding DFA and add propositions to simulate the transitions of DFA. The main difference between their approach and ours is the embedding method. It divides each time step into three modes: *world*, *sync* and *reward*. In *world* mode, an action from the NMRDP is applied. In *sync* mode, the automata states are synchronized according to the transitions of the automata, and the assignment of reward is delayed to *reward* mode. Three additional propositions control the alternation among three modes.

### 4.1 Academic Advising

**Problem Description**
We modify the academic-advising domain from benchmarks of IPPC. This problem is to train the agent to pass courses in a correct order. Some of these courses have prerequisite courses, and the pass of prerequisite courses will increase the probability of the pass of these courses. In addition, some of these courses are required to be passed. The agent's action is taking a course. It can select several courses in an instant, and the number of selected courses is determined by the maximum number of actions. After a course

is selected, it has a certain probability to pass. The agent's task is to pass all required courses within a finite horizon and must pass all corresponding prerequisite courses before passing them. From this problem description we can get a non-Markovian reward function for each required course specified by $LTL_f$ formula:

$$\varphi_c = \Diamond(passed(c)) \wedge \Box(\bigwedge_{c'}(taken(c) \wedge prereq(c',c)) \rightarrow passed(c'))$$

where $c$ is a required course, $prereq(c',c)$ holds when course $c'$ is the prerequisite of course $c$. The agent is given a reward upon the completion of a required course in the correct order of its prerequisite courses. We define the TERF as $\{(\varphi_c : 1)|c \text{ is a required course}\}$.

**Experimental Process**
DFA Transformation: The first step of this approach is to convert the $LTL_f$ formula $\varphi_c$ to DFA which is shown in Fig. 2:

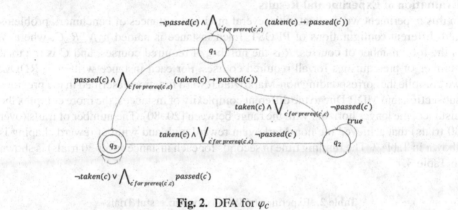

**Fig. 2.** DFA for $\varphi_c$

From Fig. 2, we can see that the state $q_3$ is an accepting state and the state $q_1$ is the initial state. moreover, once state $q_2$ holds there is no chance to transfer to state $q_3$, hence state $q_2$ is an error state. The only correct state transition process of the DFA should be $q_1 \rightarrow \cdots \rightarrow q_1 \rightarrow q_3$.

Constructing MDP: For all states of DFA $\varphi_c$, we add three propositions $f_{q_1}^c, f_{q_2}^c$ and $f_{q_3}^c$. Following the compilation rules, we can get the successor state axioms of three propositions for each course from $\varphi_c$.

$$next(f_{q_1}^c) \leftrightarrow f_{q_1}^c \wedge (\neg passed(c) \wedge \bigwedge_{c' \text{ for } prereq(c',c)} taken(c) \rightarrow passed(c'))$$

$$next(f_{q_2}^c) \leftrightarrow (f_{q_1}^c \wedge (taken(c) \wedge \bigvee_{c' \text{ for } prereq(c',c)} \neg passed(c'))) \vee f_{q_2}^c$$

$$\vee (f_{q_3}^c \wedge (taken(c) \wedge \bigvee_{c' \text{ for } prereq(c',c)} \neg passed(c')))$$

$$next(f_{q_3}^c) \leftrightarrow (f_{q_1}^c \wedge (passed(c) \wedge \bigwedge_{c' \text{ for } prereq(c',c)} (taken(c) \rightarrow passed(c'))))$$

$$\vee (f_{q_3}^c \wedge (\neg taken(c) \vee \bigwedge\nolimits_{c' \, for \, prereq(c',c)} passed(c')))$$

The reward function is defined as:

$$R = \sum\nolimits_{c \; is \; a \; required \; course} \tau_{f_{q_3}^c}$$

Optimizing reward function: According to our approach, three propositions $\{prev\_f_{q_1}^c, prev\_f_{q_2}^c, prev\_f_{q_3}^c\}$ for each course $c$ need to be augmented. We can optimize the reward function by assigning potentials $\beta(f_{q_1}^c) = 2$, $\beta(f_{q_2}^c) = -50$, $\beta(f_{q_3}^c) = 50$. Then we can define the shaping reward function as:

$$R' = \sum\nolimits_{c \; is \; a \; required \; course} \tau_{f_{q_3}^c} + \gamma (2\tau_{f_{q_1}^c} - 50\tau_{f_{q_2}^c}$$
$$+ 50\tau_{f_{q_3}^c}) - (2\tau_{prev\_f_{q_1}^c} - 50\tau_{prev\_f_{q_2}^c} + 50\tau_{prev\_f_{q_3}^c})$$

**Evaluation of Experimental Results**

In this experiment we conduct with several modified instances of benchmark problems and different configurations of PROST. Each instance is named $p\_N\_R\_C$, where $N$ is the total number of courses, $R$ is the number of required courses, and $C$ is the total number of prerequisites for all required courses. For each instance written in RDDL, we compile the corresponding non-Markovian reward function described in the previous subsection into MDP. Due to the different complexity of instances, the more complex the instance, the longer horizon, with the range between [20, 80]. The number of trails (over 30 trials) that achieved the non-Markovian reward with and without reward shaping is shown in Table 2. The running time in seconds for each instance (over 30 trials) is shown in Table 3.

**Table 2.** Experimental Results for Successful Trials

| Planner | Instance | | | | | |
|---|---|---|---|---|---|---|
| | IPPC 2014 | | IPPC 2011 | | UCTSTAR | |
| | No RS | RS | No RS | RS | No RS | RS |
| $p\_10\_3\_6$ | **30** | **30** | **30** | **30** | **30** | **30** |
| $p\_10\_7\_15$ | 29 | **30** | 29 | **30** | 28 | **30** |
| $p\_15\_4\_3$ | 29 | **30** | 29 | **30** | 27 | **28** |
| $p\_15\_7\_16$ | 3 | **30** | 2 | **29** | 1 | **27** |
| $p\_20\_8\_14$ | 2 | **26** | 2 | **28** | 0 | **27** |
| $p\_20\_10\_23$ | 0 | **27** | 0 | **27** | 0 | **26** |

*(continued)*

**Table 2.** (*continued*)

| Planner | Instance | | | | | |
|---------|----------|-----|----------|-----|---------|-----|
| | IPPC 2014 | | IPPC 2011 | | UCTSTAR | |
| | No RS | RS | No RS | RS | No RS | RS |
| $p\_25\_8\_15$ | 0 | **28** | 0 | **26** | 0 | **28** |
| $p\_25\_9\_22$ | 0 | **27** | 0 | **27** | 0 | **27** |
| $p\_30\_11\_19$ | 0 | **26** | 0 | **28** | 0 | **27** |

**Table 3.** Experimental Results for Running Time

| Instance | Planner | | | | | |
|----------|---------|-----|----------|-----|---------|-----|
| | IPPC 2014 | | IPPC 2011 | | UCTSTAR | |
| | No RS | RS | No RS | RS | No RS | RS |
| $p\_10\_3\_6$ | 349.9 | **347.9** | 351.4 | **348.8** | 346.2 | **344.3** |
| $p\_10\_7\_15$ | 290.2 | **262.2** | 292.6 | **264.7** | 277.0 | **271.4** |
| $p\_15\_4\_3$ | 481.4 | **473.9** | 479.2 | **473.1** | 488.4 | **477.9** |
| $p\_15\_7\_16$ | 513.4 | **468.4** | 474.0 | **465.9** | 492.3 | **471.5** |
| $p\_20\_8\_14$ | 1073.6 | **1035.6** | 1077.2 | **1040.8** | 1062.7 | **1041.3** |
| $p\_20\_10\_23$ | 1029.7 | **964.5** | 1039.8 | **966.9** | 1001.8 | **961.1** |
| $p\_25\_8\_15$ | 2217.8 | **2152.4** | 2267.1 | **2144.8** | 2280.6 | **2155.7** |
| $p\_25\_9\_22$ | 2318.0 | **2187.6** | 2389.8 | **2190.3** | 2339.6 | **2191.5** |
| $p\_30\_11\_19$ | 2322.9 | **2189.7** | 2344.6 | **2192.4** | 2403.5 | **2194.4** |

The first column of the Table 2 and Table 3 lists all instances. Each row records the number of successful trails of the corresponding instance by different planners. The results are divided into two groups, with or without reward shaping (No RS and RS). Better results are marked in bold for each planner. In Table 2, since the first three instances are relatively simple, the successful trails are all close to 30. However, for other complex instances, the success rate is very low (zero or near zero) without reward shaping, while the successful trails with reward shaping are all close to 30.

We can see that the state-of-the-art MDP planners struggle to generate good solutions in the compiled MDP without reward shaping. They are only able to solve the instances that are relatively simple. The lack of guidance causes MDP planners myopic lookahead. We note that there is an abrupt decrease in the performance for complex instances since the size of compiled MDP is large. Without reward shaping, MDP planners are forced to expand a large-size search tree for compiled MDPs, either the restricted memory is run out or search depth exceeds the horizon. Moreover, due to the fact that planners can only obtain rewards when the proposition representing the accepting state holds, and the look ahead cannot serve any useful information (close to blind search). Reward shaping can provide guidance (immediate rewards) for planners when DFAs transform from one state to another. The closer a state to (resp. far away) an accepting state, the more positive (resp. negative) rewards are obtained. Therefore, these rewards can serve abundant information to make planners achieve the non-Markovian reward.

In Table 3, the running time of RS is shorter than No RS for all instances. As the complexity of the instance becomes higher, the running time is shortened even more. We can infer that RS is helpful for guiding the search. In general, the average running time is reduced by 4.97% for IPPC 2014, 4.88% for IPPC 2011 and 3.95% for UCTSTAR.

**Table 4.** Experimental Results for Different Approaches

| Instance | Approach | | | | | |
|----------|----------|---|---|---|---|---|
| | IPPC 2014 | | | | | |
| | Running Time (s) | | Successful Trials | | Length | |
| | A1 | A2 | A1 | A2 | A1 | A2 |
| $p\_10\_3\_6$ | **347.9** | 459.9 | **30** | 30 | **6.6** | 11.4 |
| $p\_10\_7\_15$ | **262.2** | 366.8 | **30** | 27 | **12.7** | 13.1 |
| $p\_15\_4\_3$ | **473.9** | 525.9 | **30** | 27 | **9** | 15.2 |
| $p\_15\_7\_16$ | **468.4** | 798.9 | **30** | 27 | **22.1** | 25.6 |
| $p\_20\_8\_14$ | **1035.6** | 1154.5 | **26** | 26 | **28.9** | 33.2 |
| $p\_20\_10\_23$ | **964.5** | 1119.5 | **27** | 24 | **22.4** | 26.5 |
| $p\_25\_8\_15$ | **2152.4** | 2336.4 | **28** | 25 | **35.1** | 41.89 |
| $p\_25\_9\_22$ | **2187.6** | 2467.9 | **27** | 0 | **39** | × |
| $p\_30\_11\_19$ | **2189.7** | 2458.1 | **26** | 0 | **43.2** | × |

Finally, we compare our approach (A1) with that of [11] (A2) in Table 4. The column "Length" means the average length of the solutions in 30 trials. The selected MDP planner is IPPC 2014. Compared to A2, A1 does not need to divide each time step into three different modes. Therefore, the horizon and the solutions of A2 are both tripled so that the search tree is far larger to a great extent. Although A2 has triple horizon, only one third of actions (which are applied in *world* mode) are related to the solution. Other actions are used to synchronize the transitions of DFA and assign the reward. Table 4 compares running time, successful trials and quality of solutions for A1 and A2. For all instances, the experimental results of A1 are better than A2. In the last two instances, the excessively long horizon prevents the planner from finding the solutions via A2, hence the step of solutions is marked as ×. But the successful trials for A1 are still close to 30. The running time of A1 is 178.41 s less than that of A2 on average. Comparing the quality, the average length of solutions for A2 is 4.17 steps more than that for A1.

Remarkably, the successful trials are increased and running time is decreased after optimizing the reward function. Hence reward shaping can enhance the performance of MDP planners to achieve the non-Markovian reward. Furthermore, our approach is better than [11] in the metrics of running time, successful trails and quality of solutions.

## 4.2  Triangle Tireworld

**Problem Description**

We conduct second experiment with a modification of the triangle-tireworld domain from [17]. The basic idea is that a car can move between different kinds of locations (white or black) via roads, with the task being to move car from 'start' to 'goal'. Moreover, the car must move between black and white locations in turn ('black' to 'white' or 'white' to 'black') until arriving at 'goal'. There is a chance of getting a flat tire (which need to be fixed in the next instant) for each move. A visual representation of this problem is shown in Fig. 3.

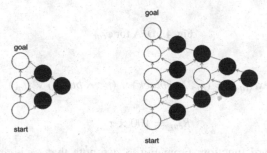

**Fig. 3.**  Visual Representation of Modified Triangle Tireworld

From the problem description above we can define the non-Markovian reward specified by $LTL_f$ formula:

$$\varphi_{car} = \Box((black \wedge \neg goal) \rightarrow O(\neg black)) \wedge \Box((\neg black \wedge \neg goal) \rightarrow O(black)) \wedge \Diamond(goal)$$

where *black* means the car is in a black location and *goal* means the car has arrived at 'goal'. We define the TERF $\{(\varphi_{car}, 100)\}$.

**Experimental Process**

DFA Transformation: The corresponding DFA $A_{\varphi_{car}}$ for $\varphi_{car}$ is shown as follows (Fig. 4):

Constructing MDP: We augment extra propositions $\{f_{q_1}, f_{q_2}, f_{q_3}, f_{q_4}, f_{q_5}\}$ corresponding to the states of $A_{\varphi_{car}}$ $\{q_1, q_2, q_3, q_4, q_5\}$. According to $A_{\varphi_{car}}$, the successor state axioms of these propositions and the reward function can be defined.

$$next(f_{q_1}) = false$$

$$next(f_{q_2}) = (f_{q_1} \wedge \neg goal \wedge \neg black) \vee (f_{q_3} \wedge \neg goal \wedge \neg black) \vee (f_{q_4} \wedge \neg goal \wedge \neg black)$$

$$next(f_{q_3}) = (f_{q_1} \wedge goal) \vee (f_{q_2} \wedge goal \wedge black) \vee (f_{q_4} \wedge goal \wedge \neg black)$$

$$next(f_{q_4}) = (f_{q_1} \wedge \neg goal \wedge black) \vee (f_{q_3} \wedge \neg goal \wedge black) \vee (f_{q_2} \wedge \neg goal \wedge black)$$

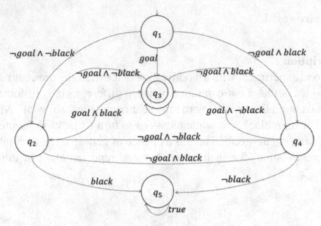

**Fig. 4.** DFA for $\varphi_{car}$

$$next(f_{q_5}) = (f_{q_2} \wedge \neg black) \vee (f_{q_4} \wedge black) \vee (f_{q_5})$$

$$R_{car} = 100 \times \tau_{f_{q_3}}$$

Optimizing reward function: From Fig. 3, we note that $q_3$ is an accepting state and $q_1$ is the initial state. Once $q_5$ holds, there is no chance for $A_{\varphi_{car}}$ to transform to$q_3$, hence $q_5$ is an error state. The correct state transition process of the DFA should be$q_1 \rightarrow q_2 \rightarrow q_4 \rightarrow q_2 \rightarrow q_4 \rightarrow \cdots \rightarrow q_2 \rightarrow q_4 \rightarrow q_3$. According to our approach, propositions $\{prev\_f_{q_1}, prev\_f_{q_2}, prev\_f_{q_3}\}$ need to be augmented. We can optimize the reward function by assigning potentials$\beta(f_{q_1}) = 0$, $\beta(f_{q_2}) = 500$, $\beta(f_{q_3}) = 1000$, $\beta(f_{q_4}) = 500$, $\beta(f_{q_5}) = 0$. Then the shaping reward function can be defined as:

$$R'_{car} = 100 \times \tau_{f_{q_3}} + \gamma \left( 500 \times f_{q_2} + 1000 \times f_{q_3} + 500 \times f_{q_4} \right)$$
$$- \left( 500 \times \tau_{prev\_f_{q_2}} + 1000 \times \tau_{prev\_f_{q_3}} + 500 \times \tau_{prev\_f_{q_4}} \right)$$

**Evaluation of Experimental Results**
The planners we use are the same as the first experiment. Each instance is named $p\_L\_R$, where $L$ is the number of locations and $R$ is the number of roads. There are different horizons (the range is $[10, 20]$) for different instances. Experimental results are summarized in Table 5, Table 6 and Table 7.

**Table 5.** Experimental Results for Successful Trials

| Instance | Planner | | | | | |
|---|---|---|---|---|---|---|
| | IPPC 2014 | | IPPC 2011 | | UCTSTAR | |
| | No RS | RS | No RS | RS | No RS | RS |
| p_6_8 | 30 | **30** | 30 | **30** | 30 | **30** |
| p_15_24 | 30 | **30** | 30 | **30** | 30 | **30** |
| p_28_66 | 30 | **30** | 30 | **30** | 30 | **30** |
| p_45_80 | 0 | **30** | 0 | **30** | 0 | **30** |
| p_66_160 | 0 | **30** | 0 | **30** | 0 | **30** |

**Table 6.** Experimental Results for Running Time

| Instance | Planner | | | | | |
|---|---|---|---|---|---|---|
| | IPPC 2014 | | IPPC 2011 | | UCTSTAR | |
| | No RS | RS | No RS | RS | No RS | RS |
| p_6_8 | 2.21 | **2.20** | **272.65** | 273.04 | **1.62** | 2.16 |
| p_15_24 | **6.25** | 6.67 | 275.39 | **257.89** | **6.27** | 6.64 |
| p_28_66 | 108.28 | **105.68** | 459.86 | **459.62** | **106.10** | 106.35 |
| p_45_80 | **538.36** | 569.68 | 915.42 | **907.18** | **565.39** | 584.21 |
| p_66_160 | **1049.7** | 1052.74 | 1477.2 | **1440.8** | 1062.7 | **1041.3** |

**Table 7.** Experimental Results for Different Approaches

| Instance | Approach | | | |
|---|---|---|---|---|
| | IPPC 2014 | | | |
| | Running Time (s) | | Successful Trials | |
| | A1 | A2 | A1 | A2 |
| p_6_8 | **2.20** | 6.28 | **30** | 30 |
| p_15_24 | **6.67** | 16.92 | **30** | 27 |
| p_28_66 | **105.68** | 108.86 | **30** | 24 |
| p_45_80 | **569.68** | 663.42 | **30** | 27 |
| p_66_160 | **1052.74** | 1382.01 | **26** | 23 |

From Table 5, we note that PROST solve the former three instances which are relatively simple without reward shaping while solving all instances with reward shaping. Obviously, reward shaping can effectively guide search for MDP planners. In Table 7, the running time via A1 is shorter than that via A2 in all instances. In this experiment, we do not compare the length of solutions since every instance has only one solution.

Overall, results of the second experiment are basically consistent with the first. The comparison between RS and No RS shows that reward shaping can improve the performance. The successful trials of RS is 30 in all instances, while that of No RS is 0 in the last two instances. But the running time of the two approaches is at the same level. Moreover, Table 7 indicates the results of A1 are better than A2 in all instances.

## 5  Summary and Discussion

NMRDP provides a powerful framework for modelling decision-making problems with historical behavior-based rewards. In this paper, we propose an approach to achieve non-Markovian rewards which is specified by temporal logic $LTL_f$. In particular, we propose an embedding method to transform the non-Markovian reward into Markovian rewards which can be solved by off-the-shelf MDP planners. Finally, we show the feasibility of this approach through experiments over MDP benchmarks from IPPC. The proposed approach will also work for other rewards specified in any formal language for which there is a corresponding automata form such as finite variant of Past $LTL$ (PLTL) [18] and Golog [19]. In the future, we will extend our approach to deep reinforcement learning.

## References

1. Li, J., Pu, G., Zhang, Y., et al.: Sat-based explicit ltlf satisfiability checking. Artif. Intell. **289**, 103369 (2020)
2. Sanner, S.: Relational dynamic influence diagram language (RDDL): Language description. Unpublished ms. Australian National University **32**, 27 (2010)
3. Li, X., Vasile, C.I., Belta, C.: Reinforcement learning with temporal logic rewards. In: 2017 IEEE/RSJ International Conference on Intelligent Robots and Systems (IROS), pp. 3834–3839. IEEE (2017)
4. Icarte, R.T., Klassen, T., Valenzano, R., et al.: Using reward machines for high-level task specification and decomposition in reinforcement learning. In: International Conference on Machine Learning. PMLR, pp. 2107–2116 (2018)
5. Puterman, M.L.: Markov Decision Processes: Discrete Stochastic Dynamic Programming. Wiley 2014)
6. Thiébaux, S., Kabanza, F., Slanley, J.: Anytime state-based solution methods for decision processes with non-Markovian rewards. arXiv preprint arXiv:1301.0606, 2012
7. Bonet, B., Geffner, H.: mGPT: a probabilistic planner based on heuristic search. J. Artif. Intell. Res. **24**, 933–944 (2005)
8. Pulver, H., Eiras, F., Carozza, L., et al.: PILOT: Efficient planning by imitation learning and optimisation for safe autonomous driving. In: 2021 IEEE/RSJ International Conference on Intelligent Robots and Systems (IROS), pp. 1442–1449. IEEE (2021)
9. Keller, T., Eyerich, P.: PROST: probabilistic planning based on UCT. In: Twenty-Second International Conference on Automated Planning and Scheduling (2012)
10. Geißer, F., Speck, D., Keller, T.: An analysis of the probabilistic track of the IPC 2018. In: ICAPS 2019 Workshop on the International Planning Competition (WIPC), pp. 27–35 (2019)
11. Camacho, A., Chen, O., Sanner, S., et al.: Non-Markovian rewards expressed in LTL: Guiding search via reward shaping (extended version). In: GoalsRL, a Workshop Collocated with ICML/IJCAI/AAMAS (2018)

12. Lucas, S.M., Reynolds, T.J.: Learning deterministic finite automata with a smart state labeling evolutionary algorithm. IEEE Trans. Pattern Anal. Mach. Intell. **27**(7), 1063–1074 (2005)
13. Brafman, R., De Giacomo, G., Patrizi, F.: LTLf/LDLf non-Markovian rewards. In: Proceedings of the AAAI Conference on Artificial Intelligence, vol. 32, no. 1 (2018)
14. Ng, A.Y., Harada, D., Russell, S.: Policy invariance under reward transformations: Theory and application to reward shaping. Icml **99**, 278–287 (1999)
15. Sohrabi, S., Baier, J.A., Mcilraith, S.A.: Proceedings of the Twenty-Fifth AAAI Conference on Artificial Intelligence Preferred Explanations: Theory and Generation via Planning (2014)
16. Ng, A.Y., Harada, D., Russell, S.: Theory and application to reward shaping. In: Proceedings of the Sixteenth International Conference on Machine Learning (1999)
17. Little, I., Thiebaux, S.: Probabilistic planning vs. replanning. In: ICAPS Workshop on IPC: Past, Present and Future (2007)
18. Bacchus, F., Boutilier, C., Grove, A.: Rewarding behaviors. In: Proceedings of the National Conference on Artificial Intelligence, pp. 1160–1167 (1996)
19. Levesque, H.J., Reiter, R., Lespérance, Y., et al.: GOLOG: a logic programming language for dynamic domains. J. Logic Program. **31**(1–3), 59–83 (1997)

# A JPSL Based Model Checking Approach for Java Programs

XinFeng Shu[(⊠)], YanLin Li, and WeiRan Gao

School of Computer Science and Technology, Xi'an University of Posts
and Telecommunications, Xi'an 710061, China
shuxf@xupt.edu.cn

**Abstract.** In order to verify the correctness of Java programs, a model
checking approach that accurately verifies the properties of Java is advocated. To this end, an algorithm is defined to use (Java Property Specification Language, JPSL) to accurately describe the properties of Java
programs to be verified and convert them into automata, then use the
On-The-Fly strategy to design algorithm to verify the object-oriented
abstract syntax tree constructed by Java programs, which in turn can
be verified with the model checking tool JMC. In addition, an example is
given to illustrate how the method works. This method makes full use of
the precise constraint ability of JPSL properties on the property range
and the advantages of the On-The-Fly strategy.

**Keywords:** JPSL · Java · Program verification · Model checking

## 1 Introduction

As the main software development language and theory in the software industry
in the past two decades, The Java programming language and its theory have
always been the focus of attention of practitioners in the software industry. Java
object-oriented methods and design patterns have been widely used in artificial
intelligence frameworks, databases, distributed large-scale software systems, etc.
With the increasing structural complexity of Java large-scale software systems,
how to ensure the security, reliability, and correctness of such systems Sexuality
is an important issue of academic concern.

Software testing [1] is the mainstream verification method in the field of
software verification. This method has great advantages, but it is also limited
by the fact that the affections of the test depends entirely on the design of the
test cases. The scale of modern software is getting bigger and bigger, and it
is developing towards the trend of hardware dependence, distribution and high
concurrency. The runtime status of such systems cannot be determined, and
software testing cannot meet the verification requirements of such software.

This research is supported by the Key Research and Development Projects of Shaanxi
Province (No. 2020GY-210), and the Equipment Pre-research Key Laboratory Foundation (No. JZX7Y202001SY000901).

Different from software testing methods, formal methods [1–5] use mathematical methods to model the system and the expected properties of the system, then use mathematical derivation and logical operations to prove whether the system satisfies the expected properties. The biggest difference between formal methods and software testing is to use mathematical derivation to prove the verification process, the verification process has strict theoretical support. Some formal methods can also locate the path of system errors in a more detailed and dynamic manner in the process of software design and implementation, and ensure the correctness of the software in time, without the need for software testing after a certain unit of the software or the entire system has been fully implemented. Verify that the system or a unit has no errors. Formal verification technology is based on mathematical reasoning, which can cover all possible paths of the system during verification, so this method has a good effect on making up for the deficiencies of software testing.

Model checking is one of the main methods of formal methods. During verification, a finite state transition model S of the system to be verified needs to be established first, and the properties to be verified are described as temporal logic formula $F$, and then the algorithm is automatically passed with the support of model checking tools. Exhaustively traverse the execution path of the system S to detect whether the property $F$ holds, and if the property does not hold, a counterexample path can be given to help engineers and technicians locate and debug errors. Model checking has been applied to the analysis and verification of computer hardware, communication protocols, control systems, security authentication protocols, etc., and has achieved remarkable success, and has radiated from academia to industry. The great advantage of model checking is that it automates the validation process.

Program verification mainly uses traditional model checking tools such as SPIN [6] or NuSMV [7]. During verification, it is necessary to convert the Java source program into SPIN's Promela [8] model or NuSMV's SMV [9] model, and describe the properties to be verified. Then verify the logic formulas such as Linear-time Temporal Logic (LTL) [10] or Computation Tree Logic (Computation Tree Logic, CTL) [11]. Because the model description strategy of Promela and SMV is very different from the Java source code, the model conversion process often needs to be done manually. As the software system becomes more and more complex and the expressive ability of modeling languages such as Promela and SMV is limited, it is difficult to ensure the consistency between the abstract model of the model checking system and the original software design.

At the same time, since the system modeling languages of model checking tools are all specific scripting languages, e.g., Promela and MSV of such as SPIN and NuMSV respectively, engineers and technicians need to be proficient in this language to conduct system modeling, and the built model does not have intuitive visibility and is complex. System modeling is very difficult, and it is difficult to ensure the correctness of the model itself. In addition, the description of the properties to be verified mainly uses logical formulas such as LTL and CTL, and engineers and technicians are still required to be proficient in the syntax and semantics of the corresponding logic system, and combine the established abstract model of the system to be verified with the properties to be verified in the Java source code. And there is a lack of a special property description method suitable for engineers and technicians to directly describe the object-oriented software code. Therefore, it is urgent to design a new Java model checking method.

In order to solve the problems existing in the existing model checking methods in modeling and describing the properties of Java program systems, and verifying requirements, an algorithm is defined to use JPSL to accurately describe the properties of Java programs to be verified and convert them into automata, then use the On-The-Fly strategy to design algorithm to verify the object-oriented abstract syntax tree constructed by Java programs. which in turn can be verified with the model checking tool JMC. In addition, an example is given to illustrate how the method works. This method makes full use of the precise constraint ability of JPSL properties on the property range and the advantages of the On-The-Fly strategy.

The rest of this paper is organized as follows. In the next section, a brief introduction to the Java language and the Java Property Specific Language are given. In Sect. 3, the transformation from JPSL properties to automata and the algorithm of model checking for automata constructed from JPSL properties and object-oriented syntax trees constructed by Java programs based on the On-The-Fly strategy are introduced. In Sect. 4, an example is given to illustrate how the JMC model checker based on this method works. Finally, conclusions are given in Sect. 5.

## 2   Preliminaries

### 2.1   Java Property Specific Language

The basic grammatical components of JPSL [12] include class attributes, method parameters, local variables, or first-order logic formulas formed. With specific labels and sentence patterns (JPSL keywords), classes are described by adding labels to program codes. Class , methods, program code fragments, and statements and temporal characteristics that need to be satisfied at a particular position. The following introduces the specific definitions of the JPSL language. Table 1 shows the JPSL recursive definitions. The JPSL statement is marked in the Java source program in the form of property//@JPSL (...), JPSL_Prop is the time series property expression; Pred is the relational expression composed of Exp; Exp is the arithmetic operation expression composed of Java class attributes and variables.

Class statements, function statements, and code statements of JPSL are marked with //@JPSL (content="JPSL_Prop") before classes, functions, and code statements; code segment statements are marked by //@JPSL (content= "SEC_BEGIN JPSL_Prop ")...// @JPSL (content="SEC_END") contains the constraint code segment; the position of the statement property marker is before any statement in the program method code. All four types of statements support describing the temporal property of program execution.

**Table 1.** JPSL Definitions

| Types | Symbols | definitions |
|---|---|---|
| Statements | JPSL_Stmt | ::= //@JPSL (content="JPSL_Prop")<br>\|//@JPSL (content="SEC_BEGIN JPSL_Prop")...<br>// @JPSL (content="SEC_END") |
| Properties | JPSL_Prop | ::= Pred \| SEQ(JPSL_Prop1, ..., JPSL_Propn)<br>\| REPEAT(JPSL_Prop) \| SOMETIMES (JPSL_Prop)<br>\| ALWAYS (JPSL_Prop) \| PRE (Pred) \| POST (Pred)<br>\| JPSL_Prop1 and JPSL_Prop2 |
| Predicate | Pred | ::= Exp1(< \| <= \| == \| > \| >=)Exp2 \| !Pred \| Pred1 \|\| Pred2 \| Pred1 &&Pred2 |
| Expression | Exp | ::= const \| v \| obj.attr \| this.attr \| class.attr \| Exp1 (+ \| − \|\|/\|%) Exp2 |

## 2.2 Labeled Normal Form Graph

Labeled Normal Form Graph (LNFG) is an important tool to solve the problem of satisfiability determination of propositional projection temporal logic formula, and it is a special form of automaton. References [14,15] have proved that any propositional projection temporal logic formula P can be equivalently transformed into a Label Normal Form, $V_{j=1}^{n_0} (p_{ej} \land \varepsilon) \lor V_{i=1}^{n} (p_{ci} \land \circ P_i)$, in which the $p_{ej}$ and $p_{ci}$ is a state formula composed of atomic formulas; the successor formula called is a general propositional projection temporal sequence. logical formula. Using the LNFG of propositional projection temporal logic, the successor formulas of and are continuously expanded, so that the LNFG expansion relationship of $P$ and the successor formula constitutes a directed graph, namely LNFG.

The LNFG of formula $P$ is a quadruple $G = (CL(P), EL(P), v_0, V_f)$, where $CL(P)$ is the vertex set, $EL(P)$ is the arc set, and $v_0 \in CL(P)$ is The initial vertex named $P$, $V_f$ is the set of two-tuples formed by the vertex and the label. Each vertex in $CL(P)$ is a propositional projection temporal logic formula; the arc from vertex $R$ is a triple $\langle R, r_s, Q \rangle$; for any vertex $R \in CL(P)$, let the LNFG of R be $V_{j=1}^{n_0} (r_{ej} \land \varepsilon) \lor V_{i=1}^{n} (r_{ci} \land \circ R_i)$, then $\varepsilon \in CL(P)$ and for every $1 \leq j \leq n_0$, there is $\varepsilon \in CL(P)$ and $\mathbb{K}_i \in Z(1 \leq i \leq n)$ for every $1 \leq i \leq n$; vertices in $V_f$ and their labels are described as two-tuples $(Q, \mathbb{K}_1, \ldots, \mathbb{K}_n)$, where $K_i \in Z(1 \leq i \leq n)$ is an integer that identifies the Chop expansion cycle.

Based on the LNFG technique, it has been proved that $P$ is satisfiable if and only if the LNFG of $P$ either has a finitely acceptable path from the initial vertex $P$ to the vertex, or there exists an infinite path from the initial vertex $P$ Acceptable path, all vertices in the infinite loop that it eventually falls into cannot have the same label (that is, an acceptable cycle), thus solving the satisfiability judgment of the propositional projection temporal logic formula. The relevant proof details and judgment algorithm are shown in the literature [14,15].

For example, the LNFG of the propositional projection temporal logic formula $p$; $q$ is shown in Fig. 1. The initial vertex is represented by two concentric circles, and the vertex is a black solid circle. The formula is satisfiable because there are several finitely acceptable paths from the initial vertex $p$; $q$ to the vertex, and there is an infinitely acceptable path from the initial vertex $p$; $q$ and looping down to the vertex true. There is also an infinite path that falls into the vertex true; $q$ and performs an infinite loop, but since the only vertex in the loop is marked with 1, it is not a valid infinitely acceptable path.

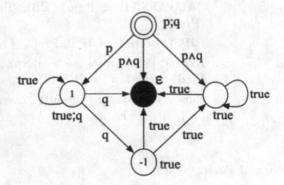

**Fig. 1.** LNFG of PPTL formula $p$; $q$

In essence, the LNFG can be regarded as a special automaton that can accept completely regular languages. The vertex $\varepsilon$ is the acceptance condition for the automaton to accept finite strings, and the acceptable cycles on the connected component vertices are the acceptance conditions for infinite strings. The LNFG can be equivalently transformed into an extended Büchi automaton [15]. For the convenience of describing the model checking algorithm, in the following, the LNFG is directly referred to as an automaton.

## 2.3   JPSL to PPTL

The grammatical structure of commonly used sequential logic LTL, CTL, etc. is complex, and the semantics are difficult to be understood and mastered by engineers, which increases the difficulty of model checking. In order to solve this problem, the properties to be verified are described by directly embedding the JPSL language into the Java program, which is convenient for engineers to verify the properties of the program. JPSL [12] has four types of properties, namely class properties, function properties, and statement properties. Fragment properties, sentence properties. According to the requirements, different types of JPSL properties are used to mark the source program, which can realize the refined verification of model checking, especially whether the part of the program satisfies the expected properties can be verified.

This section designs the rules of JPSL annotation, and provides the accurate annotation method of JPSL in Java programs, including the annotation position and annotation form, combined with case descriptions, the annotation rules are as follows:

Annotation Rule 1: After describing the properties of all objects of a class from creation to destruction, use JPSL statements to describe them, and annotate them in the Java source code before the corresponding class definitions, referred to as "class properties".

Labeling Rule 2: Describe the properties of a function during execution using JPSL statements, and annotate them in the Java source code with comments before the corresponding function definition, referred to as "function properties".

Annotation Rule 3: Describe the properties of a code fragment in a function during execution using JPSL statements, and annotate it in the Java source code with comments on the start and end statements of the corresponding statement fragment, referred to as "code segment";

Labeling Rule 4: Describe the properties of a statement in the function before the execution period, using JPSL statements, and annotate them on the corresponding statement nodes in the Java source code by way of comments, referred to as "statement properties".

The model checking technology studied in this paper constructs a LNFG structure for PPTL [19] formulas. First, it is necessary to convert the JPSL statements suitable for the description of the properties of Java source programs into PPTL formulas. This section analyzes and designs this process and defines a conversion algorithm. Implement JPSL statement to PPTL formula conversion.

The conversion strategy is to convert the JPSL property statement into the PPTL time series property formula. For the predicate formula in the formula, due to its indeterminacy, PPTL replaces the predicate formula with a new and unique atomic proposition, and constructs the state transition arc as The automaton structure of atomic propositions or atomic propositional formulas, using the map two-tuple structure is the set of atomic proposition descriptions of the atomic propositions contained in the PPTL formulas and the predicate formulas they represent, the JPSL formulas can be processed recursively using a recursive algorithm until complete conversion For the PPTL formula, the recursively designed transformation strategy is as follows.

(1) For the predicate formula $e_1[<\ |\ <=\ |\ ==\ |\ >\ |\ >=]e_2$, the map is $(p, \{p : e_1[<\ |\ <=\ |\ ==\ |\ >\ |\ >=]e_2\})$;

(2) For the property statement SEQ $(\text{Prop}_1, ..., \text{Prop}_n)$, convert $\text{Prop}_n$ to $(\text{pptl\_prop}_1, ..., \text{pptl\_prop}_n, \text{map}_1)$, and $ppt_l\text{\_prop}_1$ to $(\text{pptl\_prop}_1)^+$, the atomic proposition description set map is $\text{map}_1 \cup ... \cup \text{map}_n$;

(3) For the property statement REPEAT $(\text{Prop}_1)$, convert Prop1 to $(\text{pptl\_prop}_1, \text{map}_1)$, convert $\text{pptl\_prop}_1$ to $(\text{pptl\_prop}_1)^+$, and the atomic proposition indicates that the set map is $\text{map}_1$;

(4) For the property statement SOMETIMES $(\text{Prop}_1)$, convert $\text{Prop}_1$ to $(\text{pptl\_prop}_1, \text{map}_1)$, convert $\text{pptl\_prop}_1$ to $\text{pptl\_prop}_1$, and the atomic proposition description set map is $\text{map}_1$;

(5) For the property statement ALWAYS (Prop$_1$), convert Prop$_1$ to (pptl_prop$_1$, map$_1$), convert pptl_prop$_1$ to pptl_prop$_1$, and the atomic proposition description set map is map$_1$;

(6) For the property statement PRE (Prop$_1$), convert Prop$_1$ to (pptl_prop$_1$, map$_1$), convert pptl_prop$_1$ to pptl_prop$_1$, and the atomic proposition indicates that the set map is map$_1$;

(7) For the property statement POST (Prop$_1$), convert Prop1 to (pptl_prop$_1$, map$_1$), convert pptl_prop$_1$ to $(\varepsilon \rightarrow$ pptl$_{prop}$1$)$, and the atomic proposition indicates that the set map is map$_1$;

(8) For the property statement !Prop$_1$, convert Prop$_1$ to (pptl_prop$_1$, map$_1$), convert pptl_prop$_1$ to ¬pptl_prop, and the atomic proposition indicates that the set map is map$_1$;

(9) For the property statement Prop$_1$&&Prop$_2$, convert Prop$_1$ and Prop$_2$ into (pptl_prop$_1$, map$_1$), (pptl_prop$_2$, map$_2$), the semantic conversion result is pptl_prop$_1$ $\wedge$ pptl_prop$_2$, and the atomic proposition description set map is map$_1$map$_2$;

(10) For the property statement Prop$_1$||Prop$_2$, convert Prop$_1$ and Prop2 into (pptl_Prop_1, map$_1$), (pptl_Prop$_2$, map$_2$), the semantic conversion result is pptl_Prop$_1$ $\vee$ pptl_Prop$_2$, and the atomic proposition description set map is map$_1$map$_2$;

The technology described in the previous content converts the JPSL statement into the corresponding PPTL formula, but PPTL cannot directly enter the model checking. Based on the model checking algorithm idea of automata, in the Java model checking technology, the PPTL formula needs to be negated and constructed as a non-automatic machine of properties.

Finally we need to convert the PPTL formula to LNFG and input it as a property automaton into the model checking algorithm, the algorithm for converting the PPTL formula to LNFG has been given and proved in the literature [14, 15].

## 2.4   Java Source Code to OOAST

OOAST [16] is used to represent the semantic and syntactic content of object-oriented programs, and its structure is shown in Fig. 2. Among them, each class node ClassNode contains three kinds of nodes, Parent, Attributes and Functions. The Parent node points to its parent node, the Attributes node points to the class attribute attr node, and the Functions node points to the method node fun.

(1) Class node: This node is a class node in the syntax tree, such as ClassNode_1 to ClassNode_n in Fig. 2. This node stores the serial number of the symbol table pointed to by the class name, which can be used to obtain the basic information of the class in the symbol table. In addition, the class node also stores the information of its associated Parent, Attributes, and Functions nodes.

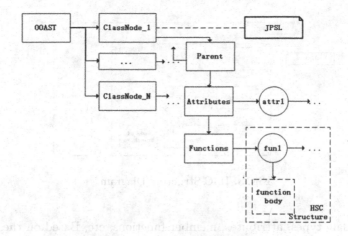

**Fig. 2.** Object-Oriented Abstract Syntax Tree Structure

(2) Parent node: This node is associated with its corresponding parent class node, and can obtain its parent class information, including the parent class attribute and method information inherited in the subclass. Other relationships between classes can also be directly converted to corresponding class attributes.

(3) Attributes node: This node is associated with the attribute node of the class, and can obtain all attribute information content of the class to which it belongs. In order to clearly represent the content of the attribute, the structure of the attr attribute node pointed to by Attributes in Fig. 2 can also only be saved The attribute name, and the type and initial value of the attribute are directly stored in the character table corresponding to the serial number of the attribute name.

(4) Functions node: This node is associated with the method node of the class, and can obtain all method information of the class to which it belongs. Due to the complex logical relationship in the method statement, the method statement structure can be converted into the Hierarchical Syntax Chart HSC (Hierarchical Syntax Chart HSC) [16] structure shown in Fig. 2, and its specific structure is shown in Fig. 3.

(5) JPSL node: This node is associated with class nodes, method nodes, and statement nodes according to different requirements, and can obtain JPSL content and constraint scope, indicating the expected properties of the code within the constraint scope of this property.

To create the OOAST for the given Java program, we first need to perform lexical parsing of the program with the lexical and syntax analysis tool JavaCC. With the tool, we only need to give the lexical and syntax rules of the subset of Java language, the lexical and syntax analyzer written in pure Java code can be automatically generated.algo Then we employee the analyzer to process the Java program, and all the syntax elements of the program can be recognized, such

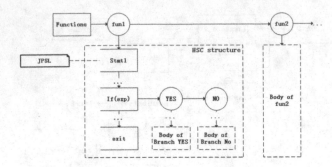

**Fig. 3.** HSC Structure Diagram

as classes, date types, attributes, member functions, etc. Based on the analysis result, it is not hard to write the rithm to create the OOAST, so the details are omitted here.

### 2.5  Multi-property Verification Problems

In order to realize the refined verification of the programs in the JPSL scope, the constraint range of the JPSL properties is solved according to its type. Since multiple JPSL properties may be marked in the Java program system participating in model checking, and even multiple JPSL properties may be marked in one Java class. In most practical application scenarios, in order to improve efficiency and save time, it is impossible to verify only one property at a time. Therefore, the Java model checking process should deal with the cases of multiproperty verification needs.

In order to solve the situation of multi-property verification, a container structure is used to store the completely finite automata and constraint ranges constructed by all JPSL properties into the same memory. The state on the above triggers the start position of the constraint range in the container. According to the start position, the non-automatic machine of the properties is located in the container, and the model checking of this properties is started. After repeated research and trade-offs, this design method is conducive to resource utilization and facilitates algorithm design.

Then define the LNFGSet<(LNFG, prop_start, prop_end)> container to store the properties of JPSL constructs, non-automatic LNFG and JPSL properties constrain the start and end positions, and use the properties of JPSL constructs in Sect. 3 to replace JPSL properties stored in JPSLSet. The position of the object can easily complete the construction of the above container, and the specific definition is given below.

**Definition 1.** When the original JPSL constraint range is from the start position of the source program to the end position, that is, the JPSL two-tuple is (jpsl, start: end), and the non-automatic property constructed by the JPSL statement is LNFG, then construct a JPSL property and its Label the range to

the property non-automatic constraint two-tuple(LNFG,prop_start:prop_end),
where prop_start =start,prop_end=end, and all property non-automatic constraint two-tuple (LNFG, prop_start, prop_end) in the Java program to be
verified stored in the set of non-automatic constraint two-tuples of properties
LNFGSet<(LNFG,prop_start,Prop _end)>.

When interpreting and executing the system model OOAST, each interpretation executes a statement, and the statement position is used to match all the
two-tuple prop_start in the LNFGSet. If the current statement corresponds to
the prop_start position, the model checking of this property is started, and the
system model is interpreted and executed. When the position of the statement
corresponds to the position of prop_end, the verification of this property ends,
and the system gives the verification result. Use LNFGSet to store the property
non-automata of all JPSL property transformations and their bounded scope in
the Java source code.

## 2.6   Model-Checking with On-The-Fly Strategy

The property construction and system modeling of Java program model checking
are ready. In the model checking verification stage, the object-oriented abstract
syntax tree and the property non-automatic machine are input into the model
checking algorithm to realize the verification.

During model checking, the On-The-Fly strategy [17] is used to provide
dynamic construction for the system model, and after executing a part of the
system model, the result after execution is obtained, the system state is constructed from the result, and then the system state is used to correspond to a
certain non-automatic properties. The state is negotiated, and the satisfiability
is judged. After a state no longer participates in the intersection operation, the
memory of the state is recovered, and the number of system operations is always
kept at a low scale, which also improves the efficiency of the algorithm. The Java
model checking algorithm described in this paper is shown in Fig. 4.

When interpreting the execution system model, each interpreting and executing a single complete statement node of the abstract syntax tree constructs the
system state for its result, and matches the prop_start and prop_end positions in
the property non-automatic constraint two-tuple set LNFGSet by the position
of the interpreting execution, Locate the non-automatic machine of properties
that should participate in the model checking operation. Starting from the initial state, perform a model checking and intersection operation between the
system state and the corresponding state of the non-automatic machine of this
property, and construct the resulting automaton according to the result of the
intersection operation. The non-automatic machine uses the node pointer to continuously search for the ejected arc, advances to the new arc, obtains the new
non-automatic machine state from the new arc, continues to perform the intersection operation or ends the program as required, recovers the memory created
by the interpretation and execution system model and releases the path whose
properties are established by the operation occupies the memory.

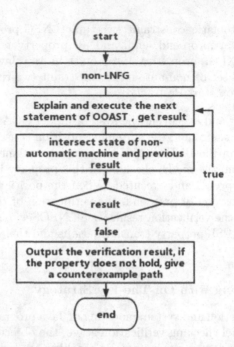

**Fig. 4.** Strategy of Java model checking algorithm

The algorithm for dynamically interpreting and executing OOAST in the algorithm flow is as follows:

**Algorithm 1: Dynamic Executing OOAST.** The algorithm traverses the entire syntax tree in pre-order starting from the root node of OOAST, determines the node type when accessing each node, and specifies the corresponding interpretation and execution rules.

(1) For the specified entry function Function node, select the first child node of the current node to start interpretation and execution.
(2) For a common statement node, the successor node of the current node is selected as the next statement node to be executed.
(3) For the if statement node, calculate the value of the conditional expression in the if statement, and select the first node corresponding to the YES and NO branches according to the true or false results as the next statement node to be executed.
(4) For the while statement node, calculate the value of the conditional expression in the while statement, if the result is true, select the first node of the YES branch as the next node to be executed, otherwise select the successor node of the while loop as the next node to be executed statement node.
(5) For the function call statement node, after calculating the value of each actual parameter expression and assigning it to the corresponding function formal parameter, the first statement of the called function is used as the next statement node to be executed.

(6) For variable assignment, declaration node, and object creation statement node, it is interpreted and executed according to the infix operation mode.

(7) For expression operations, infix operations are generally used in combination with operator priorities to perform expression operations.

(8) For special expression operations, specify special processing rules, such as $j - -$, convert them to $j = j - 1$, and then perform infix operations on them. Interpret and execute each statement node of the syntax tree according to the rules. The values in the variable stack and object heap change synchronously with the interpretation and execution, and save the result of continuously updating the memory reference to the variable stack and object heap. In the process of interpreting and executing OOAST, the system state is constructed and then the model checking and intersection operation is performed. The two are triggering conditions for each other and call each other to complete.

The second part of the model checking process in Fig. 4 is to compute the intersect state of result automata. For each node of OOAST, its corresponding line number in the source program is stored. When the OOAST statement is interpreted and executed, it is judged whether there are one or more non-automatic machine two-tuples in LNFGSet according to the statement position rowID stored by the node. The prop_start or prop_end of (LNFG, prop_start, prop_end) are equal to it. If rowi is equal to prop_start, the model checking process ModelChecking (vs, h, LNFG) of the LNFG is triggered. If rowid is equal to prop_end, the model checking process of the LNFG ends and outputs the model checking result of this property.

**Algorithm 2: Computing the Result Automata.** The function ModelChecking(vs,h,LNFG) begins after a statement on OOAST is interpreted and executed. At this time, the variable stack and the object heap are updated synchronously, and the value of the variable stack and the object heap is recorded as $rst_n$, and the With the execution of OOAST, n = 1, 2, 3, 4..., until the end of the OOAST interpretation and execution, the data is continuously updated during the execution to form a system state sequence.

(1) Use the Z3 [18] solver to perform the intersection operation between the initial system state $rst_0$ within the property constraint range and the initial state $<state_0, p_0, state_1>$ of the property non-automatic machine LNFG.

(2) If the Z3 solver obtains the SAT result, it is proved that the system can accept this state of the non-automatic automaton LNFG, and use the initial system state rst0 to construct the arc $<stmt_0, rst_0, stmt_1>$ and the arc of the non-automaton LNFG $< state_0, p_0, state_1>$ is constructed as an arc $<<stmt0,state0 >, rst_0, <stmt_1, state_1 >>$ on the result automaton rstLNFG, and $<stmt_1,state_1 >$ is pressed into cursorStack to turn (4).

(3) If the Z3 solver obtains the UNSAT result, it proves that the state on the non-automatic machine of this property is the unacceptable state of the system. At this time, backtracking is required, and the top element $<stmtx, statex>$ of the backtracking stack is taken out to judge the path from near to far.

Whether the searched node has other unsearched paths $<state_1, p_1, state_2 >$, use the intersection operation of $<state_1, p_1, state_2 >$ and $rst_1$. According to the operation result, execute (2) or (3), if the intersection of the unsearched path of the backtracking path node and rst1 always results in UNSAT, until the node on the backtracking path no longer has any unsearched path, go to (8) .

(4) Advance the LNFG node pointer to the next state, take out the arcs $<state_2,$ $p_2, state_3 >$ emitted by the next state and the state rstn updated after the OOAST interpretation is executed, and use the Z3 solver to start within the constraint range of this property The system state rstn performs the intersection operation with $<state_2, p_2, state_3 >$, and executes (2) or (3) respectively according to the operation result. When the LNFG node pointer advances to the termination state of LNFG, or the position of the statement executed by OOAST interpretation triggers the current property The position of prop_end that is not constrained by an automaton, turn (5) or (6) or (7) according to the execution of the algorithm.

(5) The LNFG node pointer is advanced to the termination state of LNFG, and the OOAST interpretation and execution just ends, the output verification result is that the system does not meet the expected property, and the counter-example path is prompted according to the content of the result automaton.

(6) The LNFG node pointer is not advanced to the termination state of LNFG, and the OOAST interpretation and execution within the property constraint ends, the output verification result is that the system does not meet the expected property, and the counterexample path is prompted according to the content of the result automaton.

(7) The LNFG node pointer is advanced to the LNFG termination state, and the OOAST interpretation and execution within the constraint is not completed, the output verification result is that the system does not meet the expected property, and the counterexample path is prompted according to the content of the result automaton.

(8) The output verification result is that the system satisfies the expected property.

The above model checking operations (1)-(8) is completed using Fig. 5.

## 2.7   Counter Example Path

In Algorithm 2, for the operation whose intersection result is SAT, the result automaton will be dynamically expanded using the corresponding state of the system state $rst_n$ and the non-automatic machine LNFG, because the result automaton and the set of counterexample paths are independent structures, and the result of SAT or UNSAT is obtained. There are different situations when there are different situations, and this section explains its decision rules in detail.

(1) The resulting automaton is composed of multiple arcs connected end to end, and has a starting state and an ending state. The type of the resulting

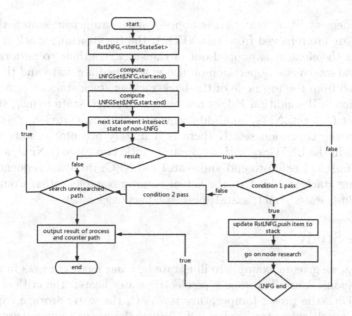

**Fig. 5.** Algorithm flowchart of Java model checking algorithm

automaton arc is $<$[stmt$_x$, state$_x$], rst$_n$, [stmt$_y$, state$_y$]$>$, where [stmt$_x$, state$_x$] and [stmt$_y$, state$_y$] represent, and stmtx and $q_x$ represent the statements and properties in the syntax tree, respectively. For the state node in the automaton, during the intersection operation, since the intersection result is SAT, the stmtx and statex states are merged, rstn represents the content on the arc, and the arc on the automaton represents $<$[stmt$_x$, state$_x$], rst$_n$, [stmt$_y$, state$_y$]$>$, [stmt$_x$, state$_x$] state is migrated to [stmt$_y$, state$_y$] state through statement execution result rstn, the state sequence in the counter example path set is $<$[stmt$_x$, state$_x$], rst$_n$,[stmt$_y$, state$_y$], rst$_{n+1}$, [stmt$_z$, state$_z$]$>$.

(2) If the Z3 solver determines the satisfiability of $<$stmt$_x$, rst$_n$, stmt$_y>$ and the arc $<$state$_x$, p$_n$, state$_y>$ of the non-automatic machine LNFG, there are two cases, one of which is that the property is not The state on the automaton LNFG is an acceptable state of the system, which satisfies the dynamic expansion result automaton condition; the other is that there is an infinitely acceptable condition c of LNFG that satisfies c is included in the union sset of the states on all automata. The following definitions describe the conditions for dynamically expanding the resulting automata to construct counterexample paths.

**Definition 2.** Condition of dynamic expansion result automaton rstLNFG, construct counterexample path condition:

Condition 1: If state [stmt$_1$, state$_1$] and arc$<$[stmt$_0$, state$_0$], rst, [stmt$_1$, stateSet$_1$]$>$, calculate the union sset of all states on the path from state [stmt$_1$, state$_1$] to state [stmt$_x$, state$_x$] in rstLNFG, if there is an infinite receiving condition c of LNFG in LNFGSet that satisfies csset, it will backtrack to the top of the stack Element [stmt, stateSet] is popped, and state [stmt, stateSet] and its associated arc are removed from rstLNFG. If the backtracking stack is still not empty after the element is popped out of the stack, continue to perform model checking and intersection operation on the unsearched arc state and the system state ejected from the top node of the backtracking stack stack.

Condition 2: If condition 1 does not hold, add a new state [$stmt_1$, $state_1$] to the state set $Q$ of rstLNFG, and add a new arc <[$stmt_0$, $stateSet_0$], rst, [$stmt_1$, $state_1$]> to the transition set. If there is a finitely acceptable state (that is, $state_1 \rightsquigarrow F$) in the LNFGSet with a non-automatic two-tuple (LNFG, start:end) that satisfies stmt1 equal to end and state1 is LNFG, the state sequence in the backtracking stack is added to the set of counterexample paths. CountExam-PathSet. Push state [stmt1, state1] onto the backtrack stack.

## 3   Case Study

In following, we give an example to illustrate how our method works in verifying a Java program. A small storage-type electric water heater, the critical temperature is 50 °C, the preset temperature is 75 °C, the water storage capacity is 80L, and the critical water level is 20L. When the water temperature is lower than 50 °C and the water level is greater than 20L, the water heater starts to heat until the water temperature reaches the preset temperature (75 °C for a fixed temperature), and when the temperature drops by 5 °C, it enters the heating state; when the water level is lower than 20L, the automatic water injection mode is turned on. Until maximum capacity is reached; cycle sequentially.

System properties are annotated in Java code through JPSL statements. As Follows, the problem is structured into three classes, namely the System class, the Water class, and the Heater class. The electric water heater is abstracted into the System class, and there are two member variables under the class, namely Heater and Water objects. Using the constructor of the System class can control the changes of the heater and water volume in the water heater, and realize the hot water function of the water heater. The property of the system is described using JPSL statements as follows:

(1) if the software designer needs the properties to be verified, it means that the water level of the water heater can never be lower than 20L. Before definition.
(2) if the software designer needs to verify the properties to indicate that the total water volume in the electric water heater is between 20L and 80L, the description is JPSL statement @JPSL PRE(watrt.vol>=20&&water.vol<=80), marked before the System() function declaration.
(3) if the software designer needs to verify the properties to indicate that the state of the electric water heater is always in repeated heating and non-heating, the start and end positions of the Heater function are marked with the start and end of the JPSL code segment respectively. Comments, described as @JPSL REPEAT(state=0, state=1), are marked before the first statement of the code segment and after the last statement.

```
public class Water {
        int vol = 0 ;
        int temper = 0;
        Water water;
        Water(){};
}
public class Heater {
        int mintemper = 50;
        int maxtemper = 75;
        int state = 0;
        Heater(Water water){
//@JPSL(content=''SEC_BEGIN REPEAT(state=0,state=1)'')
                if(water.temper<this.mintemper){
                        this.state = 1;
                        water.temper = water.temper+1;
                        if(water.temper!=this.maxtemper)
                          {
                          this.state = 0;
                        }else{
                          water.temper= water.temper+1;
                        }
                }else{
                        water.temper=water.temper-5;
                        water.vol = water.vol-2;
                        //@JPSL(content=''SEC_END'')
                }
        }
}
}
//@JPSL(content=''ALWAYS(!(water.vol<20))'')
public class System {
        Water water;
        Heater heater;
//@JPSL(content=''PRE(water.vol>=20&&water.vol<=80)'')
        System(){
                this.water = new Water();
                this.water.vol = 10;
                this.heater=new Heater(this.water);
        }
}
```

The constructor System() of the System class is the execution entry function of the electric water heater. The constructor of the Heater object is executed this.Heater = new Heater(this.water), and is marked with the JPSL code segment property statement @JPSL SEC_BEGIN REPEAT(state=0, state=1) and the annotation @JPSL SEC_END A property of the code segment in the function, indicating that the statement segment keeps the state of the electric water heater in repeated heating and non-heating.

**Fig. 6.** The OOAST structure constructed by JMC

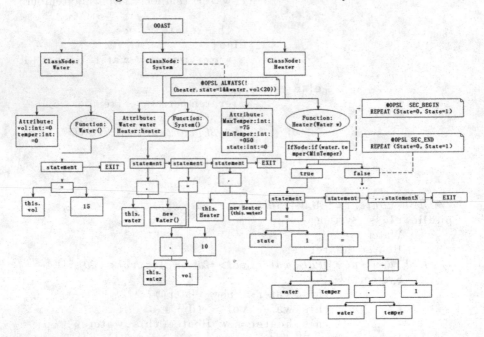

**Fig. 7.** The logical structure of OOAST

Then, use the JMC tool to perform lexical and syntactic analysis on the Java program marked with JPSL, construct an object-oriented abstract syntax tree with additional JPSL properties, and perform complete and consistent verification. The abstract syntax tree constructed in this case using the JMC tool is shown in the Fig. 6, the OOAST logical structure is shown in Fig. 7.

Next, convert each JPSL statement in the OOAST into a PPTL property formula two-tuple (pptl_prop, map), and construct the corresponding property non-automaton LNFG after negating the PPTL formula pptl_prop.

Taking the JPSL properties marked on the System class as an example, the original JPSL properties are:

$$@JPSL\ ALWAYS(!(water.vol < 20))$$

After conversion, the 2-tuple of the PPTL property formula is:

$$(\Box(\neg p), p : water.vol < 20)$$

Among them, $\Box(\neg p)$ is the PPTL property formula obtained by conversion, and the atomic proposition p represents the predicate formula water.vol<20. Negate the PPTL property formula $\Box(\neg p)$ to be $\Diamond p$, and construct a property non-automatic machine $G = (CL(P), EL(P), v0, Vf)$ as shown in Fig. 8, where $CL(P) = \{q_1, q_2, q_3, q_4\}$, $EL(P) = \{< q_1, true, q_2 >, < q_2, true, q_2 >, < q_2, p, q_3 >, < q_3, true, q_4 >, < q_3, true, q_4 > . < q_1, p, q_4 >, < q_4, true, q_4 >\}$, $q1, \{(q_2)[1], (q_3)[-1], (q_4[1])\}\}$, the properties of non-automatic machines constructed using JMC are shown in Fig. 8.

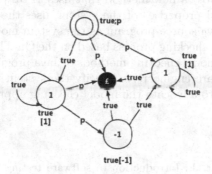

**Fig. 8.** Non-Automata by JMC

Finally, run the JMC tool to execute OOAST to dynamically generate the system states, and compute the intersection automata with the LNFG of the JPSL statement according to its constraint range. The final result is shown in Fig. 9. There is an acceptable path in the automaton, the system does not meet the expected properties, the system is insecure, and an error occurs from the first line of the source program. The water heater filling procedure described by the current model cannot meet the minimum water requirement of 20L for heating mode.

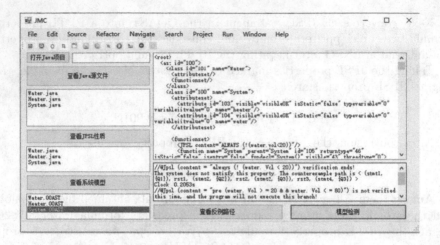

**Fig. 9.** Verification result and counterexample path

## 4   Conclusion

In this paper, we propose a new method that uses JPSL properties to precisely constrain the expected properties of the system, uses the abstract syntax tree constructed by the Java source program as the system model, and incorporates the two into the model checking process based on the On-The-Fly strategy. Compared to the existing model checking methods of Java programs, JPSL can easily be mastered by software engineers to specify the system properties while programming, and helps to advocate the model checking approach to the industry.

## References

1. Ammann, P., Offutt, J.: Introduction to software testing. Cambridge University Press (2008)
2. Shu, X., Duan, Z., Hongwei, D.: A decision procedure and complete axiomatization for projection temporal logic. Theor. Comput. Sci. **819**, 50–84 (2020)
3. Wolper, P.: The Meaning of "Formal." Int. J. Softw. Tools Technol. Transfer **1**(1-2), 6–8 (1997)
4. Wing, J., Woodcock, J.: The first world congress on formal methods in the development of computing systems. Form Aspects Comput. **12**, 145–146 (2000)
5. Dodani, M.: Formal methods for object-oriented software engineering. Ann. Softw. Eng. **2**, 121–160 (1996)
6. Kammüller, F.: Formal modeling and analysis with humans in infrastructures for IoT health care systems. In: Tryfonas, T. (ed.) HAS 2017. LNCS, vol. 10292, pp. 339–352. Springer, Cham (2017). https://doi.org/10.1007/978-3-319-58460-7_24
7. Clarke, E.M., Henzinger, T.A., Veith, H.: Introduction to model checking. In: Handbook of Model Checking, pp. 1–26. Springer, Cham (2018). https://doi.org/10.1007/978-3-319-10575-8_1

8. Baier, C., Haverkort, B.R., Hermanns, H., et al.: Model-checking algorithms for continuous-time Markov chains. IEEE Trans. Software Eng. **29**(06), 524–541 (2003)
9. Cui, J., Duan, Z., Tian, C., Hongwei, D.: A novel approach to modeling and verifying real-time systems for high reliability. IEEE Trans. Reliability **67**(02), 481–493 (2018)
10. Probst, C.W., Kammüller, F., Hansen, R.R.: Formal modelling and analysis of socio-technical systems. Lect. Notes Comput. Sci. **9560**, 54–73 (2015)
11. Liu, W.W., Song, F., Zhang, T.H.R., et al.: Verifying ReLU neural networks from a model checking perspective. J. Comput. Sci. Technol. **35**, 1365–1381 (2020)
12. Li, X.: Research on technologies of model checking Java program with MSVL and JPSL, Master Thesis, Xi'an University of Posts and Telecommunications (2021)
13. Arnold, K., Gosling, J., Holmes, D.: Java programming language (4th Edition). Addison-Wesley Professional (2005)
14. Duan, Z., Tian, C., Zhang, N.: A canonical form based decision procedure and model checking approach for propositional projection temporal logic. Theoret. Comput. Sci. **609**, 544–560 (2016)
15. Shu, X., Zhang, N.: An efficient decision procedure for propositional projection temporal logic. In: Du, D.-Z., Duan, Z., Tian, C. (eds.) COCOON 2019. LNCS, vol. 11653, pp. 503–515. Springer, Cham (2019). https://doi.org/10.1007/978-3-030-26176-4_42
16. Shu, X., Luo, N., Wang, B., Wang, X., Zhao, L.: Model checking java programs with MSVL. In: Duan, Z., Liu, S., Tian, C., Nagoya, F. (eds.) SOFL+MSVL 2018. LNCS, vol. 11392, pp. 89–107. Springer, Cham (2019). https://doi.org/10.1007/978-3-030-13651-2_6
17. Ben-Ari, M.: On-the-fly garbage collection: new algorithms inspired by program proofs. In: Nielsen, M., Schmidt, E.M. (eds.) ICALP 1982. LNCS, vol. 140, pp. 14–22. Springer, Heidelberg (1982). https://doi.org/10.1007/BFb0012753
18. Mcmillan, K.L.: Interpolants from Z3 proofs. In: 2011 International Conference on Formal Methods in Computer-aided Design (FMCAD) Inc, pp. 19–27 (2011)
19. Shu, X., Zhang, N., Wang, X., Zhao, L.: Efficient decision procedure for propositional projection temporal logic. Theor. Comput. Sci. **838**, 1–16 (2020)

# Model Analysis and Tool Implementation

# Implementation of Matlab matfun Toolkit Based on MSVL

Xueqing Feng, Nan Zhang(✉), and Zhenhua Duan(✉)

Institute of Computing Theory and Technology, ISN Laboratory, Xidian University,
Xi'an 710071, China
{xueqingfeng,nanzhang}@xidian.edu.cn, zhhduan@mail.xidian.edu.cn

**Abstract.** The matfun toolkit of the scientific computing software Matlab contains more than 40 commonly used matrix computing related functions, which have important applications in artificial intelligence, big data and other fields. This paper makes use of the modeling, simulation and verification language MSVL to imitate all basic functions in the matfun function library, and gives several representative function algorithms and implementation details. Finally we use these functions to design and implement a practical application.

**Keywords:** Matlab · Linear Algebra · matfun Toolkit · MSVL · Simulation · Application

## 1 Introduction

Matlab is a software widely used in scientific computing. It has dozens of toolkits, among which matfun (matrix and numerical linear algebra function library) contains more than forty functions commonly used in matrix operations, including the familiar functions of basic matrix operations (rank, det, inv, etc.), and some more complex functions for extracting matrix features (lu, eig, svd, etc.). These functions are widely used in many fields related to numerical computing. However, because Matlab software has certain intellectual property, therefore, it is necessary for us to develop a software toolkit with similar functions and have its own intellectual property.

MSVL is a modeling, simulation, and verification language that can be used to model, simulate, and verify hardware and software systems. It can be used to verify Web services, Petri nets, C programs, concurrent systems, and virtual memory management systems.

The reason why we choose MSVL as the language to implement Matlab functions is two-fold: (1) MSVL can be used to implement and verify functions in Matlab; (2) The developed applications using the new Matlab could also be verified in a convenient way.

The contributions of the paper are as follows: (1) We use the simulation function of MSVL to implement the matfun toolkit, including forty functions of five modules i.e. matrix analysis, linear equations, eigenvalues and singular values, matrix functions,

---

The research is supported by the National Natural Science Foundation of China under Grant No. 61133001, 61572386, 61420106004 and 91418201.

and decomposition tools. (2) Implemented Principal Component Analysis (PCA) applications in the field of machine learning using the developed toolkit.

The rest of the paper is organized as follows: in the next section, the MSVL language is briefly introduced; the five modules in matfun toolkit and the main functions of each module are described. Then, a practical application of matrix computing using the functional design is implemented in Sect. 3. Finally, conclusions are drawn in Sect. 4.

## 2   The Design and Implementation of Matfun Toolkit

### 2.1   MSVL

MSVL (Modeling, Simulation, Verification Language) [1,2] is a parallel logic programming language that can be used to model, simulate, and verify hardware and software systems. It can be used to verify Web services, Petri nets, C programs, concurrent systems, virtual memory management systems, etc. MSVL is based on PTL (Projection Temporal Logic) [3–7].

MSVL can be compiled and executed as well as interpreted in a convenient way. In this paper, MSVL compiler (MC II) is used to execute MSVL programs [8].

### 2.2   Function Implementation Method

#### 2.2.1   Matfun

The manfun toolkit in Matlab includes five modules: matrix analysis, linear equations, eigenvalues and singular values, matrix functions and decomposition tools. Each module consists of several main functions and some sub-functions encapsulated by the main functions. In the following, we will specifically introduce the approaches of implementing the main functions in each module and the relationship between some relevant functions and the main functions (Fig. 1).

#### 2.2.2   The Main Functions of Five Modules

The most important function in the matrix analysis module is rref (Gaussian elimination method), which can clearly show some characteristics of the matrix, such as the solution of the equation system, by reducing the matrix to the simplest row. Based on the rref function, rank (the rank of the matrix), det (the determinant) and so on can be implemented.

The main functions of the linear equation module include / and \ (linear equation solving), inv (matrix inverse), pinv(matrix pseudo-inverse) [9], lu (matrix lu decomposition), qr (orthogonal triangular decomposition). / and \ are unique symbols for solving linear equations in Matlab, representing right division and left division, respectively. Right division means solving linear equations xA = B and left division means solving linear equations Ax = B. The inv is a row reduction based on Gaussian elimination. The lu decomposition is an important decomposition, which can decompose the matrix A into an upper triangular matrix U and a permuted lower triangular matrix L, so that A = L * U [10]. The qr decomposition of the matrix decomposes the matrix A into the

| module | function | explanation | function | explanation |
|---|---|---|---|---|
| matrix analysis | norm | norm of a matrix or vector | null | null space orthogonal basis |
| | normest | estimation of the 2-norm of a matrix | orth | orthogonalization |
| | rank | rank of the matrix | rref | reduced row echelon format |
| | det | determinant | subspace | the angle between two sub-spaces |
| | trace | sum of elements on the main diagonal | | |
| Linear equation | /and\ | linear equation solver | qr | orthogonal triangle decomposition |
| | chol | Cholesky decomposition | condest | 1-norm condition number evaluation |
| | cond | matrix condition number | lsqnonneg | nonnegative least squares |
| | rcond | linspace inverse condition number calculation | pinv | matrix pseudo-inverse |
| | lu | Gaussian Elimination coefficient matrix | lscov | least squares with known co-variance |
| | inv | matrix inversion | | |
| Eigenvalues and Singular Values | eig | eigenvalues and eigenvectors | eigs | several eigenvalues |
| | poly | characteristic polynomial | condeig | condition numbers corresponding to eigenvalues |
| | polyeig | polynomial eigenvalues | schur | Schur decomposition |
| | hess | Hessenberg form | balance | equilibrium (improve condition number) |
| | qz | generalized eigenvalues | svd | singular value decomposition |
| matrix function | expm | matrix index | expm2 | find matrix exponent using Taylor Series |
| | expm1 | find matrix index using M-file | expm3 | find matrix index using eigenvalues |
| | logm | matrix logarithm | funm | computation of general matrix functions |
| | sqrtm | matrix square root | | |
| decomposition tool | qrdelete | remove a column from qr decomposition | cdf2rdf | complex diagonal becomes real diagonal |
| | qrinsert | Insert a column in qr decomposition | planerot | Givens plane rotation |

**Fig. 1.** matfun

form of A = Q * R, where Q is an orthogonal matrix, and R is an upper triangular matrix whose main diagonal elements are positive.

The main functions of the Eigenvalues and Singular Values module are eig (eigenvalues and eigenvectors), svd (singular value decomposition) [11]. There are many ways to decompose eigenvalues. The method used in this paper is qr iteration. The calculation method of eigenvectors uses the definition of eigenvectors $Ax = \lambda x$, and the eigenvectors can be obtained according to the eigenvalues. The expression of svd decomposition is $A = U\Sigma V^{T}$, where $\Sigma$ is all zero except for the elements on the main diagonal, and each element on the main diagonal is called a singular value [12].

The main function of the matrix function module is the solution of the matrix index. Three methods are used in this paper, namely Padé approximation [13, 14], Taylor series approximation, and eigenvalues and eigenvectors [15, 16].

The main function in the decomposition tool module is planerot (Given's plane rotation), the expression is $[G, y] = planerot(x)$, where $x$ is a column vector containing two components, and a $2 * 2$ orthogonal matrix $G$ is obtained, such that $y = G * x$ and $y(2) = 0$ [17].

```
function qr(int row,int col,float* matrix,int row1,int col1,float* Q,int row2,int col2,float* R,int RValue){
    frame(i,j,k,length)and{
        int i,j,k and skip;
        float length and skip;
        RValue:=0;
        if(row!=col)then{
            RValue:=-1
        }
        else{
            for(k:=0;k<col;k:=k+1){
                length:=0;
                for(i:=0;i<row;i:=i+1){
                    length:=length+matrix[i,k]*matrix[i,k]
                };
                R[k,k]:=sqrt(length);
                for(i:=0;i<row;i:=i+1){
                    Q[i,k]:=matrix[i,k]/R[k,k]
                };
                for(i:=k+1;i<col;i:=i+1){
                    for(j:=0;j<row;j:=j+1){
                        R[k,i]:=R[k,i]+matrix[j,i]*Q[j,k]
                    };
                    for(j:=0;j<row;j:=j+1){
                        matrix[j,i]:=matrix[j,i]-R[k,i]*Q[j,k]
                    }
                }
            }
        }
    }
};
```

**Fig. 2.** qr decomposition

```
function e_eig(int row,int col,float* matrix,int row1,int col1,float* Q,int row2,int col2,float* R,int row3,int col3,float* eig,int RValue){
    frame(i,j,k,r)and{
        int i,j,k and skip;
        int r and skip;
        RValue:=0;
        if(row!=col)then{
            RValue:=-1
        }
        else{
            for(k:=0;k<100;k:=k+1){
                for(i:=0;i<row;i:=i+1){
                    for(j:=0;j<col;j:=j+1){
                        Q[i,j]:=0;
                        R[i,j]:=0
                    }
                };
                qr(row,col,matrix,row1,col1,Q,row2,col2,R,RValue);
                MulMatrix(row2,col2,R,row1,col1,Q,row,col,matrix,RValue)
            }
        };
        for(i:=0;i<row;i:=i+1){
            eig[i,0]:=matrix[i,i]
        }
    }
};
```

**Fig. 3.** Eigenvalue Decomposition

### 2.2.3 Example of Function Implementation

The $qr$ decomposition uses Gram-Schmidt Orthogonalization [18]. The orthogonalization process is to convert any group of bases in the Euclidean space into a standard orthogonal base, and the generated standard orthogonal base is the $Q$ matrix, and the $R$ matrix can be used in the orthogonalization process calculate (Fig. 2).

The calculation of the eigenvalues is based on an iterative $qr$ decomposition [19] (Fig. 3).

# 3  Application of PCA Implementation

In many fields of research and applications, it is usually necessary to observe data containing multiple variables, and to collect a large amount of data to analyze and find rules. Although large data sets containing multivariate will provide rich information for research and application, it also increases the workload of data collection. Therefore, it is necessary to find a reasonable method to reduce the loss of information as much as possible while to reduce the indicators to be analyzed, so as to achieve the purpose of comprehensive analysis of the collected data. Since there is a certain correlation between the variables, it can be considered to change the closely related variables into as few new variables as possible, so that these new variables are uncorrelated in pairs, then less comprehensive indicators can be used to represent them respectively. Various types of information that exist in each variable. Principal component analysis (PCA) is used for dimensionality reduction of such data [20].

The main method of PCA is to map the n-dimensional features to the new k-dimensional orthogonal features, so the k-dimensional features reconstructed on the basis of the original n-dimensional features. The k-dimensional orthogonal features are called principal components.

PCA can be implemented through a covariance matrix based on eigenvalue decomposition. For example, it is necessary to reduce the dataset $X = \{x_1, x_2, \cdots, x_n\}$ to k dimensions. The specific method is as follows:

(1) De-average (decentralization)
(2) Calculate the covariance matrix $\frac{1}{n} X X^T$
(3) Use eigenvalue decomposition (eig function) to calculate the eigenvalues and eigenvectors of the covariance matrix $\frac{1}{n} X X^T$
(4) Select the largest $k$ eigenvalues, and use the corresponding $k$ eigenvectors as row vectors to form an eigenvector matrix $P$
(5) Convert the data to a new space $Y = P * X$ constructed by $k$ eigenvectors

Assuming that the matrix $\begin{bmatrix} -1 & -1 & 0 & 2 & 0 \\ -2 & 0 & 0 & 1 & 1 \end{bmatrix}$, the matrix after PCA dimension reduction given by the MSVL compiler is $\begin{bmatrix} \frac{-3}{\sqrt{2}} & \frac{-1}{\sqrt{2}} & 0 & \frac{3}{\sqrt{2}} & \frac{-1}{\sqrt{2}} \end{bmatrix}$, indicating that the original two lines of data have been reduced to one line (Fig. 4).

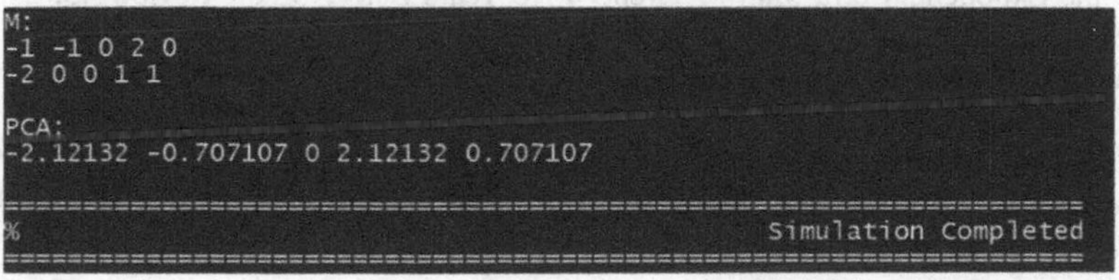

```
M:
-1 -1 0 2 0
-2 0 0 1 1

PCA:
-2.12132 -0.707107 0 2.12132 0.707107

==========================================================
%                                        Simulation Completed
==========================================================
```

**Fig. 4.** Application of PCA Implementation

## 4   Conclusion

In this paper, the functions in the matfun toolkit in Matlab are implemented by using MSVL language. The principles of the functions are studied, and the realization methods are presented. The functional capabilities are shown by implementing the commonly used dimensionality reduction method Principal Component Analysis (PCA).

## References

1. Moszkowski, B.C.: Executing Temporal Logic Programs. Cambridge University Press, Cambridge (1986)
2. Duan, Z.: Temporal Logic and Temporal Logic Programming. Science Press, Beijing (2005)
3. Duan, Z., Tian, C., Zhang, L.: A decision procedure for propositional projection temporal logic with infinite models. Acta Informatica **45**(1), 43–78 (2008)
4. Duan, Z., Yang, X., Koutny, M.: Framed temporal logic programming. Sci. Comput. Program. **70**(1), 31–61 (2008)
5. Duan, Z., Tian, C.: A practical decision procedure for propositional projection temporal logic with infinite models. Theor. Comput. Sci. **554**, 169–190 (2014)
6. Zhang, N., Duan, Z., Tian, C.: Model checking concurrent systems with MSVL. Sci. China Inf. Sci. **59**(11), 1–3 (2016)
7. Zhang, N., Duan, Z., Tian, C.: A mechanism of function calls in MSVL. Theor. Comput. Sci. **654**, 11–25 (2016)
8. Peng, Y., Duan, Z., Zhang, N.: Design and Implementation of MSVL Compiler Based on Normal Form. Xidian University (2022)
9. Pseudo-inverse Matrix. https://www.jianshu.com/p/609fa0cce409
10. Xu, D., Meng, X.: Matlab Function Library Query Dictionary. Document (2006). https://ww2.mathworks.cn/help/matlab/index.html
11. Singular Value Decomposition. https://zhuanlan.zhihu.com/p/29846048
12. Golub, G.H., Van Loan, C.F.: Matrix Computations, Sections 6.5.2-6.5.3, 4th edn., pp. 335–338. Johns Hopkins University Press, Baltimore (2013)
13. Higham, N.J.: The scaling and squaring method for the matrix exponential revisited. SIAM J. Matrix Anal. Appl. **26**(4), 1179–1193 (2005)
14. Matrix Computations. Posts and Telecom Press (2014)
15. Golub, G.H., Van Loan, C.F.: Matrix Computation, p. 384. Johns Hopkins University Press, Baltimore (1983)
16. Moler, C.B., Van Loan, C.F.: Nineteen dubious ways to compute the exponential of a matrix. SIAM Rev. **20**, 801–836 (1978). Reprinted and updated as Nineteen Dubious Ways to Compute the Exponential of a Matrix, Twenty-Five Years Later? SIAM Review 45, 2003, pp. 3–49
17. Givens Transform. https://www.cnblogs.com/reasno/p/9643529.html
18. Matlab Document. https://ww2.mathworks.cn/help/matlab/index.html
19. Linear Algebra and Its Application. China Machine Press (2020)
20. Detailed Explanation of the Principle of Principal Component Analysis (PCA). https://zhuanlan.zhihu.com/p/37777074

# Extending Visibly Pushdown Automata over Multi-matching Nested Relations

Jin Liu[1], Yeqiu Xiao[1], Haiyang Wang[1], and Wensheng Wang[2(✉)]

[1] Shaanxi Key Laboratory for Network Computing and Security Technology,
School of Computer Science and Engineering, Xi'an University of Technology,
Xi'an 710048, China
[2] Institute of Computing Theory and Technology and ISN Laboratory,
School of Computer Science and Technology, Xidian University,
Xi'an 710071, China
wwsheng889@163.com

**Abstract.** Visibly Pushdown Automata (VPAs) are a subclass of push-down automata, which can be well applied as specification formalism for verification and the model for XML streams process. The input alphabet is partitioned into three disjoint sets: call, internal and return symbols, which can determine a push, pop or no stack operation taken by VPAs respectively. Hence, the matchings of push (call) and pop (return) make languages with matching nested relations accepted. Nevertheless, it is limited to one-to-one matching. In this paper, we extend the model of VPAs over multi-matching nested relations. By a subdivision for call and return symbols, inner-calls and inner-returns are obatined to discriminate a one-to-n or n-to-one matching relation. Then, Multi-matching Visibly Pushdown Automata (MVPA) are formally defined whose stack behavior is achieved by setting a guard in the stack, which can guarantee whether a one-to-n or n-to-one matching nested relation is read without confusion. Each nondeterministic multi-matching visibly pushdown automaton is demonstrated to be transformed into a deterministic one. Moreover, the symbolic version of multi-matching visibly pushdown automata is proposed when the input alphabet is given by a Boolean algebra where there is an infinite domain.

**Keywords:** multi-matching nested relation · visibly pushdown automata · one-to-n · n-to-one · symbolic automata

## 1 Introduction

A model of nested words is proposed for describing the data with a dual linear-hierarchical structure [1]. A nested word consists of a linear sequence of positions, calls, internals and returns, augmented with matching relations connecting from calls to returns. Visibly Pushdown Automata (VPAs) are proposed over nested

This research is supported by the NSFC Grant Nos. 62202371 and 61902312.

words by Alur in [2] as a subclass of Pushdown Automata (PDAs) [3]. VPAs are well applied as the automaton model for processing XML streams [4,5] and specification formalism for verification [6,7]. The key character is that the alphabet in VPAs is partitioned into three disjoint sets of call, internal, and return symbols. Based on the partition, VPAs can push symbols into the stack by reading a call, pop the top of the stack by a return, and via an internal, VPAs only modify the state with the stack unchanged. Hence, this setting makes the stack behavior visible. In classical automata theory, there are two basic assumptions: a finite state space and a finite alphabet. The concept of automata with predicates instead of concrete symbols was first mentioned in [8] and was first discussed in [9] in the context of natural language processing. Accordingly, Symbolic Visibly Pushdown Automata (SVPAs) are proposed as an executable model for nested words over infinite alphabets [10], which are further applied in XML processing and program trace analysis [11].

Nevertheless, the models above are limited to describe only one-to-one matching structures. If a call (resp. return) is matched with multiple returns (resp. calls), a one-to-n (resp. n-to-one) multi-matching nested relation is obtained. By introducing a tagged alphabet, multi-matching nested words are defined where symbols can be calls, inner-calls, internals, inner-returns and returns. Multi-matching Nested Traceable Automata (MNTAs) are proposed to describe the languages of multi-matching nested words [12–14], which is an variant of Traceable Automata (TAs) and VPAs. In a MNTA, both of states and input symbols, which are recorded in the stack, are utilized to determine the subsequent transitions together. For a call, the current input symbol and state are pushed into the stack, while for a return they are popped. Note that the automaton traces back to the state which is popped then. As for inner-calls and inner-returns, the top stack is updated besides state transfer.

However, natural nondeterminization exists in MNTAs if there are several calls at a state. Suppose two calls $\widehat{a}$ and $\widehat{b}$ can be read at a state $q$, one cannot construct a MNTA such that $\widehat{a}$ is certain to read indeed ahead of $\widehat{b}$. In addition, the characteristic that a state is pushed at a call and finally traced back upon a return makes MNTAs accept languages always beyond a single multi-matching nested relation. With this motivation, we loosen the restriction on stack behavior of MNTAs by eliminating the record of states from the stack. Only symbols are recorded as a guard during transitions. Accordingly, Multi-matching Visibly Pushdown Automata (MVPAs) are proposed as a new model for describing multi-matching nested words. And nondeterministic MVPAs are as expressive as deterministic ones. In addition, if the input alphabet is given by a Boolean algebra where there is an infinite domain, symbolic version of multi-matching visibly pushdown automata is formally proposed.

The rest of paper is organized as follows. In Sect. 2, we revisit the definitions of multi-matching nested relations and its linear word encoding. Section 3 extends visibly pushdown automata over multi-matching relations. Multi-matching visibly pushdown automata are formally defined. Besides, a deterministic MVPA can be constructed for a nondeterministic one. When the input alphabet is given by a Boolean algebra where there is an infinite domain, symbolic version of multi-matching visibly pushdown automata is proposed in Sect. 4. Finally, conclusions are drawn in Sect. 5.

## 2  Preliminaries

In this section, we first recall the concept of multi-matching nested relations. By linear word encodings, multi-matching nested languages can be obtained.

### 2.1  Multi-matching Nested Relation

Given a linear sequence, the positions are divided into *calls*, *internals* and *returns*. To realize n-to-one and one-to-n matchings, *inner-call* and *inner-return* are introduced. Hence, n-to-one matching relation can be achieved by a call, multiple inner-calls and a return, while one-to-n by a call, multiple inner-returns and a return. Suppose pending edges are indicated by edges starting at $-\infty$ and edges ending at $+\infty$. Assume that $-\infty < i, j < +\infty$ for integers $i$ and $j$.

**Definition 1 (Multi-matching Nested Relation).** *A multi-matching nested relation $\rightsquigarrow$ of length $m$, $m \geqslant 0$, is a subset of $\{-\infty, 1, 2, \cdots, m\} \times \{1, 2, \cdots, m, +\infty\}$ such that for any $i \rightsquigarrow j$, $i' \rightsquigarrow j'$, (i) nesting edges go only forward($i < j$); (ii) nesting edges do not cross($i < i' \leqslant j < j'$ does not hold); (iii) only one end of a nesting edge can be shared with others.*

For $i \rightsquigarrow j$, $i, j$ are denoted as a call and a return respectively. Specifically, if $j = +\infty$, $i$ is called a *pending call* while $j$ is denoted a *pending return* if $i = -\infty$. Suppose there are $n$ different nesting edges sharing the same call $i$, namely $i \rightsquigarrow j_k$, where $1 \leqslant k \leqslant n$ and $1 \leqslant i < j_1 < j_2 < \cdots < j_n \leqslant m$. Among them, $i \rightsquigarrow j_n$ is the outermost nesting edge. By contrast, for each inner nesting edge, $j_h$ is identified as an *inner-return* where $1 \leqslant h < n$. Similarly, for $n$ different nesting edges sharing the same return $j$, namely $i_k \rightsquigarrow j$, where $1 \leqslant i_1 < i_2 < \cdots < i_n < j \leqslant m$, each $i_h$, $1 < h \leqslant n$, is identified as an *inner-return*. A position is an *internal* if it is neither a call (resp. inner-call) nor a return (resp. inner-return). A multi-matching nested relation is *well-matched* if there is no *pending call* or *pending return*.

### 2.2  Word Encoding

Given a multi-matching nested relation, a word can be obtained by assigning each position with a symbol. To distinguish different position categories, a tagged alphabet $\hat{\Sigma} = \Sigma_c \cup \dot{\Sigma}_c \cup \Sigma_i \cup \dot{\Sigma}_r \cup \Sigma_r$ is introduced, where $\Sigma_c = \{\stackrel{\frown}{a_1} | a_1 \in \Sigma\}$, $\dot{\Sigma}_c = \{\stackrel{\frown}{a_2} | a_2 \in \Sigma\}$, $\Sigma_i = \Sigma$, $\dot{\Sigma}_r = \{\stackrel{.}{a_3}\!\!\stackrel{\frown}{} | a_3 \in \Sigma\}$ and $\Sigma_r = \{a_4\!\!\stackrel{\frown}{} | a_4 \in \Sigma\}$ are the symbols of call, inner-call, internal, inner-return and return, respectively. $\Sigma$ is a normal alphabet. Note that $\stackrel{\frown}{a_1}$, $\stackrel{\frown}{a_2}$, $\stackrel{.}{a_3}\!\!\stackrel{\frown}{}$ and $a_4\!\!\stackrel{\frown}{}$ are indicated to be matched if and only if $a_1 = a_2 = a_3 = a_4$.

The set of all multi-matching nested words over $\hat{\Sigma}$ are denoted as $MNW(\hat{\Sigma})$. Note that due to the requirement of symbol matching, it can be obtained $MNW(\hat{\Sigma}) \subset \hat{\Sigma}^*$.

# 3  Multi-matching Visibly Pushdown Automata

## 3.1  Model

**Definition 2 (Multi-matching Visibly Pushdown Automata, MVPA).**
*A multi-matching visibly pushdown automaton is a tuple $M = (Q, Q_0, F, \hat{\Sigma}, \Gamma, \delta)$, where*

- $Q$, $Q_0 \subseteq Q$, $F \subseteq Q$ *are finite sets of states, initial states, final states respectively;*
- $\hat{\Sigma} = \Sigma_c \cup \dot{\Sigma}_c \cup \Sigma_i \cup \dot{\Sigma}_r \cup \Sigma_r$ *is a finite set of input symbols, where $\Sigma_c$, $\dot{\Sigma}_c$, $\Sigma_i$, $\dot{\Sigma}_r$ and $\Sigma_r$ denote call, inner-call, internal, inner-return and return symbols, respectively;*
- $\Gamma \subseteq (\Sigma_c \cup \dot{\Sigma}_c \cup \dot{\Sigma}_r) \times \Xi \cup \{\bot\}$ *is a finite set of stack elements including a special bottom-of-stack symbol $\bot$, where $\Xi$ is a finite alphabet; and*
- $\delta$ *is a finite set of transitions consisting of the following four parts:*

$$\delta_c \subseteq Q \times \Sigma_c \times Q \times (\Sigma_c \times \Xi)$$
$$\delta_i \subseteq Q \times \Sigma_i \times Q$$
$$\delta_u \subseteq Q \times \Gamma \times (\dot{\Sigma}_c \cup \dot{\Sigma}_r) \times Q \times \Gamma$$
$$\delta_r \subseteq Q \times \Gamma \times \Sigma_r \times Q$$

The transitions in $M$ can be classified into four categories. Let $q, q' \in Q$, $\gamma, \gamma' \in \Gamma$, $\overset{\frown}{a} \in \Sigma_c$, $\dot{\overset{\frown}{a}} \in \dot{\Sigma}_c$, $i \in \Sigma_i$, $\dot{\overset{\frown}{a}} \in \dot{\Sigma}_r$ and $\overset{\frown}{a} \in \Sigma_r$. For convenience, we use notation $a/b$ to denote $a$ or $b$.

1. call transition (push transition): $(q, \overset{\frown}{a}, q', \overset{\frown}{a}\xi) \in \delta_c$
   When reading a call $\overset{\frown}{a}$ at state $q$, $M$ turns to state $q'$, meanwhile both the call $\overset{\frown}{a}$ and the symbol $\xi \in \Xi$ are pushed into the stack.
2. internal transition: $(q, i, q') \in \delta_i$
   For an internal $i$, the operation is similar to the usual finite automata, $M$ only updates the state from $q$ to $q'$ without the stack modified.
3. update transition: $(q, \gamma, x, q', \gamma') \in \delta_u$
   (a) Upon an inner-call $x = \dot{\overset{\frown}{a}}$, it is noteworthy that the symbol of the top stack must be $\overset{\frown}{a}$ or $\dot{\overset{\frown}{a}}$ stating that it is the same as or matched with the input symbol. Then, the state is updated to $q'$ and the top of the stack modifies from $\gamma = \overset{\frown}{a}\xi/\dot{\overset{\frown}{a}}\xi$ to $\gamma' = \dot{\overset{\frown}{a}}\xi'$ where $\xi, \xi' \in \Xi$. Hence, this transition is denoted as a call update one.
   (b) As for an inner-return $x = \dot{\overset{\frown}{a}}$, it is similar to the case of inner-calls. Besides $M$ turns to $q'$, the top of the stack is modified from $\gamma_1 = \overset{\frown}{a}\xi/\dot{\overset{\frown}{a}}\xi$ to $\gamma_2 = \dot{\overset{\frown}{a}}\xi'$ where $\xi, \xi' \in \Xi$.
4. return transition (pop transition): $(q, \gamma, \overset{\frown}{a}, q') \in \delta_r$
   (a) In a return transition with the input return $\overset{\frown}{a}$, suppose that the top of the stack is $\gamma = x\xi$. Symbol $x$ can only be one of $\overset{\frown}{a}$, $\dot{\overset{\frown}{a}}$ or $\dot{\overset{\frown}{a}}$, since $x$ must be matched with $\overset{\frown}{a}$. Then $M$ turns to $q'$ and $\gamma$ is popped.
   (b) In particularly, when the stack is empty, i.e. $\gamma = \bot$, only the state is updated and the stack remains unchanged.

Formally, a stack $\sigma$ is a finite word over the set $\Gamma$. All stacks constitute the set $St = (\Gamma\backslash\{\bot\})^* \cdot \{\bot\}$. Let $|\sigma|$ stand for the length of $\sigma$. Especially, when $\sigma = \bot$, $|\sigma| = 0$; otherwise $|\sigma| > 0$.

A *configuration* of $M$ is a pair $(q, \sigma)$ where $q \in Q$ and $\sigma \in St$. Given a word $w = w_1 w_2 \cdots w_n$ with multi-matching nest relations, $w$ can be accepted by $M$ if there exists a run of $M$ on $w$. A *run* $\rho$ is defined as a non-empty sequence of configurations, i.e. $\rho = (q_0, \sigma_0) \xrightarrow{w_1} (q_1, \sigma_1) \xrightarrow{w_2} \cdots \xrightarrow{w_n} (q_n, \sigma_n)$, where $q_0 \in Q_0$ is an initial state and $\sigma_0 = \bot$. $\rho$ is accepted by $M$ if $q_n \in F$ is a final state and $\sigma_n \in (\Sigma_c \times \Xi)^* \cdot \{\bot\}$. In another word, when $M$ terminates, no inner-call or inner-return symbols are allowed to exist in the stack, since only well-matched or pending calls/returns are considered. The case of a call and multiple inner-calls without a return (or multiple inner-returns and a return without a call) is illegal. The set of multi-matching nested words that are accepted by $M$ constitutes the language $L(M)$.

## 3.2   Determinization

Given a multi-matching visibly pushdown automaton $M = (Q, q_0, F, \hat{\Sigma}, \Gamma, \delta)$, $M$ is called to be deterministic if $q_0$ is the unique initial state in $M$. Besides, for each transition $q \in Q$, $\gamma \in \Gamma$ and $x \in \hat{\Sigma}$, there is at most one transition for $\delta(q, \gamma, x)$.

As shown in [2], the main idea of transformation from a nondeterministic MVPA to an equivalent deterministic one is the subset construction with call transitions postponed handling. To do this, two components $S$ and $R$ are introduced, where $S$ is a set of *summary edges* that keeps track of what transitions are possible from a call transition to a matched return one, and $R$ is a set of reachable states by using the summary information. However, in MVPAs, update transitions require special treatments.

Let $w = w_1 \ulcorner a w_2 x w_3$ accepted by a MVPA $M$, where $w_1$, $w_2$ and $w_3$ are well-matched words where there are no pending calls or returns. One can construct an equivalent deterministic MVPA. After reading call $\ulcorner a$, the stack of $M$ is now $(\ulcorner a \lceil S_1, R_1 \rfloor) \bot$ and $M$ turns to state $\lceil S, R \rfloor$. All possible pairs $(q, q')$ are included in $S_1$ such that $M$ can get on $w_1$ from $q$ with empty stack $\bot$ to $q'$ with empty stack $\bot$. $R_1$ contains all reachable states by $M$ from any initial state on $w_1$. Then, several situations are taken into consideration.

1. If $x \in \Sigma_c$ is a new call, the stack then is $(x \lceil S_2, R_2 \rfloor)(\ulcorner a \lceil S_1, R_1 \rfloor) \bot$. $S_2$ contains all pairs such that the stack of $M$ updates from $\ulcorner a \xi \bot$ to $\ulcorner a \xi \bot$. $R_2$ records reachable states by $M$ on $w_2$.
2. When $x = \ulcorner a \in \Sigma_c$ is an inner-call, the stack is updated to $(\ulcorner a \lceil S_1', R_1 \rfloor) \bot$. Then $S_1' = S_1 \cup \{q, q'\}$ where $(q, q')$ records the summary such that $M$ can get from $q$ with $\ulcorner a \xi \bot$ to $q'$ with $\ulcorner a \xi \bot$.
3. On the basis of the second case, suppose the inner symbol $x$ is read for the second time, namely $w = w_1 \ulcorner a w_2 x w_3 x$. Similarly, the new updated stack is $(\ulcorner a \lceil S_1'', R_1 \rfloor) \bot$. $S_1'' = S_1' \cup \{q, q'\}$ where $(q, q')$ records the summary such that $M$ can get $w_2$ from $q$ with $\ulcorner a \xi \bot$ to $q'$ with $\ulcorner a \xi \bot$.

4. When the matched return $\overline{a}$ is read with $x$ be inner-call $\overleftarrow{a}$, that means the
   word is $w = w_1 \overleftarrow{a} w_2 \overleftarrow{a} w_3 \overline{a}$. $\overleftarrow{a}\lfloor S_1'', R_1 \rfloor$ is popped. And state is updated by
   using the current summaries $S_1''$ and $S$ along with a call transition on $\overleftarrow{a}$, a
   call update transition on $\overleftarrow{a}$ and a return transition on $\overline{a}$.

Note that the treatment for an inner-return is similar to the analysis above
for an inner-call. Accordingly, we present the determinization procedure in detail
as below.

**Theorem 1.** *Given a multi-matching visibly pushdown automaton $M$, an equivalent deterministic one $M_D$ can be constructed such that they can accept the same
language, i.e. $L(M) = L(M_D)$.*

*Proof.* For a multi-matching visibly pushdown automaton $M = (Q, Q_0, F, \hat{\Sigma},$
$\Gamma, \delta)$, one can acquire an equivalent deterministic one $M_D = (Q', Q_0', F', \hat{\Sigma},$
$\Gamma', \delta')$ according to the following constructions.

First, the set of states in $M_D$ is expanded as the set $Q' = 2^{Q \times Q} \times 2^Q$. The set
$2^{Q \times Q}$, denoted by $S$, records the summary edges within a multi-matching nested
relation accepted by $M$, i.e. from a call to an inner-call/inner-return/return
or from an inner-call (resp. inner-return) to an inner-call/return (resp. inner-
return/return), while a reachable state set can be calculated by $2^Q$, called $R$.
For convenience and clarity, we denote $Q' = \lceil S, R \rfloor$.

Let $Id_X$ indicate the set $\{(q, q) | q \in X\}$. Then, the set of initial states can
be obtained as $Q_0' = \{\lceil Id_Q, Q_0 \rfloor\}$. A state $\lceil S, R \rfloor$ is a final one if $q_f \in R$ where
$q_f \in F$. Hence, $F' = \{\lceil S, R \rfloor | R \cap F \neq \varnothing\}$.

For the set of stack elements, let $\Gamma' = \{\Sigma_c \cup \dot{\Sigma}_c \cup \dot{\Sigma}_r\} \times S \times R$ where
$\Xi = S \times R$.

For each symbol $x \in \hat{\Sigma}$, the top of stack $\gamma' \in \Gamma'$ and state $\lceil S, R \rfloor \in Q'$, the
set of transitions $\delta'$ is constructed as follows:

**Call.** When $x = \overleftarrow{a} \in \Sigma_c$ is a call, one can construct a call transition $(\lceil S, R \rfloor, \overleftarrow{a},$
$\lceil Id_{R'}, R' \rfloor, \overleftarrow{a}\lceil S, R \rfloor) \in \delta_c'$ where

$$R' = \{q' \mid \exists q \in R, \xi \in \Xi, \text{ s.t. } (q, \overleftarrow{a}, q', \overleftarrow{a}\xi) \in \delta_c\}.$$

**Internal.** For an internal $x = i \in \Sigma_i$, there is a transition $(\lceil S, R \rfloor, i, \lceil, S', R' \rfloor) \in$
$\delta_i'$ where

$$S' = \{(q, q') \mid \exists q'' \text{ s.t. } (q, q'') \in S \text{ and } (q'', i, q') \in \delta_i\},$$
$$R' = \{q' \mid \exists q \in R \text{ s.t. } (q, i, q') \in \delta_i\}.$$

**Update.** There are two cases for inner symbols.
  – **Call Update.** With regard to an inner-call $x = \overleftarrow{a} \in \dot{\Sigma}_c$, one can
    construct $(\lceil S, R \rfloor, \overleftarrow{a}\lceil S_1, R_1 \rfloor / \overleftarrow{a}\lceil S_1, R_1 \rfloor, \overleftarrow{a}, \lceil Id_{R'}, R' \rfloor, \overleftarrow{a}\lceil S_2, R_2 \rfloor) \in \delta_u'$
    where

$$R' = \{q' \mid \exists q \in R, \xi, \xi' \in \Xi, \text{ s.t. } (q, \overleftarrow{a}\xi / \overleftarrow{a}\xi, q', \overleftarrow{a}\xi') \in \delta_u\},$$
$$S_2 = S_1 \cup S,$$
$$R_2 = R_1.$$

The pair $(q, q') \in S$ records the summary such that $M$ can get after a call or call update transition, in which the state is updated to state $q$ with stack $\gamma = {}^{\curvearrowleft}a\xi / {}^{\curvearrowleft}a\xi$, to a call update transition from $q'$ with stack $\gamma' = {}^{\curvearrowleft}a\xi'$.

- **Return Update.** Similarly, when $x = \vec{a} \in \dot{\Sigma}_r$, $(\lceil S, R \rfloor, {}^{\curvearrowleft}a \lceil S'', R'' \rfloor / \vec{a} \lceil S'', R'' \rfloor, \vec{a}, \lceil Id_{R'}, R' \rfloor, \vec{a} \lceil S'', R'' \rfloor) \in \delta'_u$ can be constructed, where

$$R' = \{q' \mid \exists q \in R, \xi, \xi' \in \Xi, \text{ s.t. } (q, {}^{\curvearrowleft}a\xi / \vec{a}\,\xi, q', \vec{a}\,\xi') \in \delta_u\},$$
$$S_2 = S_1 \cup S,$$
$$R_2 = R_1.$$

**Return.** When a return $x = \vec{a}$ is read, any type of call, inner-call, inner-return or return symbol can be met at the top of the stack since they are all matched with $x$. Especially, the stack can also be empty. Hence, four cases are taken into consideration as follows. Suppose the return transition is constructed as $(\lceil S, R \rfloor, y \lceil S'', R'' \rfloor, \vec{a}, \lceil S', R' \rfloor) \in \delta'_r$. *Update* is a set of state pairs in $S$.

- If $y = {}^{\curvearrowleft}a$, let

$$Update = \{(q, q') \mid \exists q_1, q_2 \in Q, \xi \in \Xi \text{ s.t. } (q, {}^{\curvearrowleft}a, q_1, {}^{\curvearrowleft}a\xi) \in \delta_c, (q_1, q_2) \in S$$
$$\text{and } (q_2, {}^{\curvearrowleft}a\xi, \vec{a}, q') \in \delta_r\}.$$

Then the two components of the state $(S', R')$ satisfy conditions

$$S' = \{(q, q') \mid \exists p \text{ s.t. } (q, p) \in S'' \text{ and } (p, q') \in Update)\}$$
$$R' = \{q' \mid \exists q \text{ s.t. } q \in R'' \text{ and } (q, q') \in Update\}.$$

In this case, the matching nested relation has only a one-to-one matching structure.

- When $y = {}^{\curvearrowleft}\dot{a}$, it indicates that an n-to-one matching relation is currently read. The set *Update* is defined as:

$$Update = \{(q_0, q) \mid \exists q \in Q, (q_i, q'_i) \in S'', (q_S, q'_S) \in S, \xi, \xi' \in \Xi, 0 \leqslant i \leqslant n,$$
$$n \geqslant 1, \text{ s.t. } (q'_0, {}^{\curvearrowleft}a, q_1, {}^{\curvearrowleft}a\xi) \in \delta_c (i = 0),$$
$$(q'_i, {}^{\curvearrowleft}a\xi / {}^{\curvearrowleft}\dot{a}\xi, {}^{\curvearrowleft}\dot{a}, q_{i+1}, {}^{\curvearrowleft}\dot{a}\xi') \in \delta_u (0 < i < n),$$
$$(q'_n, {}^{\curvearrowleft}\dot{a}\xi, {}^{\curvearrowleft}\dot{a}, q_S, {}^{\curvearrowleft}a\xi') \in \delta_u,$$
$$(q'_S, {}^{\curvearrowleft}\dot{a}\xi, \vec{a}, q) \in \delta_r\}.$$

The value of $n$ needs to be larger than 1, since in this case, there is at least one call update transition in the run from a call transition to a return transition. Based on *Update*, the state $(S', R')$ is calculated by:

$$S' = \{(q, q') \mid \exists p \text{ s.t. } (q, p) \in S'' \text{ and } (p, q') \in Update)$$
$$R' = \{q' \mid \exists q \text{ s.t. } q \in R'' \text{ and } (q, q') \in Update\}\}$$

– For $y = \overleftarrow{a}$, it is similar to the case of a call update transition. One can easily acquire each component by

$$Update = \{(q_0, q) \mid \exists q \in Q, (q_i, q_i') \in S'', (q_S, q_S') \in S, \xi, \xi' \in \Xi, 0 \leqslant i \leqslant n,$$
$$n \geqslant 1, \text{ s.t. } (q_0', {}^{\prec}a, q_1, {}^{\prec}a\xi) \in \delta_c(i = 0),$$
$$(q_i', {}^{\prec}a\xi/\overrightarrow{a}\,\xi, {}^{\prec}a, q_{i+1}, \overrightarrow{a}\,\xi') \in \delta_u(0 < i < n),$$
$$(q_n', \overrightarrow{a}\,\xi, \overrightarrow{a}, q_S, \overrightarrow{a}\,\xi') \in \delta_u,$$
$$(q_S', \overrightarrow{a}\,\xi, \overrightarrow{a}, q) \in \delta_r\},$$
$$S' = \{(q, q') \mid \exists p \text{ s.t. } (q, p) \in S'' \text{ and } (p, q') \in Update)$$
$$R' = \{q' \mid \exists q \text{ s.t. } q \in R'' \text{ and } (q, q') \in Update\}\}$$

– If the stack is empty, then $(\lceil S, R \rfloor, \perp, \overrightarrow{a}, \lceil S', R' \rfloor) \in \delta_r'$ where

$$S' = \{(q, q') \mid \exists q'' \text{ s.t. } (q'', \perp, \overrightarrow{a}, q') \in \delta_r\}$$
$$R' = \{q' \mid \exists q \in R \text{ s.t. } (q, \perp, \overrightarrow{a}, q') \in \delta_r\}.$$

# 4   Symbolic Multi-matching Visibly Pushdown Automata

In this section, the definitions of symbolic alphabets are presented first. Then symbolic multi-matching visibly pushdown automata are formally defined.

## 4.1   Notations

The conventional notations of symbolic visibly pushdown automata is used in [10,11]. First, let symbol $\Psi$ be a *label theory* including a recursively enumerable set of formulas. $\Psi$ is closed under Boolean operations. Notation $\mathbb{P}_x(\Psi)$ represents the set of unary predicates in $\Psi$ where the subscript $x$ is set as the unique free variable in $\mathbb{P}_x(\Psi)$. Similarly, $\mathbb{P}_{x,y}(\Psi)$ signifies the set of binary predicates where there are only two free variables $x$ and $y$. For two predicates $\varphi_1$ and $\varphi_2$, we can obtain that:

1. if $\varphi_1, \varphi_2 \in \mathbb{P}_x(\Psi)$, $\varphi_1 \wedge \varphi_2$ and $\neg\varphi_1 \in \mathbb{P}_x(\Psi)$ are also both unary predicates;
2. if $\varphi_1 \in \mathbb{P}_x(\Psi) \cup \mathbb{P}_{x,y}(\Psi)$ and $\varphi_2 \in \mathbb{P}_{x,y}(\Psi)$, $\varphi_1 \wedge \varphi_2$ and $\neg\varphi_2 \in \mathbb{P}_{x,y}(\Psi)$ are both binary predicates.

We define $IsSat(\varphi)$ as the satisfiability of the predicate $\varphi \in \mathbb{P}_x(\Psi)$. $\varphi$ is satisfiable, if there exists a *witness* $a$ such that $\varphi$ is true when variable $x$ is substituted by $a$, i.e. $[\![\varphi[x/a]]\!] = true$. Similarly, when $\varphi \in \mathbb{P}_{x,y}(\Psi)$, $[\![\varphi[x/a, y/b]]\!] = true$ when $x$ and $y$ are substituted by $a$ and $b$ respectively. If for each predicate $\varphi \in \Psi$, it is decidable to check whether $IsSat(\varphi)$ is true or not, then we say the label theory $\Psi$ is decidable.

## 4.2   Model

Next we propose the model of symbolic multi-matching visibly pushdown automata which is defined as follows.

**Definition 3 (Symbolic Multi-matching Visibly Pushdown Automata, SMVPA).** *A symbolic multi-matching visibly pushdown automaton is a tuple* $\mathbb{M} = (Q, Q_0, F, \hat{\Sigma}, \Gamma, \Psi, \delta)$, *where*

1. $Q$ *is a finite set of states;*
2. $Q_0 \subseteq Q$ *is the set of initial states;*
3. $F \subseteq Q$ *is the set of final states;*
4. $\hat{\Sigma} = \Sigma_c \cup \dot{\Sigma}_c \cup \Sigma_i \cup \dot{\Sigma}_r \cup \Sigma_r$ *is a finite set of input symbols;*
5. $\Gamma \subseteq (\Sigma_c \cup \dot{\Sigma}_c \cup \dot{\Sigma}_r) \times \Xi \cup \{\bot\}$ *is a finite set of stack elements including a special bottom-of-stack symbol* $\bot$;
6. $\Psi$ *is a label theory; and*
7. $\delta = \delta_c \cup \delta_i \cup \delta_u \cup \delta_r$ *is the set of transitions consisting of four parts:*

$$\delta_c \subseteq Q \times \mathbb{P}_x \times Q \times \Gamma$$
$$\delta_i \subseteq Q \times \mathbb{P}_x \times Q$$
$$\delta_u \subseteq Q \times \Gamma \times \mathbb{P}_{x,y} \times Q \times \Gamma$$
$$\delta_r \subseteq Q \times \Gamma \times \mathbb{P}_{x,y} \times Q$$

A *configuration* of $\mathbb{M}$ is a pair $(q, \sigma)$ where $q \in Q$ and $\sigma \in St$. Given a word $w = w_1 w_2 \cdots w_n$ with multi-matching nest relations, $w$ can be accepted by $\mathbb{M}$ if there exists a run of $\mathbb{M}$ on $w$. A *run* $\rho$ is defined as a non-empty sequence of configurations, i.e. $\rho = (q_0, \sigma_0) \xrightarrow[\varphi_1]{w_1} (q_1, \sigma_1) \xrightarrow[\varphi_2]{w_2} \cdots \xrightarrow[\varphi_n]{w_n} (q_n, \sigma_n)$, where $q_0 \in Q_0$ is an initial state and $\gamma_0 = \bot$. For $0 < i \leqslant n$, each configuration $(q_i, \sigma_i)$, where $q_i \in Q$ and $\gamma_i \in \Gamma$, satisfies one of the following cases:

1. call     if $w_i = \,^\frown a$ is a call, there is $(q_{i-1}, \varphi_i, q_i, w_i\xi) \in \delta_c$ where $w_i \in [\![\varphi_i]\!]$, $\varphi_i \in \mathbb{P}_x$ and $\sigma_i = w_i\xi \cdot \sigma_{i-1}$;
2. internal     if $w_i = i$ is an internal, there is $(q_{i-1}, \varphi_i, q_i) \in \delta_i$ where $w_i \in [\![\varphi_i]\!]$, $\varphi_i \in \mathbb{P}_x$ and $\sigma_i = \sigma_{i-1}$;
3. update
    (a) if $w_i = \,^\frown \dot{a}$ is an inner-call, there is $(q_{i-1}, \gamma_{i-1}, \varphi_i, q_i, \gamma_i) \in \delta_u$ where $(w_{i-1}, w_i) \in [\![\varphi_i]\!]$, $\varphi_i \in \mathbb{P}_{x,y}$, $\sigma_{i-1} = \,^\frown a\xi\sigma' / \,^\frown \dot{a}\xi\sigma'$, $\sigma_i = \,^\frown \dot{a}\xi\sigma'$ and $\sigma' \in St$;
    (b) it is similar for an inner-return $w_i = \dot{a}^\frown$. The difference is that $\sigma_{i-1} = \,^\frown a\xi\sigma' / \dot{a}^\frown \xi\sigma'$ and $\sigma_i = \dot{a}^\frown \xi\sigma'$;
4. return
    (a) with regarding to a return $w_i = a^\frown$, there is $(q_{i-1}, \gamma_{i-1}, \varphi_i, q_i) \in \delta_r$ where $(w_{i-1}, w_i) \in [\![\varphi_i]\!]$, $\varphi_i \in \mathbb{P}_{x,y}$ $\sigma_{i-1} = \,^\frown a\xi\sigma' / \,^\frown \dot{a}\xi\sigma'$ and $\sigma_i = \dot{a}^\frown \xi\sigma'$;
    (b) specifically, when the stack is empty, i.e. $(q_{i-1}, \bot, \varphi_i, q_i) \in \delta_r$, there is $\sigma_{i-1} = \sigma_i = \bot$, $w_i \in [\![\varphi_i]\!]$, and $\varphi_i \in \mathbb{P}_x$.

A run $\rho = (q_0, \sigma_0) \xrightarrow[\varphi_1]{w_1} (q_1, \sigma_1) \xrightarrow[\varphi_2]{w_2} \cdots \xrightarrow[\varphi_n]{w_n} (q_n, \sigma_n)$ is accepted by $\mathbb{M}$ if $q_n \in F$ is a final state and $\sigma_n \in (\Sigma_c \times \varXi)^* \cdot \{\bot\}$.

Given a symbolic multi-matching visibly pushdown automaton $\mathbb{M}$, $\mathbb{M}$ is called to be deterministic if $q_0$ is the unique initial state in $\mathbb{M}$, besides, the transition set $\delta$ satisfies the following conditions:

1. for any two call transitions $(q_1, \varphi_1, q_1', \gamma_1) \in \delta_c$ and $(q_2, \varphi_2, q_2', \gamma_2) \in \delta_c$: if $q_1 = q_2$ and $IsSat(\varphi_1 \wedge \varphi_2)$, there is $q_1' = q_2'$ and $\gamma_1 = \gamma_2$;
2. for any two internal transitions $(q_1, \varphi_1, q_1') \in \delta_i$ and $(q_2, \varphi_2, q_2') \in \delta_i$: if $q_1 = q_2$ and $IsSat(\varphi_1 \wedge \varphi_2)$, there is $q_1' = q_2'$;
3. for any two call/return update transitions $(q_1, \gamma_1, \varphi_1, q_1', \gamma_1') \in \delta_u$ and $(q_2, \gamma_2, \varphi_2, q_2', \gamma_2') \in \delta_u$: if $q_1 = q_2$, $\gamma_1 = \gamma_2$ and $IsSat(\varphi_1 \wedge \varphi_2)$, $q_1' = q_2'$ and $\gamma_1' = \gamma_2'$ hold;
4. for any two return transitions $(q_1, \gamma_1, \varphi_1, q_1') \in \delta_u$ and $(q_2, \gamma_2, \varphi_2, q_2') \in \delta_u$: if $q_1 = q_2$, $\gamma_1 = \gamma_2$ and $IsSat(\varphi_1 \wedge \varphi_2)$, there is $q_1' = q_2'$; especially, if the stack is empty, the difference from the former case is that $\gamma_1 = \gamma_2 = \bot$.

## 5   Conclusion

In this paper, we extend the model of visibly pushdown automata over multi-matching nested relations. Different categories of transitions are determined according to a fixed partition of input tagged alphabet. Then, languages with one-to-one, one-to-n and n-to-one relations can be described. Besides, each non-deterministic multi-matching visibly pushdown automaton is demonstrated to be transformed into a deterministic one. In addition, if the input alphabet is given by a Boolean algebra where there is an infinite domain, symbolic version of multi-matching visibly pushdown automata is formally proposed. In the future, we will further investigate the closure properties and decision problems of multi-matching visibly pushdown automata and the symbolic version. Moreover, how visibly pushdown automata over multi-matching nested relations can be well applied in more fields are further explored.

## References

1. Alur, R., Madhusudan, P.: Adding nesting structure to words. J. ACM (JACM) **56**(3), 1–43 (2009)
2. Alur, R., Madhusudan, P.: Visibly pushdown languages. In: Proceedings of the Thirty-Sixth Annual ACM Symposium on Theory of Computing, pp. 202–211 (2004)
3. Hopcroft, J.E., Motwani, R., Ullman, J.D.: Introduction to Automata Theory, Languages, and Computation, 2nd edn. Pearson Education, London (2000). ISBN 0-201-44124-1
4. Kumar, V., Madhusudan, P., Viswanathan, M.: Visibly pushdown automata for streaming XML. In: Proceedings of the 16th International Conference on World Wide Web (WWW 2007), 1053C1062 (2007)

5. Debarbieux, D., Gauwin, O., Niehren, J., et al.: Early nested word automata for XPath query answering on XML streams. Theor. Comput. Sci. **578**, 100–125 (2015)
6. Chaudhuri, S., Alur, R.: Instrumenting C programs with nested word monitors. In: International SPIN Workshop on Model Checking of Software, pp. 279–283 (2007)
7. Driscoll, E., Thakur, A., Reps, T.: OpenNWA: a nested-word automaton library. In: International Conference on Computer Aided Verification, pp. 665–671 (2012)
8. Watson, B.W.: Implementing and using finite automata toolkits. In: Extended Finite State Models of Language, pp. 19–36. Cambridge University Press, New York (1999)
9. van Noord, G., Gerdemann, D.: Finite state transducers with predicates and identities. Grammars **4**(3), 263–286 (2001)
10. D'Antoni, L., Alur, R.: Symbolic visibly pushdown automata. In: International Conference on Computer Aided Verification (CAV 2014), pp. 209–225 (2014)
11. Margus, V., Pieter, H., Benjamin, L., et al.: Symbolic finite state transducers: algorithms and applications. In: Proceedings of the 39th Annual ACM SIGPLAN-SIGACT Symposium on Principles of Programming Languages (POPL 2012), pp. 137–150 (2012)
12. Liu, J.. Duan, Z., Tian, C.: Transforming multi-matching nested traceable automata to multi-matching nested expressions. In: Proceedings of the 14th International Conference on Combinatorial Optimization and Applications (COCOA 2020), pp. 320–333 (2020)
13. Liu, J., Duan, Z., Tian, C.: Multi-matching nested relations. Theor. Comput. Sci. **854**, 77–93 (2021)
14. Liu, J., Duan, Z., Tian, C.: Multi-matching nested languages. Chin. J. Electron. **31**(1), 137–145 (2022)

# Schedulability Analysis of Rate-Monotonic Algorithm on Concurrent Execution of Digraph Real-Time Tasks

Jin Cui[1]([🖂]), Xu Lu[2], Guangliang Yu[3], and Bin Yu[2]

[1] Xi'an Shiyou University, Xi'an 710065, People's Republic of China
cuijin_xd@126.com
[2] ICTT and ISN Laboratory Xidian University, Xi'an 710071,
People's Republic of China
{xulu,yubin}@mail.xidian.edu.cn
[3] Beijing Institute of Control Engineering, Beijing 100190, People's Republic of China
ygl_222@126.com

**Abstract.** Rate-monotonic algorithm is a classical algorithm for scheduling periodical tasks. Lots of work has been carried out to analyze the schedulability of RMS algorithm. While most of the work focus on the classical Liu and Layland task model. In this paper, we propose an approach to testing the schedulability of RMS algorithm on digraph task models. Our approach has higher efficiency since we just analyze schedulability of subtasks in the scheduling point set of one time interval rather than all possible cases.

**Keywords:** Schedulability analysis · Digraph real-time tasks · Rate-monotonic algorithm · Real-time systems · Concurrent execution

## 1 Introduction

In real-time systems, concurrent execution of multi-tasks with static priorities is common. Tasks are scheduled according to the pre-assigned priority during the execution process. RMS (Rate-monotonic Scheduling) algorithm is a classical static priority scheduling algorithm for periodic tasks. The priorities of tasks are assigned according to their periods and a task with smaller period runs in a higher priority. RMS algorithm was proposed by Liu and Layland in 1973 and shown to be optimum among all fixed priority scheduling algorithms.

Different formal models have been proposed to represent the running of tasks in real-time systems. The formal models include Liu and Lanyland model [1], the sporadic tasks model [2], multiframe (MF) model [3], generalized multiframe (GMF) model [4], and digraph task model [5,6]. In the digraph task model, vertices represent subtasks and edges indicating the control flow among subtasks.

This research is supported by Special Scientific Research Project No. 21JK0844 of Education Department of Shaanxi Province.

Analyzing the schedulability of concurrent execution of multi-tasks in digraph models is an important work in the design stage of real-time systems.

Schedulability of different task models have been studied where the first work is carried out by Liu and Layland in 1973. Liu and Layland focus on periodic tasks with hard deadlines being equal to the task periods [1], they derive the optimal static priority scheduling algorithm: rate-monotonic scheduling (RMS) algorithm. They proved that using RMS, the periodic task set of size $n$ will be able to meet all deadlines all of the time if the total utilization is not greater than $n(2^{(1/n)} - 1)$, a quantity which decreases monotonically from 0.83 when $n = 2$ to $log_e 2 = 0.693$ as $n \to \infty$.

Based on the theoretical results of Liu and Layland, several approaches for deciding the feasibility of periodic tasks are proposed, such as response time analysis [7,8], scheduling point analysis [9,10], and model checking approach [11–13]. By means of calculating the processor demand, researchers in [14] give a necessary and sufficient condition for deciding the feasibility of Liu and Layland task model scheduled using RMS algorithm. John Lehoczky et al calculate the processor demand at the time points where tasks are released.

In [15,16], feasibility analysis of recurring real-time task model is studied for static priority scheduling. In [15], the request bound function and demand bound function for each digraph task are used to test whether a digraph task is schedulable or not. In [16], the schedulability of a task is tested using the request function defined for each path of a digraph task. And the critical request function is searched to test whether a digraph task is schedulable. The work in [15,16] is similar to ours from two aspects: on one hand, we all focus on static priority digraph tasks; on the other hand, the request function is used in all approaches.

In this paper, we study the schedulability of RMS algorithm on digraph real-time tasks. Our request function is defined for a subtask of digraph task. And we just check the scheduling points of all cases for a critical instant of each subtask. Suppose that $d$ denotes the relative deadline of a subtask, we can limit the time interval to the first $d$ time units and just check the scheduling points in the first $d$ time units. Thus our approach has the advantage of higher efficiency.

The remainder of the paper is organized as follows. The next section gives an introduction to the digraph real-time task model, which is followed by the schedulability analysis process in Sect. 3. Finally, conclusions and future work are drawn in Sect. 4.

## 2   The Digraph Task Model

A digraph task $T$ is denoted as a directed graph $G(T) = <V, E>$, the set of vertices $V = \{v_1, \ldots, v_n\}$ represents the subtasks of $T$. Each vertices $v_i$ is labeled with an ordered pair $\langle e(v_i), d(v_i) \rangle$ with $e(v_i)$ and $d(v_i)$ being its execution time and deadline respectively. Each edge $(u, v)$ is labeled with a positive real number $p(u, v)$ for the minimum inter-release separation time, which means that when task $T$ is started, $v$ is released $p(u, v)$ time units right after $u$ is released. $G(T)$

72 J. Cui et al.

may have a source vertex $v$ and a sink vertex $v'$, which means that a complete execution of task $T$ starts from $v$ and ends when $v'$ finishes its execution. Figure 1 shows an example of a digraph task containing six subtasks.

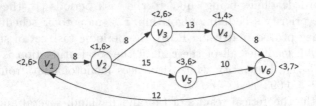

**Fig. 1.** Digraph task $T$: an example with six different subtasks

An execution of a task $T$ corresponds to a potentially infinite path $\pi = (\pi_1, \pi_2, \ldots)$ in $G(T)$. Each visit to a vertex along a path of $G(T)$ triggers the release of a subtask. For a path $\pi$, the number of vertices is denoted as $|\pi|$, $\pi_1$ is called the initial vertex and $\pi_{|\pi|}$ the final or last vertex. Further, we use $\pi_{(i,j)}$ to denote a sub-path of $\pi$ and $\pi_{(i,j)} = (\pi_i, \pi_{i+1}, \ldots, \pi_j)$ with, $1 \le i \le j \le |\pi|$. For a path $\pi$, we define the following notations:

$$len(\pi_i, \pi_j) \overset{def}{=} \sum_{l=i}^{j-1} p(\pi_l, \pi_{l+1})$$
$$el(\pi_i, \pi_j) \overset{def}{=} \sum_{l=i}^{j} e(\pi_l)$$
$$dl(\pi_i, \pi_j) \overset{def}{=} len(\pi_i, \pi_j) + d(\pi_j)$$

Actually, $len(\pi_i, \pi_j)$ denotes the absolute release time of $\pi_j$ in path $\pi$ with the assumption that $\pi_i$ is released at $t = 0$; $el(\pi_i, \pi_j)$ means the time requirement for executing the sub-path $\pi_{(i,j)}$ of $\pi$; and $dl(\pi_i, \pi_j)$ means the absolute deadline for executing the sub-path $\pi_{(i,j)}$ of $\pi$. When $i = 1$, $len(\pi_i, \pi_j)$, $el(\pi_i, \pi_j)$ and $dl(\pi_i, \pi_j)$ can also be written as $len(\pi_j)$, $el(\pi_j)$ and $dl(\pi_j)$ respectively for simplicity.

Assume $v_1$ is a source node of $G(T)$, $\pi = (v_1, \ldots, v_1)$ is an execution path of $G(T)$, and $v_1$ dose not occur in $\pi$ except for the initial and final position, then we say path $\pi$ is a cycle of $G(T)$ and $len(\pi_{|\pi|})$ is called the period of the cycle. For example, in Fig. 1, $\pi = (v_1, v_2, v_3, v_4, v_6, v_1)$ and $\pi' = (v_1, v_2, v_5, v_6, v_1)$ are cycles of task $T$, the periods of $\pi$ and $\pi'$ are $len(\pi_{|\pi|}) = 49$ and $len(\pi'_{|\pi'|}) = 45$ respectively. Moreover, if $G(T)$ has only one cycle, we call $len(\pi_{|\pi|})$ is the period of $T$. In the rest of the paper, we mainly focus on digraph tasks with only one cycle.

A digraph task system $\tau = \{T_1, \ldots, T_n\}$ consists of $n$ independent tasks. We assume $T_i$ has $m_i$ subtasks, and denote its $j$-th subtask as $v_{ij}$ or $T_{ij}$ for $1 \le i \le n, 1 \le j \le m_i$ alternatively in the rest of the paper.

# 3   Schedulability Analysis for Digraph Task Models

RMS algorithm is a classical scheduling algorithm for periodic tasks. It was proposed by Liu and Layland in 1973 and shown to be optimum among all fixed priority scheduling algorithms. In this paper, we generalize RMS algorithm to schedule digraph tasks with only one cycle. Thus, for a digraph task system $\tau = \{T_1, \ldots, T_n\}$, the priorities of tasks are assigned according to their periods and a task with smaller period runs in a higher priority.

**Critical Instant.** A digraph task consists of one or more subtasks. A release of a subtask generates a job of that subtask. For digraph tasks with one cycle, jobs of each subtask are released periodically. In a digraph task system $\tau = \{T_1, \ldots, T_n\}$, we say task $T_i$ is schedulable if and only if all of its subtask $T_{ij}$ are schedulable. In digraph task $T_i$, a subtask $T_{ij}$ is schedulable if and only if all jobs released by $T_{ij}$ are schedulable. In other word, if there exists one job of a subtask $T_{ij}$ violates its deadline, then $T_{ij}$ is unschedulable, which indicates task $T_i$ as well as digraph task system $\tau$ is unschedulable. The definition as well as a theorem of the critical instant for a subtask is given as follows.

**Definition 1 (Critical Instant).** *A critical instant for a subtask is defined to be a time instant at which a request for that subtask will have the largest response time.*

**Theorem 1.** *A critical instant for any subtask occurs only when the subtask is requested simultaneously with requests from all higher priority subtasks.*

It is obvious that the schedulability of a digraph task $T$ depends on the schedulability of its subtasks. Thus the key is to determine whether each subtask in a digraph task is schedulable separately, which is equivalent to determine whether all jobs of a subtask violates their deadline or not. We only need to consider whether the job of a subtask in the worst case violates its deadline or not. From Theorem 1, we can infer that the worst case for a subtask occurs when it is requested simultaneously with requests from all higher priority subtasks. Actually, at most one subtask of a higher priority task is released at each time point, which leads to that the number of cases for a critical instant of a subtask is multiplies of the number of subtasks in each higher priority tasks. Thus we need to further find out the worst case from these cases. For example, in a digraph real-time system $\tau$, we assume that $T_1, \ldots, T_i$ are the tasks with higher priority than $T$, and a subtask $v$ in $T$ is released at time point $t = 0$. Assume $v_{1s_1}, \ldots, v_{is_i}$ are subtasks of $T_1, \ldots, T_i$ respectively. The time instant when $v$ is released simultaneously with $v_{1s_1}, \ldots, v_{is_i}$ is a critical instant of $v$. If $T_1, \ldots, T_i$ has $m_1, \ldots, m_i$ subtask respectively, then there may be $m_1 m_2 \ldots m_i$ cases occurs at a critical instant of $v$. We need to find out the worst case where the response time for $v$ is the maximum from the $m_1 m_2 \ldots m_i$ cases.

**Request Bound Function.** Let $v$ be a subtask in $T$ and the execution time and deadline of s $v$ is $c$ and $d$ respectively. Request bound function $rf_v(t)$ means the number of time requested to execute subtask $v$ at time point $t$. It can also be seen as the workload of the processor at time point $t$. The request bound function $rf_v(t)$ which corresponds to execute subtask $v$ during time interval $[0, d]$ consists of the request bound $c$ of $v$ as well as the interference it encounters due to higher priority tasks $T_1, \ldots, T_i$. Note that $v$ is released simultaneously with one of subtasks in $T_1, \ldots, T_i$ respectively. Theorem 2 shows how to define request bound function $rf_v(t)$ for $v$ in the digraph task system $\tau$. The correctness of the definition is also proved.

**Theorem 2**

$$rf_v(t) = c + \sum_{j=1}^{i} (\lfloor \frac{t}{p_j} \rfloor c_j + el(v_{s_j}^j, \ldots, v_{x_j}^j))$$

where $s_j, x_j$ are numbers of subtasks in $T_j$, $s_j, x_j \in \{1, 2, \ldots, m_j\}$; $v_{s_j}^j$ is the subtask in $T_j$ that is released simultaneously with subtask $v$ in $T$; $len(v_{s_j}^j, \ldots, v_{x_j}^j) \leq t \% p_j < len(v_{s_j}^j, \ldots, v_{x_j+1}^j)$.

**Proof:** Since $T_1, \ldots, T_i$ are tasks in $\tau$ with higher priorities than $T$, which may interfere the execution of $T$. We can observe that at any time instance $t$, there are $\lfloor \frac{t}{p_j} \rfloor$ complete iterations of higher priority tasks that occupy $\lfloor \frac{t}{p_j} \rfloor c_j$ number of processor time. In addition, jobs of $T_{js_j}, \ldots, T_{jx_j}$ are also released during the interval $[\lfloor \frac{t}{p_j} \rfloor c_j, t]$ that occupies $el(v_{s_j}^j, \ldots, v_{x_j}^j)$ number of processor time. Therefore, at time instance $t$, the number of time requested to execute subtask $v$ in $T$ is $rf_v(t) = c + \sum_{j=1}^{i} (\lfloor \frac{t}{p_j} \rfloor c_j + el(v_{s_j}^j, \ldots, v_{x_j}^j))$.                                   □

From Theorem 2, we can see that the value of $rf_v(t)$ is affected by $t$ and $s_j, (j = 1, \ldots, i)$. There are $m_j$ possible values for each $s_j$, thus for $rf_v(t)$, there are $m_1 m_2 \ldots m_i$ cases of combination for the value of $s_j$ with $j = 1, \ldots, i$. To test schedulability of subtask $v$ in $T$, we consider each case separately using the scheduling points test approach.

**Scheduling Point Set.** A scheduling point is a time instant at which there exists a job of a subtask in higher priority tasks being released. The value of $rf_v(t)$ changes only at the scheduling point, thus we just check $t$ at all scheduling point rather than all $t \in [0, d]$.

Let $SD$ be the set of time points at which jobs of subtasks in $T_1, \ldots, T_i$ being released in time interval $[0, d]$. We divide $SD$ into two parts, one is $SD_I$ denoting the scheduling points in time interval $[0, \lfloor \frac{d}{p_j} \rfloor \cdot p_j)$, and another is $SD_R$ denoting the scheduling points in time interval $[\lfloor \frac{d}{p_j} \rfloor \cdot p_j, t]$.

The path $\pi_j = (v_{s_j}, v_{1+s_j \% m_j}, \ldots, v_{1+(s_j+m_j-2)\% m_j}, v_{1+(s_j+m_j-1)\% m_j})$ is a cycle of $G(T_j)$ starts from vertex $v_{s_j}$ for each task $T_j$ in $T_1, \ldots, T_i$. We can see that there are $a_j = \lfloor \frac{d}{p_j} \rfloor$ complete cycles and one incomplete cycle $\pi_j' = (v_{s_j}, \ldots, v_{x_j})$ in time interval $[0, d]$. On the path $\pi'' = (\pi_j)^{a_j} \cdot \pi_j'$, $t \in \{len(\pi''(1)), \ldots, len(\pi''(|\pi''|))\}$ are the scheduling points for task $T_j$ in time interval $[0, d]$, we denote the set as $SD_j$. Thus it is not difficult to obtain that $SD = SD_1 \cup \ldots \cup SD_i$.

For subtask $v$ in $T$, with the concept of critical instant, request bound function, and scheduling point set, we obtain an approach to testing the scheduability of $v$ in $T$ of digraph task system $\tau$. We assume $v$'s execution time is $c$ and its deadline is $d$, the basic checking process is as follows: for each case of a critical instant, if $\exists t \in SD, rf_v(t) \leq t$ holds, we say subtask $v$ in $T$ is schedulable; otherwise, $v$ in $T$ is unschedulable. If $v$ is unschedulable, the checking process terminates; otherwise, we need to further check other cases until a case indicating that $v$ is unscheduable or all cases are checked. If for all cases $v$ is scheduable, we say subtask $v$ is schedulable, otherwise, $v$ is unschedulable thus $T$ as well as the digraph system $\tau$ is unschedulable. To check whether $T$ is schedulable, we need to test whether each subtask in $T$ is schedulable or not by repeating the process above.

# 4    Conclusion and Future Work

This paper studies the schedulability of concurrent execution of multi-tasks in digraph model using RMS algorithm. An efficient approach is provided to judge the feasibility of concurrent digraph tasks with RMS algorithm. Our work focuses on recurrent behaviour on single path, thus the branch structure is not considered. As a future work, we will consider complex structure of tasks for schedulability analysis. And we also plan to implement a tool to decide the schedulability of digraph task systems automatically.

# References

1. Liu, C.L., Layland, J.W.: Scheduling algorithms for multiprogramming in a hard-real-time environment. J. ACM (JACM) **20**(1), 46–61 (1973)
2. Mok, A.K.-L.: Fundamental design problems of distributed systems for the hard-real-time environment. Ph.D. thesis, Massachusetts Institute of Technology (1983)
3. Moyo, N.T., Nicollet, E., Lafaye, F., Moy, C.: On schedulability analysis of non-cyclic generalized multiframe tasks. In: 2010 22nd Euromicro Conference on Real-Time Systems, pp. 271–278. IEEE (2010)
4. Baruah, S., Chen, D., Gorinsky, S., Mok, A.: Generalized multiframe tasks. Real-Time Syst. **17**(1), 5–22 (1999)
5. Stigge, M., Ekberg, P., Guan, N., Yi, W.: The digraph real-time task model. In: 2011 17th IEEE Real-Time and Embedded Technology and Applications Symposium, pp. 71–80. IEEE (2011)
6. Baruah, S.: The non-cyclic recurring real-time task model. In: 2010 31st IEEE Real-Time Systems Symposium, pp. 173–182. IEEE (2010)
7. Baruah, S.K., Burns, A., Davis, R.I.: Response-time analysis for mixed criticality systems. In: 2011 IEEE 32nd Real-Time Systems Symposium, pp. 34–43. IEEE Computer Society (2011)
8. Nasri, M., Nelissen, G., Brandenburg, B.B.: Response-time analysis of limited-preemptive parallel DAG tasks under global scheduling. In: 31st Conference on Real-Time Systems, pp. 21–1 (2019)
9. Bini, E., Buttazzo, G.C.: Schedulability analysis of periodic fixed priority systems. IEEE Trans. Comput. **53**(11), 1462–1473 (2004)

10. Anssi, S., Tucci-Piergiovanni, S., Kuntz, S., Gérard, S., Terrier, F.: Enabling scheduling analysis for AUTOSAR systems. In: 2011 14th IEEE International Symposium on Object/Component/Service-Oriented Real-Time Distributed Computing, pp. 152–159. IEEE (2011)
11. Cui, J., Duan, Z., Tian, C.: Model checking rate-monotonic scheduler with TMSVL. In: 2014 19th International Conference on Engineering of Complex Computer Systems, pp. 202–205. IEEE (2014)
12. Cui, J., Cong, T., et al.: Verifying schedulability of tasks in ROS-based systems. J. Comb. Optim. **37**, 901–920 (2019)
13. Cui, J., Duan, Z., et al.: A novel approach to modeling and verifying real-time systems for high reliability. IEEE Trans. Reliab. **67**(2), 481–493 (2018)
14. Lehoczky, J., Sha, L., Ding, Y.: The rate monotonic scheduling algorithm: exact characterization and average case behavior. In: RTSS, vol. 89, pp. 166–171 (1989)
15. Baruah, S.K.: Dynamic-and static-priority scheduling of recurring real-time tasks. Real-Time Syst. **24**(1), 93–128 (2003)
16. Stigge, M., Yi, W.: Combinatorial abstraction refinement for feasibility analysis of static priorities. Real-Time Syst. **51**(6), 639–674 (2015)

# Formal Specification and Testing

# Formalization of Natural Language into PPTL Specification via Neural Machine Translation

Chunyi Li, Jiajun Chang, Xiaobing Wang(✉), Liang Zhao, and Wenjie Mao

School of Computer Science and Technology, Xidian University, Xi'an 710071, Shaanxi, China
{cyli_322,jjchang,wjmao}@stu.xidian.edu.cn,
xbwang@mail.xidian.edu.cn, lzhao@xidian.edu.cn

**Abstract.** Propositional Projection Temporal Logic (PPTL) has been widely used in formal verification, and its expressiveness is suitable for the description of security requirements. However, the expression and application of temporal logic formulas rely on a strong mathematical background, which is difficult for non-domain experts, thus bridging the chasm between natural language descriptions and formal languages is urgently needed. This paper proposes an innovative architecture for neural machine automatic translation named NL2PPTL, which transforms natural language into PPTL specification via utilizing data preprocessing, encoder-decoder network and stack sequentially. To evaluate the performance of our method, the experimental verification is realized on real datasets. The experiment conducted shows that our method has effectiveness on temporal logic specification generation.

**Keywords:** Neural machine translation · Propositional projection temporal logic · Formal specification · Formal verification

## 1 Introduction

In furtherance of ensuring the provision of highly reliable systems in industrial applications such as unmanned aerial vehicles [16], 5G [37], aerospace [3], military industry [22], nuclear power [23], and autonomous driving [24], analysis and verification of the security requirements have to be paid attention. In general, security requirements are described by informal natural language with ambiguity and contradiction, which increases the possibility of causing unexpected dysfunction possibly. More advanced approaches based on engineering security requirements, experts bring forward many unified described language for engineers, such as linear-time temporal logic (LTL) [21], computation tree logic(CTL) [9], scene description language (SDL) [11], security requirement language (SRL) [1], PPTL [7], application vulnerability description language (AVDL) [28], etc. They can describe the global properties and behavior

Supported by National Natural Science Foundation of China (61972301, 61672403), Key Research and Development Program of Shaanxi Province of China (2020GY-043), Shaanxi Innovative Research Team for Key Science and Technology (2019TD-001), and Xi'an Science and Technology Project (22GXFW0025).

S. Liu et al. (Eds.): SOFL+MSVL 2022, LNCS 13854, pp. 79–92, 2023.
https://doi.org/10.1007/978-3-031-29476-1_7

of the system abstractly. Especially, formal language theory has long employed in modeling system behavior and describing temporal logic of system properties, which can reduce errors by reducing ambiguity and imprecision and by making some instances of inconsistency and incompleteness obvious [2]. In comparison to natural language, the obvious advantages of PPTL are readily apparent: Firstly, PPTL can abstractly and normatively describe and verify the behavior and performance of systems, for example, security requirements in design and implementation of the software. Meanwhile, mature formal tools have been developed based on PPTL, where the target language can be analyzed directly. Next, It have been successfully used in scenarios such as model checking, theorem proving and formal verification which improves the reliability and safety of software [39,40]. Last but not least, PPTL has been proved to have the same expressiveness as full regular expressions [31] and an efficient decision algorithm [27]. In specific, it integrates projection, temporal and classical logic, whose expressiveness is more powerful than common logical language. However, in reality, the formal language is not easy for non-professional experts.

By this motivation, the semi-automatic and automatic generation method for formal description have been explored at least momentarily. Transforming natural language text into machine understandable meaning representation (MR) [12], such as machine executable language SQL, C/C++ and formal specification LTL, CTL. Igor Buzhinsky [5] assessed universal classifications which is roughly corresponds to rule-based and statistical approaches in NLP. The first class is employing formal language theory directly. Like some traditional methods, special transformation rules or expert templates are defined to generate the target language [30]. These ways are complicated and require a lot of manual intervention by experts, so that the scope of the study is limited by the number and description ability of templates. In order to improve the accuracy, complex templates are proposed which lead to higher costs on demand analysis. The generation performance is also limited by the enumeration schemes defined by experts, which fundamentally cannot express the diversified requirements of systems. Inspired by grammatical analysis in NLP, then structured English grammar [36] is proposed, which includes common cases originally summarized by complex templates. Generally, the advanced grammatical tagging technology is directly used, and tagging accuracy is positively correlated with automatic conversion accuracy. With the rapid development of NLP, this issue can be solved priority. The second class is statistical machine translation approaches. Motivated by developments in statistical machine methods, the trained deep network is utilized to automatically construct generation rules [41]. Especially, neural machine translation has gained in popularity. In such circumstances, translations are not generated by prescriptive rules anymore, but relatively are generated on the basis of statistical deep neural network models, whose parameters are trained on bilingual text corpora [4]. In view of the fact that a logical formula is capably disposed to expressed via a tree-like structure, so the sequence-to-tree method [19] or other constraint decoding techniques [13] are the most suitable. Nevertheless, the generation quality requires reliable datasets, a refined model and expert support, in the meantime, the over-fitting problem and information loss are urgent to be solved.

In this paper, we propose an automatic generation method, which converts the natural language into PPTL through Seq2Seq (Sequence to Sequence) model. It encodes the text into a fixed vector and generates a prediction target logical fomula with the context information. In specific, the existing PPTLGenerator tool [32] is used to create datasets firstly during the data preprocessing, which converts the source natural language into the corresponding target logic formula. Secondly, a specific encoder-decoder network is constructed and trained with relatively few parameters and training instances. Specifically, it compresses the input sequence into the fixed-length vector, and a parametric model is fitted to generate the corresponding PPTL formula without nested relationships via searching for maximizing conditional probabilities. Finally, the stack is utilized to print out the complete PPTL formula with nested relationships through defining the priority of the symbols during pop operation. We summarize our contributions as follows:

(1) Our proposed method can neglect various sentence patterns compared to semantic analysis, and effectively extract the temporal logic of security requirements.
(2) The productions is uncomplicated with demonstrating a good scalability, where the encoder-decoder network can be replaced by other neural translation models.
(3) The generation of the PPTL specification builds a bridge between security requirements and formal methods. Compared with other logic description languages, the generated PPTL specification has more powerful expression ability and richer application scenarios.
(4) We comprehensively evaluate the effectiveness and efficiency of the method on several requirements in various open-source practical applications.

This paper focuses on solving the above problems mentioned. The remainder of this paper is organized as follows. Section 2 introduces the theoretical basis. Section 3 describes notations and discusses our proposed method. Section 4 presents the experimental results. Section 5 discusses the related work. The conclusion and future works are provided in Sect. 6.

## 2 Theoretical Basis

In this section, we first give the formal definitions of PPTL and then introduce the notations of sentence element used in this paper, which are the basis of our research on PPTL specification generation.

### 2.1 PPTL

PPTL is a temporal logic based on a sequence of states. It is an improvement on the pioneer work of ITL (interval temporal logic), which extends interval temporal logic from finite state interval to infinite. The core temporal operators are $\bigcirc$ (next) and $prj$ (projection).

(1) PPTL syntax

$$P = p|\neg P| P_1 \wedge P_2 \mid \bigcirc P|(P_1, \ldots, P_m)prjP \tag{1}$$

Let $Prop$ represent the set of atomic propositions where $p$ denotes an atomic proposition and $p \in Prop$. $P, P_1, \ldots, P_m$ stand for PPTL formulas. If a formula without temporal operators is called a state formula, otherwise a temporal formula. Simultaneously, some derived formulas and common temporal logic operators are given below, where $tt \overset{def}{=} p \lor \neg p$ and $p_1; p_2 = (p_1, p_2) \, prj \, \varepsilon$.

$$\varepsilon \overset{def}{=} \neg \bigcirc tt \qquad\qquad \Diamond P \overset{def}{=} tt; P$$
$$\Box P \overset{def}{=} \neg \Diamond \neg P \qquad final(P) \overset{def}{=} \Box(\varepsilon \to P)$$

(2) PPTL semantics

   *(State)*: State $s$ is defined as a mapping relation $Prop \to B$ between $Prop$ and the boolean set $B = (true, false)$. The value of atomic proposition $p$ in state $s$ is recorded as $s[p]$. If $s[p] = true$, it indicates that $p$ is true on $s$, otherwise it is false.

   *(Interval)*: Interval $\sigma$ denotes a sequence of $s$, the length of which is $|\sigma|$. $\sigma$ is divided into two types: finite interval and infinite interval. In specific, when a finite number of states exists in the interval, $|\sigma| = c - 1$ and $c$ is the number of states. Otherwise, when there are infinite states, $|\sigma| = \omega$ and $\omega$ is infinity. In order to express the two types of interval uniformly, Let $N_\omega$ represent $N_0 \cup \{\omega\}$, where $N_0$ is the set of non-negative integers. Obviously $\omega = \omega$, any $i \in N_0$ satisfies $i < \omega$. Let $\preccurlyeq$ represents $\leqslant -\{(\omega, \omega)\}$ and $\sigma = <s_0, s_1, \ldots, s_{|\sigma|}>$, and it indicates that $\sigma_{(i \ldots j)}(0 \leqslant i \preccurlyeq j \leqslant |\sigma|)$ is the subinterval of $\sigma$. Interval operator $\cdot$ can combine two intervals $\sigma = <s_0, s_1, \ldots, s_{|\sigma|}>$ and $\sigma' = <s'_0, s'_1, \ldots, s'_{|\sigma|}>$ to $\sigma \cdot \sigma' = <s_0, s_1, \ldots, s_{|\sigma|}, s'_0, s'_1, \ldots, s'_{|\sigma|}>$ when $\sigma$ is finite.

   *(Interpretation)*: Interpretation $I$ is defined by the triple $(\sigma, k, j)$ to indicate the interpretation of the PPTL formula, where $k$ and $j$ are integers which satisfy $0 \leqslant k \preccurlyeq j \leqslant |\sigma|$. The satisfiable relationship $| =$ between $I$ and $P$ is defined by induction as:

$I| = p \quad iff \quad s_k[p] = I^k_{prop}[p] = true$
$I| = \neg P \quad iff \quad I \neq P$
$I| = P_1 \land P_2 \quad iff \quad I| = P_1 \quad and \quad I| = P_2$
$I| = \bigcirc P \quad iff \quad k < j \quad and \quad (\sigma, k+1, j)| = P$
$I| = (P_1, \ldots, P_m) \, prj P$
$iff \quad exist \quad k = r_0 \leqslant \cdots \leqslant r_{m-1} \preccurlyeq r_m \leqslant j, (\sigma, r_{l-1}, r_l)| = P_l \ is \ tenable$
$for \quad all \quad 1 \leq l \leq m \quad and \quad (\sigma', 0, |\sigma'|)| = P \quad when:$
(1) $r_m < j \quad and \quad \sigma' = \sigma \downarrow (r_0, \ldots, r_m) \cdot \sigma(r_{m+1}, \ldots, j)$
(2) $r_m = j \quad and \quad \sigma' = \sigma \downarrow (r_0, \ldots, r_h), 0 \leqslant h \leqslant m$

## 2.2  PPTLGenerator

At present, only a few of the requirements are involved with open-source. Meanwhile, the conversion of PPTL specification in manual manner is potentially highly cost-effective. Hence, the scale and non-shared properties of datasets severely hinders the extraction of specification using deep networks. To solve this issue, we borrow the tools from previous work and convert the requirements into PPTL formulas as the target language. In specific, the PPTLGenerator tool uses common NLP techniques including part-of-speech tags (POS), the tool Stanford NLP, the language dictionary WordNet to achieve extraction of the PPTL formula. It is worth noting that the target language of dataset used in this paper is interception from the postorder traversal of the syntax tree, which specifically deletes the nested parentheses to maintain statement sequence in reference to infix expressions. For instance, brackets are temporarily discarded so as not to affect the accuracy of Seq2Seq translation.

## 3   Neural Machine Translation

Traditional translation models based on statistics borrow typical n-gram models with information seriously lost, while neural machine translation analyzes word embedding representations. From the point of view of statistics, the conditional probability of the target sentence $y$ is maximized with a source sentence $x$ given in neural machine translation, namely stated $argmax_y p(y|x)$, the framework of NL2PPTL is shown in Fig. 1 including encoder network, decoder network, stack and GRU (Gated Recurrent Unit) [6] modules. Firstly, we use an existing text corpus to convert each text into a sequence of integer indices with corresponding vectors, all punctuation is stripped by default, then a vectorized sequence of space-separated words is input into the encoder-decoder network. With the purpose of effectively capture the semantic association between long sequences and alleviate the phenomenon of gradient explode or gradient vanishing, GRU also known as gated recurrent unit structure, is introduced into

**NL2PPTL Framework**

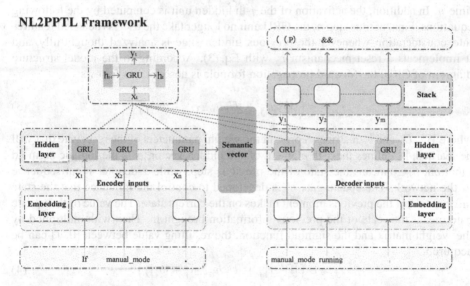

**Fig. 1.** An instance is from the dataset. The source language is "If manual_mode is running and start_auto_control_button is pressed, next auto_control_mode is running"., and the object language is "manual_mode __ running && start_auto_control_button __ pressed implication then auto_control_mode __ running". Eventually, $((P)\&\&(Q)) - > ()(R)$ is obtained through the basic operation in stack.

our translation network, which is also a variant of traditional RNN (Recurrent Neural Network) same as LSTM (Long Short-Term Memory). The output of the decoder is pushed into the stack, then pop operation is performed to obtain the final PPTL specification.

## 3.1   Encoder Network

The role of the encoder is to transform a variable-length input sequence into a fixed-length semantic variable $c$. Our method integrates state-of-the-art third-party module libraries and improves on the classic encoder-decoder architecture that exhibits great advantage in several sequence-to-sequence applications. Then input sequence is solved by the tokenizer module, then the occurrence of words is counted to generate a corpus-driven dictionary to support the vector representation of text based on lexicographic order, which is denoted as $x = x_1, x_2, ..., x_n$. When the input sequence is completed, the last hidden state $c$ is retained. The hidden layer state $h_n$ at a certain time of the encoder side is only related to the hidden state $h_{n-1}$ at the previous time and the current input $x_n$, The formula is derived as follows:

$$h_n = GRU(x_n, h_{n-1}) \tag{2}$$

The GRU unit adaptively remembers and forgets its state according to the input signal of the unit. We define $j = 1, ...k$ represents the symbol that takes a value at time $n$. In addition, the activation of the $j$-th hidden unit is computed by the following equations. First, at time step $n$, the GRU unit no longer take the useless detected features into consideration whenever the previous hidden state is analyzed thoughtfully, and it implements a reset mechanism $r_j$ with Eq. (3). According to the model structure diagram of GRU, the forward propagation formula is described as follows:

$$r_j = \sigma \left( [W_r x]_j + [U_r h_{n-1}]_j + [b_r]_j \right) \tag{3}$$

where $W_r$, $U_r$ and $b_r$ matrices represent the weight parameters of the reset gate that will be learned, $[\cdot]$ defines the $j$-th element of the hidden vector, $\sigma$ is the logistic sigmoid function, $h_{n-1}$ means the state of the previous step, while $x$ denotes input sequence of the network. The update gate $z_j$ is developed to control the influence that the state information of the previous moment makes on the current state. The value of the update gate means the scale of the previous information brought in. Then with multiplied by the weight matrix and the sigmoid function, the resulting value between [0, 1] can be acquired.

$$z_j = \sigma \left( [W_z x]_j + [U_z h_{n-1}]_j + [b_z]_j \right) \tag{4}$$

Then a new candidate set $\tilde{h}_{j,n}$ is computed according to the reset gate $r_j$, which also gets involved in controlling the balance among the input, memory and output value, defined by the following equation.

$$\tilde{h}_{j,n} = \psi \left( [W x]_j + [U(r \odot h_{n-1})]_j + [b_h]_j \right) \tag{5}$$

where the hyperbolic tangent activation function $\psi$ is applied, and $\odot$ is a special multiplication of vectors element-wise multiplication. The final semantic vector $c$ is derived from the vector representation $h_{j,n}$ at the last time step $n$.

$$h_{j,n} = z_j h_{j,n-1} + (1 - z_j)_j \tilde{h}_{j,n} \tag{6}$$

## 3.2 Decoder Network

The output of the Decoder is a fixed-dimensional vector. Each embedding vector matches to a corresponding word in the corpus-driven dictionary. Specifically, the probability of the target word is calculated referring to the similarity between the embedding vectors. Finally, the fixed-length vector is converted into a variable length target sequence $y = y_1, y_2, ..., y_m$. Unlike previous classical statistical models that rely on word frequency for prediction, our network pays more attention to the semantic and syntactic features of sentences. So as to predict the output of the next moment $m$ in the sequence, the probability distribution model of the sequence is defined as the conditional distribution $p(y_m | y_{m-1}, y_{m-2}, ..., y_1)$ in the $m$ time step, whose polynomial is defined as follows:

$$p(y_{j,m} | y_{m-1}, y_{m-2}, ..., y_1, c) = Softmax(Wh_m + b) \tag{7}$$

Dissimilar to the encoder, the information about the hidden layer state vector representation $c$ is stored in the sequence $x_n, x_{n-1}, ..., x_1$, which encodes the entire input sequence $x$. Therefore, the output of each moment maintaining the information of $c$ will be in consideration. The calculation of the hidden state on the decoder side is:

$$h_m = GRU(h_{m-1}, y_{m-1}, c) \tag{8}$$

$$p(y_{j,m}) = Softmax(h_{m-1}, y_{m-1}, c) \tag{9}$$

where $p(y_{j,m})$ is the output of the decoder network at time step $m$, and the GRU unit is also applied here. Meanwhile, the loss function of model training is:

$$loss = max_\Theta \frac{1}{m} \sum_m^1 logp(y_m | x_n) \tag{10}$$

It is worth noting that the output sequence $y$ is not the ideal PPTL specification, which will be pushed directly onto the stack in reverse order. Then, the priority of each temporal logic operator is defined, such as $\bigcirc$ (next) and $<>$ (sometimes). When the operator is popped, the previously popped word sequence is packed into independent propositional proposition like $P, Q, R...$ nested by parentheses. Until the end-of-sentence symbol pops up, the final PPTL formula is obtained.

## 4  Experiments

We firstly select five real-world security requirements to form a larger effective dataset. Then PPTLGenerator is utilized to generate corresponding PPTL formulas. The processed sentence patterns cover five temporal operators and basic sentence patterns. The requirements are described as follows:

(1) CARA: The system detects the patient's blood pressure, pulse and other vital signs and makes a series of medical information prompt operations.
(2) ELEVATOR: The scene of the rescue robot used. The responsibility of the robot is to find the injured and take them to the doctor's position in the corresponding department.
(3) ROBOT: The shopping apps, item handling apps, online booking apps, messaging apps, and local bulletin board apps.
(4) TELEPROMISE: The rules for the operation of fixed lifting equipment on prescribed floors.
(5) 3GPP: The 3rd generation partnership Project in technical specification group services and system aspects for security architecture and procedures for 5G system (Table 1 and Figs. 2, 3).

**Table 1.** Effective conversion in integrated datasets

| Dataset | Dataset size | Successfully generated |
| --- | --- | --- |
| CARA | 67 | 51 |
| ELEVATOR | 16 | 16 |
| ROBOT | 76 | 54 |
| TELEPROMISE | 77 | 53 |
| 3GPP | 11 | 9 |

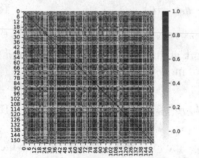

**Fig. 2.** Data diversity in the training set          **Fig. 3.** Data diversity in the validation set

As shown in the reference table, we used the PPTLGenerator tool to obtain 183 valid data. The quatity of data is not suitable for neural network training, but multiple datasets are integrated with a certain diversity. We use a heat map to analyze the similarity of its internal data, as shown in the figure below. In detail, the cosine similarity is utilized to measure data diversity, and the threshold is set to 0.5. The implementation results show that the similarity reaches 38% and 47% in the training set and validation set respectively, which alleviates the degree of overfitting to a certain extent. Meanwhile, we increase the number of training epochs upto 4000 with 32 batch size and 256 embedding size, and randomly divide the data set into nearly 2:8: a training set and a validation set, which achieves a good performance with overfitting problem. The principle of complete matching is applied as an indicator, in other words, the source language corresponds to the target language one-to-one, and the BLEU score [20] of successfully translated PPTL is 0.6917 in our experiment. As an instance, the translation result and the score of BLEU evaluation are put into github via randomly selecting 10 vaild data in the validation result.[1]

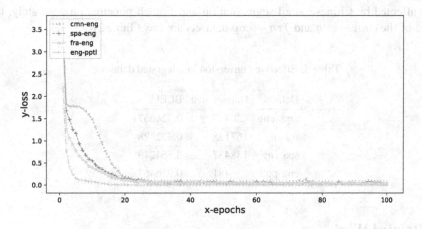

**Fig. 4.** Training loss

Data in other experiment is selected from the open-source dataset a PROMISE software engineering repository dataset made publicly available, in order to encourage repeatable, verifiable, refutable, or improvable predictive models of software engineering. Among them, 625 pieces of data exist, of which 413 pieces of data have been successfully converted into the target language in the dataset. The parameter design is the same as that of the above experiment. Through our neural translation model, we obtained a BLEU score of 0.5617.

The quantity of datasets we collect does not meet the requirements of neural network training, so the data enhancement method (DA) [17] is adopted, which aims to generate additional synthetic training data named $eng - pptl$ in insufficient scenarios. We adopt the method based on logic rules, with giving two proposition texts $x^a$ and $x^b$ whose value are true, a new text $\tilde{x}$ can be generated by $and$ operation. The method based on data logic can ensure the effectiveness of the enhanced data. It can also be considered as a part of the same distribution of the original data, which has similar semantics in machine translation. Meanwhile, we also analyzed relevant datasets in the field of neural network translation. In specific, we select three common languages with their translation from $tatoeba.org$, the translation files of which are Chinese to English named $cmn - eng$ with 28447 data, French to English named $fra - eng$ with 167138 data, and Spanish to English named $spa - eng$ with 138437 data. Another experiment is

---

[1] https://github.com/luoluohuaci/NL2PPTL_NMT.

showed in the Fig. 4 with the 128 batchsize and 100 epochs, we can observe that the loss value of the synthetic text is smaller than other datasets due to the repeated occurrence of some contents, which also makes our model reach the convergence state quickly. In order to avoid the disappearance of the gradient, we use the random gradient strategy to make the model still have small fluctuations in the convergence state. For convenience, the obtained the BLEU scores [20] are shown in the table. The scoring strategy is more favorable for matching successful long sentences, so the synthetic dataset $eng - pptl$ gets higher scores than other datasets derived from daily social statistics. At the same time, affected by Chinese word segmentation and French punctuation separately, the scores of the $cmn - eng$ and $fra - eng$ datasets are low (Table 2).

**Table 2.** Effective conversion in integrated datasets

| Dataset | Dataset size | BLEU |
| --- | --- | --- |
| cmn-eng | 28447 | 0.324667 |
| fra-eng | 167138 | 0.372328 |
| spa-eng | 138437 | 0.564249 |
| eng-pptl | 36481 | 0.986467 |

## 5   Related Work

In this section, the current researches on the automatic conversion method for formal representation generation are given, which mainly consist of automatic description generation. Finally, the value and advantages of our research are introduced.

In the field of automatically generated MR, the first method is to employ formal language theory directly [5]. Leila Kosseim [30] et al. use a template to directly map problems described in natural language to SQL statements through syntactic analysis. Sourav Mandal [18] et al. propose a model to store the extracted information of mathematical word problem content in a predefined template. Then, an object-oriented paradigm is utilized to model the template, and form an automatic mapping to executable Java code. Mller Wolfgang [10] et al. defined a formal specification template, which can realize natural language text to CCTL (Clocked CTL), and gave a specification for generating clock CTL formulas for model checking. Hu Kai [14] et al. design a set of code generation templates from AADL to the object platform, where templates represent automatic code generation rules, and develop an automatic code generation tool. The above-mentioned scholars have done lots of research on the automatic generation of MR based on templates. The generation rules described in templates are fixed, and the conversion efficiency is high. However, the content format is strictly restricted. At the same time, the update and maintenance of the template requires a lot of manpower. To further increase the flexibility of the conversion rules, some technologies combine with NLP and ML. Graham Neubig [35] et al. complete the task that integrates external knowledge into the code generation process through data resampling, pre-training and fine-tuning. Tom Mitchell [29] et al. analyze the structural rules in dialogue sequences contents, constructed text features with contextual information, and apply a joint learning semantic parser to generate logical forms. The second method is to employ statistical machine translation approaches. David Sheridan [25] et al. propose a decision tree-based supervised learning algorithm and a coverage-guided mining algorithm to generate high-quality assertions. The verification engine cooperates with experts to manually assist in screening accurate assertions. Matthias Scheutz et al. [15] infer LTL formulas from the behavior trajectory of Markov's decision-making process, and solve the problem of multi-objective optimization in the LTL formula space. The technology can be empirically inferred to generate rules without manual formulation. Nevertheless, the quality of generation is affected by the degree of model training, reliable training datasets and expert support. At present, the problem of overfitting and information loss in model training has not been resolved. In conclusion, translating security requirements into PPTL is a challenge in requirements engineering and formal methods. Such as it is the basis of requirements consistency analysis, because ontology and attributes can be directly extracted from fine-grained PPTL specification. It is also the basis of model checking because the security requirements must be expressed in formal language. Our translation process [5] is based on parsing an NL requirement according to a context free grammar, and constructing a temporal representation from the binary tree.

Formal specification can be regard as target language with rigorous mathematical argumentation, which ensures no logical problems in the security requirements. It constructs the requirements into formal logical formulas for verification. The PPTL formula we choose is more expressive and gradually applied in the industry compared to other formal languages, such as security protocols, control systems, and some conventional software applications, such as currency transaction systems [34], safety-critical task scheduling systems [39], blockchain systems [40], traffic light control systems [8], Petri net [26] and other fields. Further, it is currently exploring potential applications such as neural network verification [33] and big data processing [38]. Based on the formal verification, our work realizes the automatic conversion of natural language to PPTL logical formulas, and preliminary implement the symbol modelization in formal verification work. In our paper, the machine translation model is used to realize the transformation from informal language to formal language, which can effectively improve the efficiency of formal modeling, and promote the barrier-free communication between people and machines, as well as make PPTL better applicable to various industries. In the meantime, the self-learning process of neural network replaces the transformation template and rules formulated by experts, which reduces the consumption of time and space. However, unfortunately, more research is still needed for automatic transformation to specifications in neural networks. On the one hand, it is necessary to enrich and share real datasets, and on the other hand, to explore the application of advanced models such as attention mechanism and transfer model in the transformation for informal language to real language.

## 6    Conclusion

This paper attempts to propose an automatic generation method of natural language text to PPTL temporal logic specification based on neural translation model. Meanwhile, we conduct experimental analysis on various datasets. The results show that our method can effectively generate temporal logic. In the future, we will introduce the Few-shot Learning method to expand the dataset, and also consider the attention mechanism to improve the accuracy of transformation.

# References

1. Abie, H., Aredo, D.B., Kristoffersen, T., Mazaher, S., Raguin, T.: Integrating a security requirement language with UML. In: Baar, T., Strohmeier, A., Moreira, A., Mellor, S.J. (eds.) UML 2004. LNCS, vol. 3273, pp. 350–364. Springer, Heidelberg (2004). https://doi.org/10.1007/978-3-540-30187-5_25
2. Acharya, S., Mohanty, H., George, C.: Domain consistency in requirements specification. In: Fifth International Conference on Quality Software (QSIC 2005), pp. 231–238. IEEE (2005)
3. Ameur, Y.A., Boniol, F., Wiels, V.: Toward a wider use of formal methods for aerospace systems design and verification. Int. J. Softw. Tools Technol. Transf. **12**(1), 1–7 (2010)
4. Brunello, A., Montanari, A., Reynolds, M.: Synthesis of LTL formulas from natural language texts: State of the art and research directions. In: 26th International Symposium on Temporal Representation and Reasoning (TIME 2019). Schloss Dagstuhl-Leibniz-Zentrum fuer Informatik (2019)
5. Buzhinsky, I.: Formalization of natural language requirements into temporal logics: a survey. In: 2019 IEEE 17th International Conference on Industrial Informatics (INDIN), vol. 1, pp. 400–406. IEEE (2019)
6. Cho, K., et al.: Learning phrase representations using RNN encoder-decoder for statistical machine translation. arXiv preprint arXiv:1406.1078 (2014)
7. Duan, Z.: An extended interval temporal logic and a framing technique for temporal logic programming. Ph.D. thesis, Newcastle University (1996)
8. Duan, Z., Tian, C., Yang, M., He, J.: Bounded model checking for propositional projection temporal logic. In: Du, D.-Z., Zhang, G. (eds.) COCOON 2013. LNCS, vol. 7936, pp. 591–602. Springer, Heidelberg (2013). https://doi.org/10.1007/978-3-642-38768-5_52
9. Emerson, E.A., Sistla, A.P.: Deciding full branching time logic. Inf. Control **61**(3), 175–201 (1984)
10. Flake, S., Müller, W., Ruf, J.: Structured English for model checking specification. In: MBMV, pp. 99–108 (2000)
11. Gong, Y., Chuan, C.H., Yongwei, Z., Sakauchi, M.: A generic video parsing system with a scene description language (SDL). Real-Time Imaging **2**(1), 45–59 (1996)
12. Guo, J., et al.: Towards complex text-to-SQL in cross-domain database with intermediate representation. arXiv preprint arXiv:1905.08205 (2019)
13. Hsiung, E., et al.: Generalizing to new domains by mapping natural language to lifted LTL. In: 2022 International Conference on Robotics and Automation (ICRA), pp. 3624–3630. IEEE (2022)
14. Hu, K., Duan, Z., Wang, J., Gao, L., Shang, L.: Template-based AADL automatic code generation. Front. Comput. Sci. **13**(4), 698–714 (2019)
15. Kasenberg, D., Scheutz, M.: Interpretable apprenticeship learning with temporal logic specifications. In: 2017 IEEE 56th Annual Conference on Decision and Control (CDC), pp. 4914–4921. IEEE (2017)
16. Khan, N.A., Jhanjhi, N.Z., Brohi, S.N., Nayyar, A.: Emerging use of UAV's: secure communication protocol issues and challenges. In: Drones in Smart-Cities, pp. 37–55. Elsevier (2020)

17. Li, B., Hou, Y., Che, W.: Data augmentation approaches in natural language processing: a survey. CoRR (2021)
18. Mandal, S., Naskar, S.K.: Natural language programing with automatic code generation towards solving addition-subtraction word problems. In: Proceedings of the 14th International Conference on Natural Language Processing (ICON-2017), pp. 146–154 (2017)
19. Manning, C.D., Surdeanu, M., Bauer, J., Finkel, J.R., Bethard, S., McClosky, D.: The stanford CoreNLP natural language processing toolkit. In: Proceedings of 52nd Annual Meeting of the Association for Computational Linguistics: System Demonstrations, pp. 55–60 (2014)
20. Papineni, K., Roukos, S., Ward, T., Zhu, W.J.: BLEU: a method for automatic evaluation of machine translation. In: Proceedings of the 40th Annual Meeting of the Association for Computational Linguistics, pp. 311–318 (2002)
21. Pnueli, A.: The temporal logic of programs. In: 18th Annual Symposium on Foundations of Computer Science (SFCS 1977), pp. 46–57. IEEE (1977)
22. Qureshi, Z.H.: Formal modelling and analysis of mission-critical software in military avionics systems. In: Proceedings of the Eleventh Australian Workshop on Safety Critical Systems and Software, vol. 69, pp. 67–77 (2007)
23. Sedo, S., Seong, P.H.: A comparative study of formal methods for safety critical software in nuclear power plant. Nucl. Eng. Technol. **32**(6), 537–548 (2000)
24. Seshia, S.A., Sadigh, D., Sastry, S.S.: Formal methods for semi-autonomous driving. In: 2015 52nd ACM/EDAC/IEEE Design Automation Conference (DAC), pp. 1–5. IEEE (2015)
25. Sheridan, D.: GoldMine: an integration of data mining and static analysis for automatic generation of hardware assertions (2011)
26. Shi, Y., Tian, C., Duan, Z., Zhou, M.: Model checking petri nets with MSVL. Inf. Sci. **363**, 274–291 (2016)
27. Shu, X., Zhang, N., Wang, X., Zhao, L.: Efficient decision procedure for propositional projection temporal logic. Theor. Comput. Sci. **838**, 1–16 (2020)
28. Specification, A., Bialkowski, J., Diaz, J., Buttner, A., Evan, M.R., Wittbold, J.: Application vulnerability description (2004)
29. Srivastava, S., Azaria, A., Mitchell, T.M.: Parsing natural language conversations using contextual cues. In: IJCAI, pp. 4089–4095 (2017)
30. Stratica, N., Kosseim, L., Desai, B.C.: NLIDB templates for semantic parsing. In: Natural Language Processing and Information Systems (2003)
31. Tian, C., Duan, Z.: Expressiveness of propositional projection temporal logic with star. Theor. Comput. Sci. **412**(18), 1729–1744 (2011)
32. Wang, X., Li, G., Li, C., Zhao, L., Shu, X.: Automatic generation of specification from natural language based on temporal logic. In: Xue, J., Nagoya, F., Liu, S., Duan, Z. (eds.) SOFL+MSVL 2020. LNCS, vol. 12723, pp. 154–171. Springer, Cham (2021). https://doi.org/10.1007/978-3-030-77474-5_11
33. Wang, X., Yang, K., Wang, Y., Zhao, L., Shu, X.: Towards formal verification of neural networks: a temporal logic based framework. In: Miao, H., Tian, C., Liu, S., Duan, Z. (eds.) SOFL+MSVL 2019. LNCS, vol. 12028, pp. 73–87. Springer, Cham (2020). https://doi.org/10.1007/978-3-030-41418-4_6
34. Wang, X., Yang, X., Li, C.: A formal verification method for smart contract. In: 2020 7th International Conference on Dependable Systems and their Applications (DSA), pp. 31–36. IEEE (2020)
35. Xu, F.F., Jiang, Z., Yin, P., Vasilescu, B., Neubig, G.: Incorporating external knowledge through pre-training for natural language to code generation. arXiv preprint arXiv:2004.09015 (2020)
36. Yan, R., Cheng, C.H., Chai, Y.: Formal consistency checking over specifications in natural languages. In: 2015 Design, Automation & Test in Europe Conference & Exhibition (DATE), pp. 1677–1682. IEEE (2015)

37. Zhang, J., Yang, L., Cao, W., Wang, Q.: Formal analysis of 5G EAP-TLS authentication protocol using proverif. IEEE Access **8**, 23674–23688 (2020)
38. Zhang, N., Wang, M., Duan, Z., Tian, C.: Verifying properties of mapreduce-based big data processing. IEEE Trans. Reliab. (2020)
39. Zhang, N., Yang, M., Gu, B., Duan, Z., Tian, C.: Verifying safety critical task scheduling systems in PPTL axiom system. J. Comb. Optim. **31**(2), 577–603 (2016)
40. Zhu, W.: PPTL model checking for blockchains. In: 2020 IEEE 5th Information Technology and Mechatronics Engineering Conference (ITOEC), pp. 792–795. IEEE (2020)
41. Zhu, Y., Zhang, Y., Yang, H., Wang, F.: GANCoder: an automatic natural language-to-programming language translation approach based on GAN. In: Tang, J., Kan, M.-Y., Zhao, D., Li, S., Zan, H. (eds.) NLPCC 2019. LNCS (LNAI), vol. 11839, pp. 529–539. Springer, Cham (2019). https://doi.org/10.1007/978-3-030-32236-6_48

# Testing Program Segments to Detect Runtime Exceptions in Java

Lei Rao⬤, Shaoying Liu(✉) ⬤, and Ai Liu⬤

Graduate School of Advanced Science and Engineering, Hiroshima University,
Hiroshima 739-8511, Japan
sliu@hiroshima-u.ac.jp

**Abstract.** Runtime exceptions are difficult to be detected by static analysis tools and their occurrences in runtime often cause software systems to crash or unexcepted termination. Therefore, it is necessary to detect the existence of runtime exceptions in the program before it is executed. In this paper, we describe a novel program segment testing technique for detecting potential occurrences of runtime exceptions during the program construction process. Our testing technique is characterized by three steps. The first step is to determine the target program segment in which potential runtime exceptions may occur during the program execution. The second step is to form an appropriate environment to test the program segment by determining the values of the variables. The final step is to carry out the testing and determine whether the runtime exceptions will occur and will be handled properly during the system execution. This paper also presents a case study to demonstrate that the technique is effective.

**Keywords:** Fault Detection · Program Slicing · Software Testing · Runtime Exceptions

## 1 Introduction

Software testing is an expensive and laborious endeavor, accounting for over 50% of software developments costs and even more in critical systems [1, 2]. The purpose of software testing is not only to detect defects and errors in the program, but also to measure and evaluate software quality to provide robustness for the program under test. With the increasing scale and complexity of software, it will inevitably lead to more and more faults in the program, which brings a great burden to the testing work.

Exceptions in Java can be classified into two categories. One is *checked exceptions*, and the other is *runtime exceptions*. Checked exceptions are those exceptions that are explicitly thrown before the program is executed in response to unexpected situations at runtime, and runtime exceptions are generated by the Java runtime environment when the program is running. Checked exceptions are detected by the compiler during programming and forced to be handled, either caught with a try-catch statement or declared with a throws clause to ensure that the program can still run normally when such exceptions occur. Runtime exceptions only occur while a program is running. Therefore, our goal

© The Author(s), under exclusive license to Springer Nature Switzerland AG 2023
S. Liu et al. (Eds.): SOFL+MSVL 2022, LNCS 13854, pp. 93–105, 2023.
https://doi.org/10.1007/978-3-031-29476-1_8

is how to detect the existing or potential runtime exceptions in the program at compile time. Common runtime exceptions are divided into three categories, including index exceptions, such as an attempt to access an array element using an index that is out of the boundary of the defined array; arithmetic exceptions, such as dividing by zero; and pointer exceptions, such as trying to access an object through a null reference. Since such exceptions are not required to be caught in Java, when they occur during execution, there is no exception handler available to handle them, causing the program stops [3].

In order to avoid runtime exceptions during program execution, researchers adopted various testing techniques and strategies to detect them at compile time. Software testing keeps in line with its criticality in the pre- and post-development process makes it something that should be catered with efficient strategies and techniques [4]. Common software testing techniques include white-box testing [5], black-box testing [6] and grey-box testing [7], etc., and software testing strategies include unit testing [8], integration testing [9] and system testing [10] and so on. Nonetheless for each testing requirement, we can find relatively suitable testing techniques and testing strategies, however, there are still some defects in them. For example, it is difficult for system testing to accurately perform the detection of specific exceptions. Unit testing lacks inter-procedural analysis, resulting in system and integration errors that may be missed.

Therefore, on the basis of unit testing, we retain its modularity and automation advantages, and propose a technique for testing program segments to detect the existing and potential specific exceptions, which is called *Program Segment Testing* (PST). Specially, our technique includes following functions: (1) automatically locate the statements that may trigger specific exception in a program; (2) automatically identify all variables in a segment, and slice all the fragments related to them in the program; (3) automatically reassemble them into a segment, and test it in the context of the current program to determine the occurrences of specific exceptions.

The remainder of the paper is outlined as follows. Section 2 introduces basic knowledge for understanding our technique. Section 3 presents the method we propose in detail. Section 4 applies our method to an example program to illustrate it. Section 5 compares our technique with related work. Section 6 concludes the paper and points out future directions.

## 2    Preliminary

### 2.1    Arithmetic Exceptions in Java

Arithmetic exceptions are exceptions that are thrown when an error occurs in an arithmetic, cast, or transformation operation. As shown in Fig. 1, in Java, arithmetic exceptions can be more specifically divided into three categories, including: DivideByZero exception, NotFiniteNumber exception and Overflow exception.

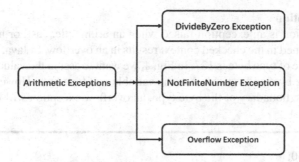

**Fig. 1.** Arithmetic exceptions in Java

## DivideByZero Exception

DivideByZero exception is an exception thrown when trying to divide an integer or decimal value by zero. As can be seen from Fig. 2, since the value of *b* is 0, when we want to output the value of *a* divided by *b*, the exception will be triggered at this time.

```
main () {
    int a = 10;
    int b = 0;
    int c = a/b;
    print(c);
}
```

**Fig. 2.** Example for DivideByZero exception

## NotFiniteNumber Exception

NotFiniteNumber exception is an exception thrown when a floating-point value is positive infinity, negative infinity or not a number (NaN). In Java, this exception occurs in operations on variables of type BigDecimal. As shown in Fig. 3, we use a variable *a* of type BigDecimal divided by *b* and set to retain four digits after the decimal point. We in turn set the rounding mode of the decimal point to UNNECESSARY, which asserts that the requested operation has an exact result without the decimal point being rounded. However, since the result is infinite at this time, the NotFiniteNumber exception will occurs.

```
main () {
    BigDecimal a = new BigDecimal (100);
    BigDecimal b = new BigDecimal (13);
    BigDecimal c = a.divide (b, 4, ROUND_UNNECESSARY);
    print (c);
}
```

**Fig. 3.** Example for NotFiniteNumber exception

**Overflow Exception**

Overflow exception is an exception raised when an arithmetic, cast, or transformation operation performed in the checked context results in an overflow. In Java, the maximum value of a variable of type byte is 127. In Fig. 4, we want to assign the value of adding the variable *a* of type byte and variable *b* to the variable *c* of type byte. However, since 150 is greater than the boundary of the byte type, an overflow exception will be triggered.

```
main () {
    byte a = 50;
    byte b = 100;
    byte c = a + b;
    print c;
}
```

Fig. 4. Example for Overflow exception

## 2.2 System Dependency Graph

System Dependency Graph (SDG) is multigraph that maps control and data dependencies between Java program statements. Statements are categorized according to whether they contribute to the constructure (i.e. methods, classes) of the program or the behavior (i.e. belong to a method body) of the program [11]. Each category has a different representation on the graph. In short, SDG is a graph that captures all the data, control as well as the inter-procedural dependencies present in a program. It consists of Procedure Dependency Graphs (PDG) for each procedure present in the program, including the main function. Various PDGs are linked together using auxiliary dependency edges.

An example program is given in Fig. 5 and its corresponding SDG is shown in Fig. 6.

```
main () {
    int a = 1;
    int b = 1;
    int c = multiply (a, b);
    print c;
}
int multiply (int a, int b){
    int c = a * b;
    return c;
}
```

Fig. 5. An example program

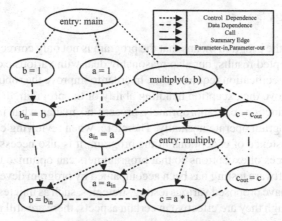

**Fig. 6.** System dependency graph for program shown in Fig. 5

## 2.3 Program Slicing

Program slicing is the computation of the set of program statements, the result of which is a program slice, which may affect the value of a certain point of interest, referred to as a slicing criterion [12]. Program slicing is an effective technique for narrowing the focus of attention to the relevant parts of a program. A slice consists of statements and predicates that have influence on the variables at a program point.

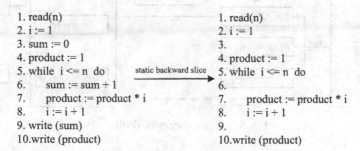

**Fig. 7.** An example program for static backward slicing

Slicing techniques has evolved rapidly since it was originally defined by Mark Weiser [12]. At first, slicing was just static, that is, only applied to the source code without other information. Then, Bogdan Korel and Janusz Laski introduced dynamic slicing, which applies to a specific execution of a program (for a given execution trace) [13].

For example, in static slicing, the slicing criterion has the form of $<i, v>$ where i the serial number of a statement in the program, and v is the variable set. We use $<10,$ product> to perform static backward slices on the program on the left in Fig. 7, and we get the slice on the right.

## 3   Methodology

The robustness of the program means that the program is not only correct, runs normally and produces excepted results, but also reasonably deal with various exceptional situations outside the specification requirements. In order to improve the robustness, it means that we must improve the exception handling ability of the program, that is, the written code, such as a function, can appropriately process no matter what input is faced to ensure that the program operate normally. Therefore, when reviewing code, in addition to locating the existence of exceptions in the program, it is also necessary to point out potential occurrences of exceptions so that programmers can optimize the code.

To this end, software testing has been accompanied by program development. Moreover, researchers have proposed various testing strategies, such as unit testing and system testing, etc. Although they are effective in certain aspects, there are still many shortcomings. First, one or a group of test sets usually cannot meet the testing requirements of all exceptions at the same time, so we consider generating specific test set for each exception and test them separately. However, there is usually only a small part of the code in a program that causes an exception to be triggered, and testing the entire program is time-consuming and inefficient. So, can we intercept code fragments that may trigger an exception and reassemble them for testing? In addition, can we achieve a prompt that a line of code will trigger a specific exception during the programming process, so as to achieve a "Correct-By-Construction" effect?

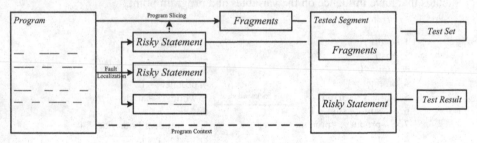

**Fig. 8.** Program Segment Testing

In order to solve the above problems, as shown in Fig. 8, we propose a *Program Segment Testing* technique, which can automatically detect the existing and potential runtime exceptions in the program. Meanwhile, to implement this technique, we give the algorithm in Algorithm 1. First, we assume that using existing automatic fault localization techniques [14], such as Tarantula [15], regular expressions [16], etc., to locate the statements in the program that may trigger runtime exceptions, which are called *Risky Statements*, and add them to the set *RS*. Next, for each statement in *RS*, it is necessary to test and determine whether it will trigger a runtime exception or whether there is a vulnerability that triggers runtime exception caused by user input. Our technique traverses all variables contained in a statement and add them to the collection *VAR*. Then, for each variable, based on the SDG, it uses program slicing technique to slice all fragments associated with this variable in the program, and combine them with the statement into a segment for testing. Final, our technique tests each segment in the context of the current program.

For each segment, if it does not contain any input from user to a variable, execute the segment directly, and the test result will show whether there is an exception in the program. Otherwise, it is necessary to generate specific test sets for the variables to test. It should be noted that the *specific* meaning is to judge which exception it may trigger according to the characteristics of the statement, so as to use the relevant testing techniques and automatic test case generation technology to generate suitable test sets [17, 18]. For example, the trigger of the DivideByZero exception must be the existence of a division operation in the statement, so the motivation for test case generation is to detect where the denominator may be equal to 0.

---

**Algorithm 1** Semi-formal algorithm for Program Segment Testing

*RS*: A set of all statements that may trigger a specific exception in a program
*SEG:* A set of segments spliced from code fragments obtained by slicing the program according to each statement in the *RS* collection
*VAR:* A set of all variables contained in each statement in the *RS* collection

**Input:** *RS*
**Output:** *Test Result*

**begin**
$RS = \{rs_1, rs_2, ..., rs_n\}$ , $SEG = \varnothing$, $VAR = \varnothing$, $i = 0$
**foreach** rs in *RS* **do**
    traverse all variables contained in it and add to *VAR*
    **foreach** v in *Var* **do**
        slice all fragments associated with v in program
        $seg_i = seg_i \cup$ fragments
    **end loop**
    $SEG = seg_i \cup SEG$
    i++;
**end loop**

**foreach** seg in *SEG*   **do**
    **if** seg does not contain any input from user to a variable
        execute seg in the context of the current program and produce a test result
    **else**
        generate specific test sets for variables to test and produce a test result
    **endif**
**end loop**
**end**

## 4   Case Study

In this paper, we use a simple case to illustrate the practical application of our method.

```
1. main () {
2.     BigDecimal a, b, c;
3.     int d, e, f, g;
4.     a = new BigDecimal (100);
5.     b = ? ;
6.     d = 5 ;
7.     e = ? ;
8.     c = divide (a, b, e);
9.     f = add (e);
10.    g = square (d, f);
11.}
12. BigDecimal divide (BigDecimal a, BigDecimal b, int e) {
13.    BigDecimal c = a.divide (b, e, RoundingMode.UNNECESSARY);
14.    return c;
15.}
16. int add (int e) {
17.    int f = e + 10;
18.    return f;
19.}
20.int square (int d, int f) {
21.    int g = Math.pow (d, f);
22.    return g;
23.}
```

**Fig. 9.** A Java example program for illustrates arithmetic exception

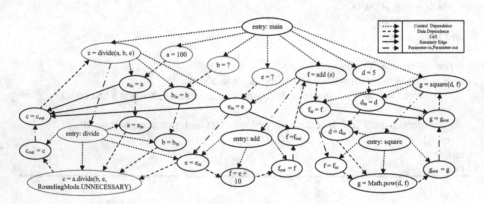

**Fig. 10.** System dependency graph for program shown in Fig. 9

The example program is given in Fig. 9 and its corresponding SDG is shown in Fig. 10. It should be noted that for the purpose of simplifying the expression, we use "?" in them to represent user input.

First of all, we can know from the fault localization technique that lines 13, 17, and 21 have the risk of triggering arithmetic exceptions. Next, it is necessary to test each statement separately to determine whether it triggers an arithmetic exception or a vulnerability that triggers an arithmetic exception caused by user input in the context of the program. The premise of testing is that there is a testable program, and operations such as variable definition, initialization, and reference are indispensable, so it is essential to intercept relevant code from other parts of the program. In addition, the root cause of the arithmetic exception is that the variables in the statement take unexpected values, so we can narrow the scope and only focus on the code related to all the variables in the statement. Our technique uses program slicing technology to accomplish this operation based on SDG.

We can see from the upper right corner of the Fig. 10 that SDG contains five different edges, each representing a different meaning. Control dependence edges represent control conditions on which the execution of a statement or expression depends; data dependence edges represent flow of data between statements or expressions; a call edge connects a call vertex to entry vertex of the called procedure's PDG; parameter-in and parameter-out edges represent parameter passing: parameter-in edges connect actual-in and formal-in vertices, and parameter-out edges connect formal-out and actual-out vertices. Somewhat special, SDG uses summary edges to explicitly represent the transitive flow of dependence across call sites caused by data dependences, control dependences, or both. That is, if the value associated with the actual-in vertex may affect the value associated with the actual-out vertex, a summary edge will connect them [19]. As the name implies, data dependence edges and parameter-in and parameter-out edges contain the transmission of data in the program, and call edges specify the function call relationship in the program. A risky statement corresponds to a certain vertex in the SDG. In fact, the process of constructing a segment starts from this vertex, and finds all vertexes related to it in the program through data dependencies edges, parameter-in and parameter-out edges and call edges.

we use the *divide* method with the variable $a$ of type BigDecimal to divide the variable $b$, set to retain $e$ digits after the decimal point, the rounding mode is UNNECESSARY, and assign the obtained value to $c$. After traversing this statement, we can see that it contains four variables $a$, $b$, $c$ and $e$. Then, our technique uses $<13, a>$, $<13, b>$, $<13, c>$, $<13, e>$ as the slicing criterion to slice the program respectively to obtain the four program fragments and combine them into a program segment in Fig. 11. This slicing process is represented in the SDG as starting from the red vertex and finally tracing back to the 5 blue vertexes in Fig. 10. From the characteristics of the statement, including the division operation and rounding mode for decimal point, it can be concluded that this statement may trigger the DivideByZero and NotFiniteNumber exceptions. In addition, the segment contains user input, therefore, specific test cases need to be generated for testing. For the DivideByZero exception, the goal of test cases generation is to make the denominator 0. Obviously, the denominator is $b$, and the value of $b$ is input by the user, that is, the test case. When $b$ is 0, the DivideByZero exception will be triggered.

For the NotFiniteNumber exception, since the number of decimal points is set to retain *e* and the rounding mode is UNNECESSARY, the goal of generating the test cases is to make the digits after the decimal point of the operation result greater than *e*. When the value of *b* is 3, the result is finite, so the exception fires. From the test results, we can know that this statement has vulnerabilities that trigger the DivideByZero and NotFiniteNumber exceptions. Therefore, it is necessary to remind the programmer to use a try-catch statement to capture or declare with the throws clause to prevent the program from being interrupted at runtime.

```
a = BigDecimal (100);
b = ?;
c = divide (a, b, e);
e = ?;
BigDecimal divide (BigDecimal a, BigDecimal b, int e) {
        BigDecimal c = a.divide (b, e, RoundingMode.UNNECESSARY);
        return c;
}
```

**Fig. 11.** Program segment obtained by slicing for the line 13

```
e = ?;
int add (int e){
        int f = e + 10;
        return f;
}
```

**Fig. 12.** Program segment obtained by slicing for the line 17

```
d = 5;
e = ?;
f = add (e);
int add (int e){
        int f = e + 10;
        return f;
}
int square (int d, int f){
        int g = Math.pow (d, f);
        return g;
}
```

**Fig. 13.** Program segment obtained by slicing for the line 21

Similar operations are performed on lines 17 and 21, and the obtained segments are shown in Fig. 12 and Fig. 13 respectively. The final test results show that they do have the vulnerability to trigger the overflow exception.

# 5   Related Work

**Static Fault Detection Techniques:** Static fault detection techniques are those applied to source code to detect specific faults or vulnerabilities in the source code without running the program. Based on data flow analysis, the author takes rules describing the vulnerability patterns and the source code to detect locations and paths of the pattern in the program [20]. However, there still remain many vulnerabilities that cannot be designed as rules in their specification language they designed. It is a special case of data flow analysis where any data coming from un-trusted sources, e.g., introduced by a user, is a potential problem to the system, thus it is marked as tainted [21]. Tainted data flow is monitored unless it is processed and changed to untainted. The disadvantage of taint analysis is that less information is available about the true state of the program, so information about possible execution path is necessarily less precise. In addition to the shortcomings of these static fault detection techniques, static analysis also lacks sufficient rigor, making it prone to a large number of false positives. However, PST improves the accuracy of exception detection by testing the sliced code automatically and pointing out the type and location of the existences or potential occurrences of runtime exceptions in the program.

**Automated Unit Testing:** Unit testing is the inspection and validation of the smallest testable unit in the program, which can be a class or a method. In order to automate the generation of test cases and unrestricted the constraints imposed by specialized execution platforms and resource constraints of embedded software on the application of concolic testing to embedded software, Kim et al. developed CONcrete and symBOLic (CON-BOL) testing framework to unit test large size industrial embedded software automatically [22]. Additionally, also to implement automated unit testing of embedded software, Christoph Luckeneder et al. analyzed an as-is workflow and proposed changes to the workflow for reducing costs and time needed for performing unit tests [23]. Moreover, they also presented an improved tool chain for supporting the test workflow. Although unit testing makes it easy to test part of system without waiting for the availability of other parts, it lacks inter-procedural analysis, and unit is tested separately, so it is difficult to catch all faults in the program, and integration errors are easily missed. However, based on SDG, our method starts from each statement that may trigger an exception, and uses program slicing to obtain a slice containing all program fragments that affect the variables in the statement and perform specific tests separately, which improves the accuracy and coverage of exception detection.

# 6   Conclusion and Future Work

Runtime exceptions are ubiquitous in programs and cannot be detected by the development tool, resulting in the program to crash at runtime. In this paper, based on the idea of Human-Machine Pair Programming proposed by Prof.Liu [24], we propose a novel program segment testing technique which can detect the existence and potential occurrences of runtime exceptions during the program construction process and give prompts to programmer. Our method starts from the statement that may trigger an exception, uses program slicing to slice all related fragments in the program, and reassemble them into a segment. Then, according to the characteristics of the statement, specific test cases is automatically generated, and the segment is tested in the context of the current program to determine whether it has a fault or vulnerability that triggers a specific exception.

We apply our method to Java arithmetic exceptions. Narrow the focus of attention to the relevant parts of a program by program slicing, so that a slice only consists of statements and predicates that have influence on the variables at a risky statement. The case study proves that the method is available. Our method preserves the advantages of locality and automation of automatic unit testing, makes up for its lack of inter-procedural analysis and other limitations, and achieves automatic and precise detection of arithmetic exceptions.

As mentioned earlier, there are still some issues to be done. In addition to arithmetic exception, runtime exception also includes index exception and pointer exception, etc. Therefore, we will apply PST to more exceptions to improve the functionality of PST. Then, another important work is to implement PST in software to assist programmers to optimize the program.

# References

1. Myers, G.J., Sandler, C., Badgett, T.: The Art of Software Testing. John Wiley & Sons (2011)
2. Sy, N.T., Deville, Y.: Automatic test data generation for programs with integer and float variables, pp. 13–21. IEEE (2001)
3. https://docs.oracle.com/javase/tutorial/essential/exceptions/runtime.html
4. Jamil, M.A., Arif, M., Abubakar, N.S.A., Ahmad, A.: Software Testing Techniques: A Literature Review, pp. 177–182. IEEE (2016)
5. Ostrand, T.: White-Box testing. In: Encyclopedia of Software Engineering (2002)
6. Beizer, B.: Black-Box Testing: Techniques for Functional Testing of Software and Systems. John Wiley & Sons, Inc. (1995)
7. Dadeau, F., Peureux, F.: Grey-box Testing and Verification of Java/JML, pp. 298–303. IEEE (2011)
8. Runeson, P.: A survey of unit testing practices. IEEE Softw. **23**, 22–29 (2006)
9. Jorgensen, P.C., Erickson, C.: Object-oriented integration testing. Commun. ACM **37**, 30–38 (1994)
10. Borjesson, E., Feldt, R.: Automated system testing using visual GUI testing tools: a comparative study in industry. In: 2012 IEEE Fifth International Conference on Software Testing, Verification and Validation, pp. 350–359. IEEE (2012)
11. Walkinshaw, N., Roper, M., Wood, M.: The Java System Dependence Graph, pp. 55–64. IEEE (2003)
12. Weiser, M.: Program slicing. IEEE Trans. Softw. Eng. (4) 352–357 (1984)
13. Agrawal, H., Horgan, J.R.: Dynamic program slicing. ACM SIGPlan Notices **25**, 246–256 (1990)
14. Sinha, S., Shah, H., Görg, C., Jiang, S., Kim, M., Harrold, M.J.: Fault localization and repair for Java runtime exceptions. In: Proceedings of the Eighteenth International Symposium on Software Testing and Analysis, pp. 153–164 (2009)
15. Jones, J.A., Harrold, M.J.: Empirical evaluation of the tarantula automatic fault-localization technique. In: Proceedings of the 20th IEEE/ACM International Conference on Automated Software Engineering, pp. 273–282 (2005)

16. Pytlik, B., Renieris, M., Krishnamurthi, S., Reiss, S.P.: Automated fault localization using potential invariants. arXiv preprint cs/0310040 (2003)
17. Edvardsson, J.: A survey on automatic test data generation. In: Proceedings of the 2nd Conference on Computer Science and Engineering, pp. 21–28. Citeseer (1999)
18. Candea, G., Godefroid, P.: Automated software test generation: some challenges, solutions, and recent advances. In: Steffen, B., Woeginger, G. (eds.) Computing and Software Science. LNCS, vol. 10000, pp. 505–531. Springer, Cham (2019). https://doi.org/10.1007/978-3-319-91908-9_24
19. Sinha, S., Harrold, M.J., Rothermel, G.: System-dependence-graph-based slicing of programs with arbitrary interprocedural control flow. In: Proceedings of the 21st International Conference on Software Engineering, pp. 432–441. IEEE (1999)
20. Kim, H., Choi, T.-H., Jung, S.-C., Kim, H.-C., Lee, O., Doh, K.-G.: Applying dataflow analysis to detecting software vulnerability. In: 2008 10th International Conference on Advanced Communication Technology, pp. 255–258. IEEE (2008)
21. Livshits, V.B., Lam, M.S.: Finding security vulnerabilities in java applications with static analysis. In: USENIX Security Symposium, p. 18. (2005)
22. Kim, Y., Kim, Y., Kim, T., Lee, G., Jang, Y., Kim, M.: Automated unit testing of large industrial embedded software using concolic testing. In: 2013 28th IEEE/ACM International Conference on Automated Software Engineering (ASE), pp. 519–528. IEEE (2013)
23. Luckeneder, C., Kaindl, H., Korinek, M.: Automated Unit Testing in Model-based Embedded Software Development, pp. 427–434 (2017)
24. Liu, S.: Software construction monitoring and predicting for human-machine pair programming. In: Duan, Z., Liu, S., Tian, C., Nagoya, F. (eds.) SOFL+MSVL 2018. LNCS, vol. 11392, pp. 3–20. Springer, Cham (2019). https://doi.org/10.1007/978-3-030-13651-2_1

# Inferring Exact Domains to Efficiently Generate Valid Test Cases via Testing

Chu Chen[1], Xuan Wang[1], Pinghong Ren[1(✉)], Zhenhua Duan[2], Cong Tian[2],
Xu Lu[2], and Bin Yu[2]

[1] School of Computer Science, Qufu Normal University, Rizhao, Shandong, China
**rzqfnu@yeah.net**
[2] ICTT and ISN Laboratory, Xidian University, Xi'an, Shaanxi, China

**Abstract.** Documents on popular libraries such as pyOpenSSL do not
specify parameters' domains precisely. Inexact domains hinder efficiently
generating valid test cases. In order to solve this problem, an approach
for inferring exact domains, namely IED, is put forward. IED starts from
crawling parameters' data types from online official documents. Then,
IED conducts exception testing to find tight domains based on slack
domains of data types. Finally, IED attempts to detect the extensibility
of tight bounds and outputs exact domains. Based on IED, experiments
have been conducted on 29 basic parameters of application programming
interfaces of pyOpenSSL. Experimental results show that the inferred
exact domains vary dramatically even for the same data type and reduce
the original domains of data types significantly. Thus, IED is effective
and helpful in efficiently generating valid test cases.

**Keywords:** Infer · Exact Domain · Testing · Test cases

## 1 Introduction

Efficiently generating valid test cases is critical to testing approaches and
heavily depends on programming languages. However, documents on popular
libraries, e.g., pyOpenSSL [1], do not specify parameters' domains precisely. The
lack of exact domains hampers researchers' efforts to efficiently generate valid
test cases. For example, the types of the parameters *version* in the function
*set_version(version)* and *serial* in *set_serial_number(serial)* are specified as
"int" in the document of pyOpenSSL. It seems right for testers to pass any integer to both functions to generate test cases. Unfortunately, it is not the truth.

Supported by Shandong Provincial Natural Science Foundation under Grant
ZR2020MF030 and ZR2018PF007. Also, this work is supported by CERNET Innovation Project under Grant NGII20190407, Fundamental Research Funds for the Central Universities under Grant XJS210305, Natural Science Basic Research Program of
Shaanxi under Grant 2021JQ-208, and Natural Science Foundation of Xi'an University
of Technology under Grant 413619001.

S. Liu et al. (Eds.): SOFL+MSVL 2022, LNCS 13854, pp. 106–116, 2023.
https://doi.org/10.1007/978-3-031-29476-1_9

The slack domains indicated by parameters' data types result in producing a lot of invalid test cases.

For purpose of efficiently generating valid test cases, we put forward an approach for inferring exact domains (IED) which consists of three phases as follows. First, IED crawls online official documents to obtain parameters' data types. Second, IED searches tight domains on the basis of slack bounds of data types via exception testing. Finally, IED checks whether such tight bounds are extensible, and outputs exact domains.

IED makes the following contributions: (1) IED conducts binary search to concurrently find tight lower and upper bounds relative to slack bounds of data types via exception testing; (2) IED detects the extensibility of tight bounds and determines practical tight bounds; and (3) Most exact domains inferred by IED are very small proper subsets of slack domains of data types and help testers efficiently generate valid test cases.

The remainder is arranged as follows. The next section introduces knowledge related to IED. Then, the approach namely IED and experiments are present in Sects. 3 and 4, respectively. Related work is summarized in Sect. 5. Finally, conclusion is made in Sect. 6.

## 2   Preliminaries

Our approach, namely IED, will be illustrated with its application in a popular library named pyOpenSSL, which is frequently employed to generate X.509 certificates i.e., test cases of certificate validation. Therefore, X.509 certificates and their generation are briefly introduced for a better understanding of the intuition and effectiveness of IED.

### 2.1   X.509 Certificate

An X.509 certificate is a signed data structure that binds a public key to a person, computer, or organization. Thus, X.509 certificates are mainly used in the Secure Sockets Layer or Transport Layer Security (SSL/TLS) protocol [6,9] and implementations. As Fig. 1 shows, an X.509 certificate consists of a sequence of three required parts [2]:

(1) *tbsCertificate*, which is composed of ten fields i.e., *version, serial number, signature, validity, issuer, issuer unique identifier, subject, subject unique identifier, subject public key info*, and *extensions*;
(2) *signature algorithm*, which is an identifier of a signature algorithm employed by a certification authority to sign a certificate; and
(3) *signature value*, which is a digital signature of a certificate.

Generally, the three parts i.e., *tbsCertificate, signature algorithm*, and *signature value* are necessary. Fields such as *issuer/subject unique identifier* and *extensions* are optional.

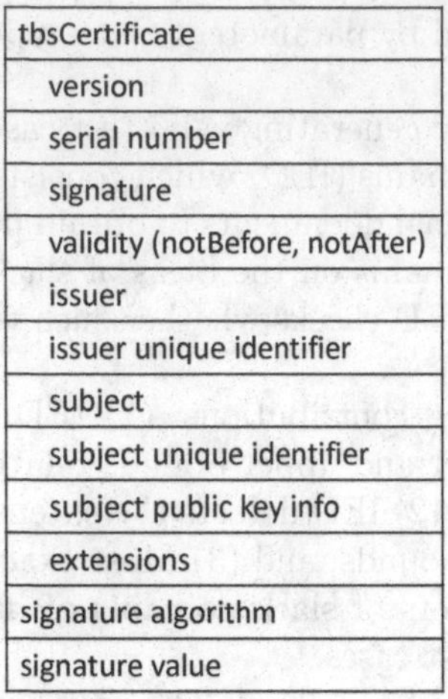

| tbsCertificate |
| --- |
| version |
| serial number |
| signature |
| validity (notBefore, notAfter) |
| issuer |
| issuer unique identifier |
| subject |
| subject unique identifier |
| subject public key info |
| extensions |
| signature algorithm |
| signature value |

**Fig. 1.** Basic structure of an X.509 certificate

## 2.2  Certificate Generation

Certificate generation employs application programming interfaces (APIs) to set values for fields shown in Fig. 1 and then sign certificates. Thus, it is critical to certificate generation whether APIs are used correctly or not. APIs have various parameters and each parameter has one data type, which is generally described in official documents related to APIs. However, domains specified by data types may not be exact and inexact domains possibly mislead testers. If testers pass invalid values to arguments, APIs are used incorrectly and test cases are not generated. If the incorrect usage of APIs frequently happens, the efficiency of certificate generation is affected. Hence, it is significant to obtain exact domains of parameters.

## 3  Inferring Exact Domains via Testing

IED starts by crawling official documents related to APIs to obtain data types of parameters. Based on slack bounds indicated by data types, IED conducts concurrent binary search and exception testing to find tight domains. Finally, IED checks the extensibility of tight bounds and outputs practical tight bounds i.e., exact domains.

### 3.1  Obtaining Data Types of Parameters

Generally, widely-used libraries offer online official documents related to APIs. Algorithm 1 crawls such documents and obtain data types of parameters. Line 2 of Algorithm 1 employs a crawler function to get contents of online official documents. Then, Lines 3–4 and 5–6 leverage regular expressions to extract static and dynamic typed APIs and data types of parameters, respectively. For static typed libraries, APIs are described in the form of $funcName(DataType_1$ $parameter_1,/; \dots )$ or $funcName(parameter_1{:}DataType_1,/; \dots )$. Thus, it is easy to leverage regular expressions to extract triples in the form of $<API, parameter$ $name, data type>$. For dynamic typed libraries, APIs are described in the form of $funcName(parameter_1, \dots )$ followed by the explanation of parameters' data type. Therefore, data types of parameters are extracted from such explanations. Finally, Line 7 of Algorithm 1 returns $\{< API, parameter, data type >\}$, in which the second element is one parameter of the first element i.e., API and the third element indicates the parameter's data type. If the number of APIs is $x$ and the average number of parameters of each API is $y$, the number of triples returned by Algorithm 1 is $x \cdot y$.

---

**Algorithm 1.** Obtaining data types of parameters

---

**Input:** Online official documents
**Output:** APIs and their parameters' data types
1: $ret \leftarrow \emptyset;$          ▷ initialize the variable 'ret' which is a set of <API, parameter, data type>
2: $con \leftarrow funcCrawler(documents);$          ▷ crawl online official documents
3: **if** APIs are static typed **then**          ▷ case: funcName(int p1, ...)
4:     $ret \leftarrow funcReStaticType(con);$
5: **else**          ▷ case: funcName(p1, ...)
6:     $ret \leftarrow funcReDynamicType(con);$
7: **end if**
8: **return** $ret;$

---

With these data types of parameters, slack domains are obtained according to the programming language specifications and x64/x86 architectures. For example, one popular data type named "int" of the Python programming language in x64 ranges from $-\infty$ to $\infty$, where the symbols $-\infty$ and $\infty$ denote bounds depending on the memory size of a host machine. Based on slack domains, tight domains will be inferred by IED in the following sub-sections.

## 3.2   Inferring Tight Domains

An element in slack domains is invalid if it triggers an exception after it is passed to an API. Such elements should be removed from slack domains to obtain tight domains. Algorithm 2 presents the method for inferring tight domains from slack domains of popular data types such as "int" and "string" in most programming languages.

Lines 1–5 of Algorithm 2 obtain a set of legal symbols. The function named *validator* in Line 3 is customized by testers. For example, testers of certificate validation in SSL/TLS implementations employ functions to generate certificates as the *validator*. For some types such as "string", the set of legal symbols is used in slack lower/upper bounds in Line 6.

---

**Algorithm 2.** Inferring a tight domain from a slack domain

---

**Input:** A parameter denoted by $par$ and its slack domain denoted by $[slackLowerBound,$ $slackUpperBound]$

**Output:** A tight domain denoted by $[tightLowerBound, tightUpperBound]$

1:  $legalSymbolSet = \emptyset;$             ▷ legalSymbolSet stores a set of legal symbols

2:  **for all** $c \in symbolSet$ **do**         ▷ symbolSet is a set of symbols in the slack domain

3:     **if** $validator(par, c^*)$ **then**         ▷ $c^*$: any element of the Kleen closure of $\{c\}$

4:        $legalSymbolSet \leftarrow legalSymbolSet \cup \{c\};$

5:        continue;

6:     **end if**

7:  **end for**

8:  $lower, upper \leftarrow slackLowerBound, slackUpperBound$ **w.r.t.** $legalSymbolSet;$

9:  $tightLowerBound, tightUpperBound \leftarrow$ **None, None**;     ▷ **tight bounds are not found**

10: **while** $lower \leq upper$ **do**

11:    **if** $tightLowerBound \neq$ **None and** $tightUpperBound \neq$ **None then**

12:      **return** $tightLowerBound, tightUpperBound;$

13:    **else**                     ▷ **tight bounds have not been found**

14:      $mid \leftarrow mean(lower, upper);$

15:      $midSuccessor \leftarrow successor(mid);$           ▷ **mid's successor**

16:      $midPredecessor \leftarrow predecessor(mid);$      ▷ **mid's predecessor**

17:      **if** $validator(par, lower)$ **and** $validator(par, upper)$ **then**

18:        **if** $tightLowerBound ==$ **None then**

19:          $tightLowerBound \leftarrow lower;$        ▷ **tight lower bound is found**

20:        **end if**

21:        **if** $tightUpperBound ==$ **None then**

22:          $tightUpperBound \leftarrow upper;$        ▷ **tight upper bound is found**

23:        **end if**

24:      **else if** $validator(par, lower)$ **then**

25:        **if** $tightLowerBound ==$ **None then**

26:          $tightLowerBound \leftarrow lower;$        ▷ **tight lower bound is found**

27:        **end if**

28:        **if** $validator(par, mid)$ **then**

29:          **if** $validator(par, midSuccessor)$ **then**

30:            $lower \leftarrow midSuccessor;$

31:            $upper \leftarrow predecessor(upper);$

32:          **else**

33:            $tightUpperBound \leftarrow mid;$      ▷ **tight upper bound is found**

34:          **end if**

35:        **else**

36:          **if** $validator(par, midPredecessor)$ **then**

37:            $tightUpperBound \leftarrow midPredecessor;$

38:          **else**

39:            $upper \leftarrow midPredecessor;$

40:          **end if**

41:        **end if**

42:      **else if** $validator(par, upper)$ **then**

43:        **if** $tightUpperBound ==$ **None then**

44:          $tightUpperBound \leftarrow upper;$        ▷ **tight upper bound is found**

45:        **end if**

46:        **if** $validator(par, mid)$ **then**

47:          **if** $validator(par, midPredecessor)$ **then**

48:            $upper \leftarrow midPredecessor;$

49:          **else**

50:            $tightLowerBound \leftarrow mid;$      ▷ **tight lower bound is found**

51:          **end if**

52:        **else**

53:          **if** $validator(par, midSuccessor)$ **then**

54:            $tightLowerBound \leftarrow midSuccessor;$    ▷ **tight lower bound is found**

55:          **else**

56:            $lower \leftarrow midSuccessor;$

57:          **end if**

58:        **end if**

59:      **else**                    ▷ **prepare for the next search**

60:        $lower \leftarrow successor(lower);$

61:        $upper \leftarrow predecessor(upper);$

62:      **end if**

63:    **end if**

64: **end while**

---

Based on the set of legal symbols, Lines 7–49 of Algorithm 2 conduct a current binary search to find tight lower and upper bounds. The *tightLowerBound* or *tightUpperBound* can be set if and only if it is None (Lines 7, 9, 16, 18, 21, and 35). Line 12 computes the arithmetic mean of *lower* and *upper*. For "string", *mid* is the length mean power of elements in the set of legal symbols. The functions *successor* and *predecessor* in Lines 13 and 14 represent a successor or predecessor of *mid*. Lines 20–33 and Lines 34–46 are similar in procedures but they search different bounds. Lines 47–49 increase *lower* and decrease *upper* for the next search iteration.

### 3.3  Checking the Extensibility of Tight Bounds

Tight bounds found by Algorithm 2 constitute tight domains. If tight lower/upper bounds are not identical to slack lower/upper bounds, practical tight domains i.e., exact domains are found. Otherwise, Algorithm 3 checks the extensibility of tight bounds to find practical tight domains.

Line 1 of Algorithm 3 sets the maximum time used in checking the extensibility of tight bounds. Lines 4–12 look for a practical tight lower bound if a tight lower bound is identical to a slack lower bound. Similarly, Lines 13–21 look for a practical tight upper bound if a tight upper bound is identical to a slack upper bound. The function *remain* in Lines 7 and 16 computes the remained time. The explanation of functions *successor* and *predecessor* is the same to that of Algorihtm 3. Finally, Line 22 outputs practical tight bounds.

## 4  Experiments

Based on the approach IED, experiments have been conducted. Experimental settings and results are presented as follows.

### 4.1  Experimental Settings

The experimental hardware consists of an Intel i5-7200U CPU and 8GB RAM while the operating system is Microsoft Windows $10 \times 64$. The supporting tools for IED is implemented in Python 3.8 and the target library is pyOpenSSL v22.0.0.

### 4.2  Parameters and Their Data Types

APIs whose parameters' data type are related to "int" and "str" are obtained from the official document of pyOpenSSL. Table 1 shows the detail. The slack bounds of the types "int" and "str" in pyOpenSSL depend on the free memory size of a host machine.

---

**Algorithm 3.** Checking the extensibility of tight bounds

---

**Input:** A parameter denoted by *par*, slack bounds denoted by $[slackLowerBound, slackUpperBound]$, and tight bounds denoted by $[tightLowerBound, tightUpperBound]$

**Output:** Practical tight bounds i.e., exact domains

1: $MaxTime \leftarrow userDefinedTime$;
2: $practicalTightLowreBound \leftarrow tightLowerBound$;
3: $practicalTightUppereBound \leftarrow tightUpperBound$;
4: **if** $slackLowerBound == tightLowerBound$ **then**
5:     $bound \leftarrow tightLowerBound$;
6:     $ret \leftarrow$ "$valid$";
7:     **while** $ret$ and $remain(\frac{MaxTime}{2}) > 0$ **do**
8:         $ret \leftarrow validator(par, bound)$;
9:         **if** $!ret$ **then**                    ▷ An exception is triggered
10:             $practicalTightLowerBound \leftarrow successor(bound)$;
11:             **break**;
12:         **end if**
13:         $bound \leftarrow predecessor(bound)$;
14:     **end while**
15: **end if**
16: **if** $slackUpperBound == tightUpperBound$ **then**
17:     $bound \leftarrow tightUpperBound$;
18:     $ret \leftarrow$ "$valid$";
19:     **while** $ret$ and $remain(\frac{MaxTime}{2}) > 0$ **do**
20:         $ret \leftarrow validator(par, bound)$;
21:         **if** $!ret$ **then**                    ▷ An exception is triggered
22:             $practicalTightUpperBound \leftarrow predecessor(bound)$;
23:             **break**;
24:         **end if**
25:         $bound \leftarrow successor(bound)$;
26:     **end while**
27: **end if**
28: **return** $practicalTightLowerBound, practicalTightUpperBound$;

---

**Table 1.** APIs' parameters and their data types

| API | Parameter | Data type |
|---|---|---|
| set_version() | version | int |
| set_serial_number() | serial | int |
| get_issuer() | C, ST, L, O, OU, CN, emailAddress, dnQualifier, title, SN, GN, initials, pseudonym, generationQualifier, DC, street, businessCategory, jurisdictionC, jurisdictionST, jurisdictionL, postalAddress, postalCode, userid, uid, UID, serialNumber, x500UniqueIdentifier | str |
| get_subject | C, ST, L, O, OU, CN, emailAddress, dnQualifier, title, SN, GN, initials, pseudonym, generationQualifier, DC, street, businessCategory, jurisdictionC, jurisdictionST, jurisdictionL, postalAddress, postalCode, userid, uid, UID, serialNumber, x500UniqueIdentifier | str |

## 4.3    Exact Domains Inferred by IED

The data types of parameters *version* and *serial* of APIs *set_version*() and *set_serial_number*() are "int", and their slack domains are identical. However, their exact domains inferred by IED are different from slack domains or each other, as shown in Table 2.

The exact domain of the parameter *version*, whose data type is "int", is $[-2^{31}, 2^{31} - 1]$. Differently, the exact domain of the parameter *serial_number*, whose data type is also "int", is $[0, \infty]$, where the symbol $\infty$ denotes the practical tight upper bound varies with the free memory size of a host machine.

**Table 2.** Tight bounds of int

| Parameter | Lower | Upper |
|---|---|---|
| version | $-2^{31}$ | $2^{31} - 1$ |
| serial_number | 0 | $\infty$ |

**Table 3.** Illegal symbols of str

| Parameter | Illegal symbols |
|---|---|
| C | } ! $ > ˜ ] # < % @ * \ ^ / ? _ [" ; { & ' \| \ t \ n \ r \ x0b \ x0c |
| ST | \ \| / ? < " * > \ t \ n \ r \ x0b \ x0c |
| L | * ? > " / \| \ t \ n \ r \ x0b \ x0c |
| O | / > * < ? " \| \ t \ n \ r \ x0b \ x0c |
| OU | " * ? < / \| \ t \ n \ r \ x0b \ x0c |
| CN | < * > ? " / \| \ t \ n \ r \ x0b \ x0c |
| emailAddress | " / < ? > * \| \ t \ n \ r \ x0b \ x0c |
| dnQualifier | * & @ < ? ˜ ^ } " % { / # \ ' [ ; ! _ > ] $ \| \ t \ n \ r \ x0b \ x0c |
| title | / > < ? " * \| \ t \ n \ r \ x0b \ x0c |
| SN | < / " > ? * \| \ t \ n \ r \ x0b \ x0c |
| GN | ? > " / < * \| \ t \ n \ r \ x0b \ x0c |
| initials | * < " ? > / \| \ t \ n \ r \ x0b \ x0c |
| pseudonym | > " * ? < / \| \ t \ n \ r \ x0b \ x0c |
| generationQualifier | > * / " < ? \| \ t \ n \ r \ x0b \ x0c |
| DC | < / ? " * > \| \ t \ n \ r \ x0b \ x0c |
| street | * " > ? / < \| \ t \ n \ r \ x0b \ x0c |
| businessCategory | / * < " > ? \| \ t \ n \ r \ x0b \ x0c |
| jurisdictionC | , # ' % : ^ . < & ( @ ] _ $ ; ? } ˜ + ) - / > = \ * " ! [ { \| \ t \ n \ r \ x0b \ x0c |
| jurisdictionST | \ / ? < * " > \| \ t \ n \ r \ x0b \ x0c |
| jurisdictionL | * " ? < / > \ t \ u \ r \ x0b \ x0c |
| postalAddress | / \ < > " * ? \| \ t \ n \ r \ x0b \ x0c |
| postalCode | / \ ? * < " > \| \ t \ n \ r \ x0b \ x0c |
| userid | " < / \ * > ? \| \ t \ n \ r \ x0b \ x0c |
| uid | * ? \ " < > / \| \ t \ n \ r \ x0b \ x0c |
| UID | \ ? " / < > * \| \ t \ n \ r \ x0b \ x0c |
| serialNumber | / ^ [ \ _ ' $ < ; % ˜ " ! > ? { # * ] } & \| \ t \ n \ r \ x0b v x0c |
| x500UniqueIdentifier | \ ? < > " \| \ t \ n \ r \ x0b \ x0c |

For parameters whose data types are "str", the exact domains given by IED are shown in Tables 3 and 4. Table 3 lists illegal elements of "str" since legal elements are so many. Table 4 shows the practical tight lower and upper bounds i.e., the minimum and maximum length of a valid string consisting of legal symbols. It can be found from Tables 3 and 4 that illegal symbols of different parameters are various and practical tight bounds vary greatly.

**Table 4.** Tight bounds of str

| Parameter | String Length | | Parameter | String Length | |
|---|---|---|---|---|---|
| | Lower | Upper | | Lower | Upper |
| C | 2 | 2 | ST | 1 | 128 |
| L | 1 | 128 | O | 1 | 64 |
| OU | 1 | 64 | CN | 1 | 64 |
| emailAddress | 1 | 128 | dnQualifier | 0 | 240 |
| titlestr | 0 | 246 | SN | 1 | 249 |
| GN | 1 | 249 | initials | 0 | 243 |
| pseudonym | 0 | 242 | generationQualifier | 0 | 232 |
| DC | 1 | 249 | street | 0 | 245 |
| businessCategory | 0 | 235 | jurisdictionC | 2 | 2 |
| jurisdictionST | 0 | 237 | jurisdictionL | 0 | 238 |
| postalAddress | 0 | 238 | postalCode | 0 | 241 |
| userid | 0 | 245 | uid | 0 | 248 |
| UID | 0 | 248 | SerialNumber | 1 | 64 |
| x500UniqueIdentifier | 0 | 231 | – | – | – |

## 4.4 Evaluation

For parameters whose data types are "int", Fig. 2 shows the evaluation of exact domains and the benchmark is $[-2^{31}, 2^{31}-1]$ which is frequently adopted by

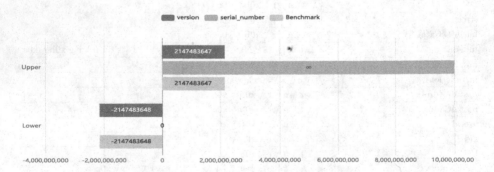

**Fig. 2.** Evaluation of slack and tight domains of int

testers. The exact domain of the parameter *version* is identical to the benchmark, resulting in helping testers avoid invalid domains $[-\infty, -2^{31} - 1]$ and $[2^{31}, +\infty]$. The exact domain of the parameter *serial_number* is different from the benchmark, resulting in helping testers avoid the invalid domain $[-\infty, -1]$.

For parameters whose data types are "str", Fig. 3 shows the percentage of legal characters. Thus, IED helps testers avoid 11%–27% symbols that will not generate valid test cases. In consideration of practical tight bounds of "str" shown in Table 4, IED improves the efficiency of generating valid test cases.

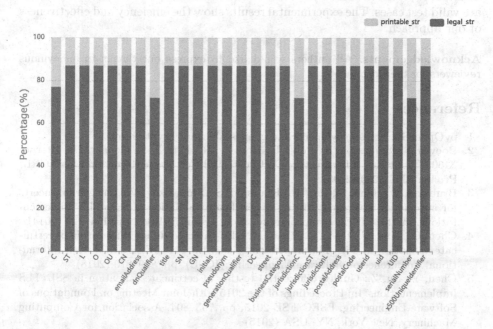

**Fig. 3.** Percentage of legal and illegal characters

## 5    Related Work

Frankencert [3] is proposed for the first time to test certificate validation logic in SSL/TLS implementations and recombines the collected certificate components to generate a new certificate. Mucert [5] uses the Markov Chain Monte Carlo (MCMC) algorithm to diversify mutation certificates. NEZHA [7] directly mutates the certificate files regardless of the certificate syntax. RFCcert [4,11] assembles certificates depending on the rules extracted from Request for Comments (RFCs). SADT [8] leverages a tree-based mutation to generate syntactically correct certificates. Work such as Frankencert requires the generation of test cases, but they do not have a well-defined domain of parameters. The performance of software testing heavily depends on the quality of the test cases, especially when the target program requires highly structured input [10]. We propose the IED to accurately test the practical tight lower and upper bounds of parameters' domains. Therefore our work helps testers generate valid test cases efficiently.

## 6   Conclusion

In this paper, we propose IED, a three-phase approach for inferring exact domains. Based on IED, experiments are performed on pyOpenSSL, and exact domains of parameters are obtained. Exact domains help testers efficiently generate valid test cases. The experimental results show the efficiency and effectiveness of our approach.

**Acknowledgements.** All authors would like to express our thanks to anonymous reviewers for their comments.

## References

1. pyOpenSSL. https://pyOpenSSL.org/en/stable/api/crypto.html
2. Boeyen, S., Santesson, S., Polk, T., Housley, R., Farrell, S., Cooper, D.: Internet X.509 Public Key Infrastructure Certificate and Certificate Revocation List (CRL) Profile. RFC 5280 (2008)
3. Brubaker, C., Jana, S., Ray, B., Khurshid, S., Shmatikov, V.: Using frankencerts for automated adversarial testing of certificate validation in SSL/TLS implementations. In: 2014 IEEE Symposium on Security and Privacy, pp. 114–129 (2014)
4. Chen, C., Tian, C., Duan, Z., Zhao, L.: RFC-directed differential testing of certificate validation in SSL/TLS implementations. In: 2018 IEEE/ACM 40th International Conference on Software Engineering (ICSE), pp. 859–870 (2018)
5. Chen, Y., Su, Z.: Guided differential testing of certificate validation in SSL/TLS implementations. In: Proceedings of the 2015 10th Joint Meeting on Foundations of Software Engineering, ESEC/FSE 2015, pp. 793–804. Association for Computing Machinery, New York, NY, USA (2015)
6. Freier, A.O., Karlton, P., Kocher, P.C.: The Secure Sockets Layer (SSL) Protocol Version 3.0. RFC 6101 (2011)
7. Petsios, T., Tang, A., Stolfo, S., Keromytis, A.D., Jana, S.: NEZHA: efficient domain-independent differential testing. In: 2017 IEEE Symposium on Security and Privacy (SP), pp. 615–632 (2017)
8. Quan, L., Guo, Q., Chen, H., Xie, X., Li, X., Liu, Y., Hu, J.: SADT: syntax-aware differential testing of certificate validation in SSL/TLS implementations. In: 2020 35th IEEE/ACM International Conference on Automated Software Engineering (ASE), pp. 524–535 (2020)
9. Rescorla, E.: The Transport Layer Security (TLS) Protocol Version 1.3. RFC 8446 (2018)
10. Rothermel, G., Untch, R.H., Chu, C., Harrold, M.J.: Test case prioritization: an empirical study. In: Proceedings IEEE International Conference on Software Maintenance - 1999 (ICSM'99). 'Software Maintenance for Business Change' (Cat. No.99CB36360), pp. 179–188 (1999)
11. Tian, C., Chen, C., Duan, Z., Zhao, L.: Differential testing of certificate validation in SSL/TLS implementations: an RFC-guided approach. ACM Trans. Softw. Eng. Methodol. **28**(4) (2019)

# Algorithms and Verification

# Testing and Verifying the Security of COVID-19 CT Images Deep Learning System with Adversarial Attack

Yang Li and Shaoying Liu[✉]

Graduate School of Advanced Science and Engineering, Hiroshima University,
Hiroshima 739-8511, Japan
{liyangfly,sliu}@hiroshima-u.ac.jp

**Abstract.** The Coronavirus disease 2019 (COVID-19) is a pandemic that occurred in December 2019 and spread globally. Most of the current research is on how to apply deep learning to detect COVID-19, but little research has been done on the security of COVID-19 deep learning systems. Therefore, we test and verify the security of COVID-19 CT images deep learning system with adversarial attack. Firstly, we build a deep learning system for recognizing COVID-19 CT images. Secondly, adding imperceptible disturbance to CT images will lead to neural network classification errors. Finally, we discuss the application of formal methods and formal verification to deep learning systems. We hope to draw more attention from researchers to the application of formal methods and formal verification to artificial intelligence.

**Keywords:** Adversarial attack · COVID-19 · Deep learning · Testing · Security · Formal methods

## 1 Introduction

COVID-19 has been a threat to the health of people around the world since its discovery. It was declared a global pandemic by the World Health Organization on March 11, 2020 [1]. COVID-19 is an acute respiratory infection caused by a new coronavirus SARS-CoV-2. Its clinical manifestations mainly include fever, cough, headache, loss of sense of smell, etc. [2]. Currently, the clinical diagnosis of the virus is based on patient epidemiology, clinical manifestations, chest CT and RT-PCR [3]. Chest CT, as the primary tool for screening and diagnosis of COVID-19, can not only detect lesions early but also stage the manifestation pattern of lesions, which can be classified into early, progressive, regressive and heavy, and critical types according to the manifestation of lesions on CT [4].

Since the emergence of COVID-19, there has been a great deal of research on it, covering a variety of fields, such as biology, chemistry, medicine, and information science [5–7]. Currently, there are many studies on the application of machine learning in COVID-19 medical image recognition and detection [8]. Ezz El-Din Hemdan [9] used deep network models with seven different architectures to classify X-ray images of COVID-19 patients and normal patients. Yifan Jiang [10] proposes a CT image synthesis approach based on a conditional generative adversarial network that can effectively generate high-quality and realistic COVID-19 CT images for deep-learning-based medical imaging tasks. However, However, there are few studies on the security of COVID-19deep learning systems.

There is no doubt that deep learning has made remarkable achievements in many fields, such as image recognition [11], object detection [12], and speech recognition [13]. In addition, deep learning has led to breakthroughs in other fields, such as disease prediction [14], protein structure modeling [15], and medical diagnosis [16]. Szegedy et al. [17] first identified interesting weaknesses of deep neural networks in image classification. They showed that despite the high correctness rate, modern deep networks are susceptible to attacks by adversarial samples. These adversarial samples are only very slightly perturbed so much so that the human visual system cannot detect such perturbations. Such an attack can cause the neural network to completely change its classification of the pictures. In addition, the same perturbation can fool so many network models. The far-reaching implications of such phenomena have attracted many researchers in adversarial attack and deep learning security.

## 2   Adversarial Attack

### 2.1   The Concept of Generating Adversarial Sample

Adversarial samples are created by superimposing subtle changes on the original data that make them acceptable to the machine learning model but imperceptible to the human eye, thus causing the machine learning model to misjudge the input data. The adversarial sample is defined mathematically as follows:

$$| \varepsilon | < \delta \, and f(x + \varepsilon) \, ! = f(x)$$

The input data $x$, machine learning model $f$, the classification result is denoted by $f(x)$. Suppose there is a small perturbation $\epsilon$ such that $f(x)$ is equal to $f(x + \epsilon)$, then $x + \epsilon$ can be called an adversarial sample.

### 2.2   The Classification of Adversarial Sample Generation Methods

**Optimization-Based Adversarial Sample Generation Algorithm.** In the training process, the loss function between the predicted and actual values of the sample data is calculated, and then the parameters of the model are adjusted by the chain rule in the backward transfer process to continuously reduce the value of the loss function, and the parameters of each layer of the model are iteratively calculated to generate the adversarial samples. Carlinr et al. [18] proposed a set of adversarial attack C&W based on optimization, considering both high attack rejection rate and low adversarial disturbance.

**Gradient-based Generation of Adversarial Sample.** The gradient of the input data is calculated first. Then the input data is updated step by step according to the meaning of the loss function to obtain the adversarial sample, such as FGSM [19], Basic Iterative

Method(BIM) [20], and PDG [21]. The specific form of the counter sample generated by FGSM is as follows:

$$x* = x + \varepsilon \cdot sign\ (\nabla_x J(x, t))$$

The original sample is $x$, $\epsilon$ is the perturbation parameter, and $\nabla x\ J(x,t)$ is the gradient, and then the adversarial sample $x*$ is generated.

**Generative Adversarial Sample Based on Generative Adversarial Network(GAN).** GAN was first proposed by Ian Goodfellow [22] in 2014 and consists of two sub-networks, the Generator network (G) and the Discriminator network (D). The Generator network optimizes itself so that the Discriminator network cannot be identified, and the Discriminator network optimizes itself to make a more accurate judgment.

# 3 Experiment

## 3.1 Datasets

The CT images datasets in this paper were obtained from publicly available datasets extracted from the medRxiv and bioRxiv preprints of COVID-19 by Xingyi Yang at the University of California, San Diego [23]. These CT images datasets are anonymized and can be applied to the study of COVID-19. The datasets contain 349 CT images that tested positive for COVID-19 and 397 CT images that tested negative for COVID-19. The datasets were divided into three categories: training set, validation set, and testing set.

## 3.2 Deep Learning Model

ResNet is the ImageNet 2015 champion model, which dramatically reduces the error rate of previous models and has low complexity, new parameters, and small calculation [24]. We use the transfer learning method to construct the COVID-19 CT images deep learning system using the pre-training model resnet50 and change the final full connection layer to two classifications (COVID-19 CT images, normal CT images).

## 3.3 Adversarial Attack

To verify the security of the deep learning model based on COVID-19 CT images, we carried out an anti-attack against it, that is, adding a slight disturbance that is imperceptible to the naked eye into the images of the test set, causing the model to be misclassified. We choose the FGSM algorithm based on gradient generation adversarial samples to attack the trained model. In addition, we adjusted different epsilon to test their interference with the model (Fig. 1).

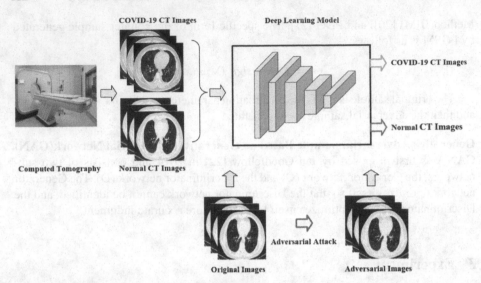

**Fig. 1.** The adversarial attack against the COVID-19 CT images deep learning system

## 4   Discussion

### 4.1   Results of Experiment

The experimental results are shown in Table 1. Before the deep learning model was attacked, the model's accuracy reached 76.27%. However, we used white box attack FGSM to attack the pre-trained deep learning model, which significantly reduced the recognition accuracy of the model, indicating that the adversarial sample successfully deceived the model, making the model unable to classify CT images correctly.

**Table 1.**   Accuracy of the COVID-19 CT images deep learning model

| Attack | Accuracy |
|---|---|
| Original | 76.27% |
| FSGM attack | 1.02% |

We attack the model with the adversarial attack algorithm FGSM. The original image with perturbation makes no difference to the naked eye but can make the deep learning model misclassify. Figure 2 shows examples of CT images from the before and after perturbation by the adversarial neural network. After slight perturbation of the original image, we obtained adversarial image that could not be distinguished by the human eye.

We analyzed and studied the impact of adversarial samples on the accuracy of the deep learning system based on COVID-19 CT images. Compared with previous studies on COVID-19, previous studies on COVID-19 and deep learning mainly focus on how to build a deep learning system with higher accuracy that can identify COVID-19 CT

original image          perturbation          adversarial image

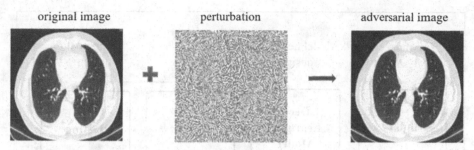

**Fig. 2.** Characteristic results of adversarial image

images, while our research focuses on testing and verifying the security of the deep learning system based on COVID-19 CT images. We find that even subtle perturbation that are hard to distinguish by the naked eye will degrade the accuracy of the deep learning image recognition system, which is more important for the judgment of medical images.

## 4.2  Formal Methods and Formal Verification

Machine learning, as represented by deep learning, has made great progress. But the shortcomings of such methods are also increasingly prominent. In particular, these are the most important issues: interpretability, generalization ability, robustness, and security. The above problems faced in artificial intelligence systems have caused concerns. Formal methods and formal verification are mainly applied in the field of software engineering, which can solve the problem of software correctness from a mathematical point of view at the root, thus saving a lot of work in code review, software testing, etc. Therefore, how to apply formal methods and formal verification in the artificial intelligence field and build verified artificial intelligence is a very meaningful topic.

For deep learning models, if we define the model system with formal methods, we can make the model have better robustness (Fig. 3). For the training data, the data can be defined and filtered by formal methods to remove some data that affect the model in advance, and for the model, the network of the model can be defined and specified by formal methods, and the adversarial samples can be used as test data to verify the robustness and security of the model. Many studies have demonstrated that adversarial attacks are a great threat to the security of deep learning systems, and if we use adversarial samples to formalize the deep learning system in advance, thus potentially improving the security and reliability of the system.

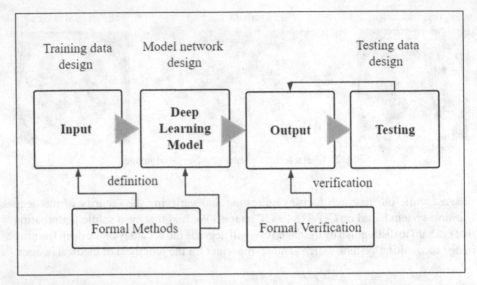

**Fig. 3.** The formal methods and formal verification with deep learning systems

## 5  Conclusion

There is no doubt that the use of deep learning in medical diagnosis is auspicious. Artificial intelligence technology has also been contributing a lot to the rapid development of medicine and health care. Then, the security of deep learning systems cannot be ignored, especially in the medical field, people's health is essential. In this article, we test and verify the security of COVID-19 CT Images Deep Learning System with adversarial attack, hoping to draw developers' attention to the security and reliability of deep learning systems, so that they can develop more secure and reliable deep learning systems.

My future research will focus on how to use formal methods to define deep learning systems, such as defining and verifying deep learning systems using formal methods to improve the security and reliability of deep learning systems.

**Acknowledgment.** The work is supported partially by JST SPRING, Grant Number JPMJSP2132.

## References

1. Li, H., Liu, Z., Ge, J.: Scientific research progress of COVID-19/SARS-CoV-2 in the first five months. J. Cell Mol. Med. **24**(12), 6558–6570 (2020)
2. Ciotti, M., Ciccozzi, M., Terrinoni, A., et al.: The COVID-19 pandemic. Crit. Rev. Clin. Lab. Sci. **57**(6), 365–388 (2020)
3. Orooji, Y., et al.: An Overview on SARS-CoV-2 (COVID-19) and other human coronaviruses and their detection capability via amplification assay, chemical sensing, biosensing, immunosensing, and clinical assays. Nano-Micro Lett. **13**(1), 1–30 (2020). https://doi.org/10.1007/s40820-020-00533-y

4. Fang, Y., Zhang, H., Xie, J., et al.: Sensitivity of chest CT for COVID-19: comparison to RT-PCR. Radiology (2020)
5. Fields, B.K.K., Demirjian, N.L., Dadgar, H., et al.: Imaging of COVID-19: CT, MRI, and PET. Sem. Nuclear Med. WB Saunders **51**(4), 312–320 (2021)
6. Tian, X.L., Peng, M., Wang, H.P., et al.: The differential diagnosis for novel coronavirus pneumonia and similar lung diseases in general hospitals. Chin. J. Tuberc. Respir. Dis. **43**(5), E035 (2020)
7. Kumar, A., Gupta, P.K., Srivastava, A.: A review of modern technologies for tackling COVID-19 pandemic. Diab. Metab. Syndr. **14**(4), 569–573 (2020)
8. Lalmuanawma, S., Hussain, J., Chhakchhuak, L.: Applications of machine learning and artificial intelligence for Covid-19 (SARS-CoV-2) pandemic: a review. Chaos Solitons Fractals **139**, 110059 (2020)
9. Hemdan, E.E.D., Shouman, M.A., Karar, M.E.: Covidx-net: A framework of deep learning classifiers to diagnose covid-19 in x-ray images. arXiv preprint arXiv:2003.11055 (2020)
10. Jiang, Y., Chen, H., Loew, M., et al.: COVID-19 CT image synthesis with a conditional generative adversarial network. IEEE J. Biomed. Health Inform. **25**(2), 441–452 (2020)
11. Simonyan, K., Zisserman, A.: Very deep convolutional networks for large-scale image recognition. arXiv preprint arXiv:1409.1556 (2014)
12. Redmon, J., Divvala, S., Girshick, R., et al.: You only look once: Unified, real-time object detection. In: Proceedings of the IEEE Conference on Computer Vision and Pattern Recognition, pp. 779–788 (2016)
13. Nassif, A.B., Shahin, I., Attili, I., et al.: Speech recognition using deep neural networks: a systematic review. IEEE Access **7**, 19143–19165 (2019)
14. Yang, H., Wei, Q., Li, D., et al.: Cancer classification based on chromatin accessibility profiles with deep adversarial learning model. PLoS Comput. Biol. **16**(11), e1008405 (2020)
15. Tunyasuvunakool, K., Adler, J., Wu, Z., et al.: Highly accurate protein structure prediction for the human proteome. Nature **596**(7873), 590–596 (2021)
16. Esteva, A., Kuprel, B., Novoa, R.A., et al.: Dermatologist-level classification of skin cancer with deep neural networks. Nature **542**, 115–118 (2017)
17. Szegedy, C., Zaremba, W., Sutskever, I., et al.: Intriguing properties of neural networks. arXiv preprint arXiv:1312.6199 (2013)
18. Carlini, N., Wagner, D.: Towards evaluating the robustness of neural networks. In: 2017 IEEE Symposium on Security and Privacy (sp). IEEE, pp. 39–57 (2017)
19. Goodfellow, I.J., Shlens, J., Szegedy, C.: Explaining and harnessing adversarial examples. arXiv preprint arXiv:1412.6572 (2014)
20. Kurakin, A., Goodfellow, I., Bengio, S.: Adversarial machine learning at scale. arXiv preprint arxiv:1611.01236 (2016)
21. Madry, A., Makelov, A., Schmidt, L., et al.: Towards deep learning models resistant to adversarial attacks. arXiv preprint arXiv:1706.06083 (2017)
22. Goodfellow, I., Pouget-Abadie, J., Mirza, M., et al.: Generative adversarial nets. Adv. Neural Inf. Process. Syst. **27** (2014)
23. Zhao, J., Zhang, Y., He, X., et al.: Covid-CT-dataset: a CT scan dataset about covid-19. arXiv preprint arXiv:2003.13865, 490 (2020)
24. He, K., Zhang, X., Ren, S., et al.: Deep residual learning for image recognition. In: Proceedings of the IEEE Conference on Computer Vision and Pattern Recognition, pp. 770–778 (2016)

# Verifying and Improving Neural Networks Using Testing-Based Formal Verification

Haiyi Liu[1], Shaoying Liu[1(✉)], Ai Liu[1], Dingbang Fang[1], and Guangquan Xu[2]

[1] Graduate School of Advanced Science and Engineering, Hiroshima University, Hiroshima 7398511, Japan
{sliu,liuai,fangdingbang}@hiroshima-u.ac.jp
[2] School of Cybersecurity, College of Intelligence and Computing, Tianjin University, Tianjin 300072, China
Losin@tju.edu.cn

**Abstract.** Neural networks have been widely used in safety-critical systems, but those safety-critical systems containing neural networks still have security risks due to the existence of adversarial examples. The security of neural networks can be ensured to some extent by verifying them. However, since the verification of neural networks is a NP-hard problem, it is still impossible to apply the verification algorithm to large-scale neural networks. For this reason, we propose TBFV-INN, a new framework for verification and improving neural networks. First, we propose a testing-based neural network pruning algorithm, which obtains the execution path of each test case in the neural network by executing them. Secondly, test-based neural network pruning divides the original neural network into several sub neural networks. Finally, for divided sub neural network, a verification algorithm is used to verify and construct the data set to retrain the neural network, thus ensuring that each sub neural network is reliable in a particular input-output interval. We show a case study to demonstrate the feasibility of the framework.

**Keywords:** Neural network · Formal verification · Software test

## 1 Introduction

In recent years, neural networks have been increasingly used in security-critical systems, such as autonomous driving [5], financial payments [8], and even aviation scheduling systems [6]. At the same time, neural networks have also been shown to be potentially vulnerable to elaborate adversarial example [25]. The neural network verification algorithm [2] can use the given formal specification to verify the neural network. Unfortunately, the neural network verification problem has been proved to be NP-hard [9], and the scale of existing neural networks is still expanding.

© The Author(s), under exclusive license to Springer Nature Switzerland AG 2023
S. Liu et al. (Eds.): SOFL+MSVL 2022, LNCS 13854, pp. 126–141, 2023.
https://doi.org/10.1007/978-3-031-29476-1_11

In general, when engineers are faced with complex tasks, they tend to build larger model structures based on experience, such as a larger number of layers of neural networks containing a larger number of neurons per layer. The reason for this is that larger neural network models are considered to be more expressive and easier to train. However, this approach also brings redundancy in the model structure, which poses a challenge to subsequently ensure the reliability of the model. For example, when we want to verify the reliability of the model, since the verification algorithm is usually NP-hard, a large number of redundant models will inevitably lead to time out. To alleviate the security problems caused by large scale neural networks, some algorithms for fast search of neural network adversarial examples have been proposed by the security community and widely used in industry [10,14,20]. To reduce the complexity of neural network adversarial examples search, some scholars have proposed pruning algorithms to reduce the size of neural networks by reducing the redundant nodes in neural networks [1,7], which facilitates the deployment of neural networks on the one hand and the testing of neural networks on the other hand to make them more stable. However, the problem of the above algorithms is that there is no formal guarantee that the neural network is reliable under a certain input-output specification. On the other hand, the formal approach community is also trying to improve the efficiency and scale of neural network verification through hardware measures such as GPUs [23] and Parallel computing [24] etc. However, the speed of verification is much slower than the growth of the number of neural network participants.

In this paper, we propose a method to construct reliable neural networks based on the combination of test and verification. Specifically, we have developed two key techniques, the first one is called testing-based neural network pruning. This technique first partitions the input and output space of the neural network using the formal specification. The original input-output space is partitioned into several subspaces, and then the training data set of the generated neural network is mapped into each subspace. Finally, the training data set mapped into the subspaces is used to prune the original neural network and generate a sub neural network for each subspace. The second technique is called validation-based neural network retraining, where formal validation of the subneural network is feasible because the subneural network is smaller in size, and we adjust the subneural network with retraining for counterexamples that exist in the subnetwork to make it converge to reliability.

This paper mainly made the following contributions:

- We propose a neural network pruning technique based on formal specification and testing. Several corresponding sub networks can be obtained from the original neural network according to the formal specification.
- We design a verification based neural network retraining algorithm. Its core technology is to construct training data sets through counterexamples. This algorithm makes the retrained neural network more reliable.

## 2  Preliminary

### 2.1  Principle of TBFV

The testing-based formal verification (TBFV) [11,12] is proposed to ensure the correctness of all traversed program paths in traditional software. The first step of TBFV is to generate a test case $T$ based on the test condition in the formal specification. The second step is to obtain a traversed program *path* by executing the test case $T$ execution program $P$, where the *path* contains a series of conditions. The third step is to verify the reliability of the *path* under the formal specification by using symbol execution or hoare logic [17].

### 2.2  Interval Arithmetic and Symbolic Execution

Interval arithmetic is an effective way to improve the stability of a program. Unlike algebraic operations with numbers as the object, the whole process of interval arithmetic is based on the interval as the object of operation, and by using the rules of interval arithmetic to abstract the rules of program operation, the purpose of analysing the program is achieved. The definitions are as follows:

The given real number $\underline{x}, \overline{x} \in R$, if the condition $\underline{x} \leq \overline{x}$ is satisfied. Then the set of closed bounded numbers. Then the set $X = [\ \underline{x},\ \overline{x}\ ] = \{x \in R \mid \underline{x} \leq x \leq \overline{x}\}$ is called a bounded closed interval. If any two intervals $X = [\ \underline{x},\ \overline{x}\ ]$ and $Y = [\ \underline{y},\ \overline{y}\ ]$ are given, Then the following operation holds on the interval.

$$X + Y = [\ \underline{x} + \underline{y},\ \overline{x} + \overline{y}\ ]$$

$$X - Y = [\ \underline{x} - \overline{y},\ \overline{x} - \underline{y}\ ]$$

$$X * Y = [\ min(\underline{xy}, \underline{x}\overline{y}, \overline{x}\underline{y}, \overline{xy}),\ max(\underline{xy}, \underline{x}\overline{y}, \overline{x}\underline{y}, \overline{xy})\ ]$$

$$if\ 0 \notin [\underline{y},\ \overline{y}],\ then\ X/Y = [\underline{x},\ \overline{x}] * [1/\underline{y}, 1/\overline{y}]$$

Symbolic execution is to use symbols to represent the input of programs, symbolically simulate the execution of each program instruction, and interpret it as a specific operation on symbolic values with semantic equivalence.

The formal specification of neural network input is usually expressed as a real closed interval. For example, the input $x_i$ of the $i$-th neurons in the input layer needs to satisfy $x_i \in [a_i, b_i]$ where interval $[a_i, b_i]$ is given by formal specification, which means that the input of the $i$-th neuron of the input layer must belong to the range of this interval. When the symbol $X_i$ is used to replace the interval of the input layer given by the formal specification, we can get,

$$X_i = [a_i, b_i]\ \ i = 1, ..., n$$

where $n$ is the number of neurons in the input layer. The process of forward propagation of neural network which needs to be verified with symbol $X_i$ is the process of neural network symbol execution.

## 2.3   Verification of Neural Networks

Deep neural network is a mapping in high-dimensional space, which can be formally expressed as $f : \mathbb{R}^n \rightarrow \mathbb{R}^m$. if there is a set of constraints $\phi$ which is the precondition of $f$ on $\mathbb{R}^n$, and existence a set of constraints $\varphi$ which is the post condition of $f$ on $\mathbb{R}^m$. Then, the problem of neural network verification is transformed into proving that $\forall x \in \mathbb{R}^n : \phi(x) \rightarrow \varphi(f(x))$ is satisfied or not.

# 3   Background and Motivation

At present, how to design the structure of deep neural network for different application scenarios is still an unsolved problem. Due to the lack of this design specification, the redundancy of neural network is widespread. Redundancy may improve the accuracy of neural network to a certain extent, but in most cases, it can only increase the training cost and reasoning cost of the network, which becomes particularly obvious in application scenarios such as edge computing, embedded systems etc. To overcome the redundancy of neural network structure, pruning has become an essential technology for neural network training and deployment. Because changes in the structure of neural networks usually lead to changes in performance, neural network pruning contains two technical challenges. The first is how to create rules to locate which neurons, or which weights should be pruned. The second is how to ensure that the pruned neural network is equivalent or similar to the original neural network.

## 3.1   Background

Up to now, there is still no formal specification to define the network structure, so the industry will rely on experience to train redundant neural networks, and then prune the redundant neural networks by sacrificing a certain accuracy. Existing neural network pruning algorithms often use a large number of test cases to test the trained neural network, and then prune the neural network according to the rules of neuron activation or weight size. Then, the pruned neural network is trained again. To achieve the same or even better effect on some test data sets. But the problem of doing so is also obvious. The test data is discrete, so the pruning algorithm driven by the test data can not guarantee that the two neural networks are completely equivalent in the continuous interval, even if the accuracy of the neural network in the test data set is exactly the same. For example, two neural networks may have different adversarial examples.

If we want the accuracy of the pruned neural network to be completely consistent with the original network, the execution path of the neural network for each test case in the input space should be known. However, the sample size of the input space to be tested to obtain the execution path is huge. Taking the fully connected neural network as an example, it is assumed that the number of neurons in the input layer is $n$ and the input space of each neuron is $m$. Then it takes $m^n$ test cases to obtain the neural network execution path corresponding to the input space through the test method. Even if we quantify the neural network input, that is, $m$ is represented by $int8$, $m^n$ tests may still be an impossible task, and worse, $n$ may also become larger with the development of training data (for example, clearer training picture data is used in CV).

## 3.2 Motivation

Formal verification is a classic technology in software engineering. Recently, the classical technology of formal verification has been applied to the verification of neural networks which detailed description in Sect. 2.3. Because the neural network is verified by analyzing the execution path of the program, intuitively, we think it can promote the pruning of the neural network.

Formally, let the fully connected neural network be a directed graph $G =< V(G), E(G), \varphi_G >$, where $V(G)$ is the set of all neurons in the neural network, $E(G)$ is the set of all edges in the neural network. $\varphi_G$ is a function from the $E(G)$ to the node ordered pair set, in short, it is the direction of edges in neural networks. Furthermore, the pruning problem can be abstracted as finding the sub-graph $G_{sub}$ of graph $G$ by using the formal verification algorithm. Specifically, we can delete some nodes and weights connected to nodes from $V(G)$. We denote the node that needs to be deleted as $V_{del}$. The edge that needs to be deleted can be denoted as $E_{del}$. Then, the sub-graph can be recorded as:

$$G_{sub} =< V_{sub} = V - V_{del}, E_{sub} = E - E_{del} >$$

After the above analysis, the neural network pruning problem is further transformed into a search problem, that is, for each input interval of the formal specification, find $G_{sub}$ in $G$ corresponding to this interval. However, the formal verification of neural networks is a NP-hard problem. The simple use of constraint solving and symbolic execution will inevitably lead to the time out of the verification algorithm when facing large-scale neural networks. In short, the current pruning method has the following two problems. First, the testing-based method can not guarantee the stability of the pruned neural network in the continuous interval. Second, the formal verification algorithm can ensure that the neural network is reliable in the continuous input-output interval of the formal specification, but how to use the verification algorithm to prune the neural network within the feasible time is still a blank. These challenges motivate us to combine the advantages of testing and verification to fill the gap of efficient formal verification of neural networks. Therefore, we propose TBFV-INN, a neural network pruning of testing-based formal verification.

## 4    Methodology

To solve the above challenges, we have introduced TBFV-INN. Section 4.1 presents an overview of TBFV-INN. There are detail about how to use test cases to prune in Sect. 4.2. Then, Sect. 4.3 describes the process of formal verification and retraining of neural networks in detail.

**Table 1.** Definitions of common symbols in this paper.

| Symbol | Significance |
|---|---|
| $NN = (V, E, W)$ | Computational graph represented by triples |
| $V\cdot$ | The set of neurons |
| $E$ | The set of directed edges |
| $W$ | The set of directed edge weights |
| $D_i = [\ \underline{d_i},\ \overline{d_i}\ ]$ | Closed interval of real numbers |
| $I = \{D_1, D_2, ...D_n\}$ | The set of $D_i$ |
| $I^p = \{D_1^p, D_2^p, ...D_n^p\}$ | The set of interval segmentation of each interval $D_i$ |
| $Tc = \{(x_1, y_1), ..., (x_m, y_m)\}$ | Training data set of neural network. |
| $TD^I = \{x_1, x_2, ...x_m\}$ | A set of inputs in a training dataset. |
| $TD^O = \{y_1, y_2, ...y_m\}$ | A set of outputs in a training dataset. |
| $ISS$ | A set is defined as an space segmentation of $I$ |
| $IS$ | An element in $ISS$ |
| $Fo$ | Output specification correspondence of $NN$ on $I$ |

## 4.1  Overview

The overview of TBFV-INN is described in Fig. 1. The proposed method includes three stages: testing-based neural network pruning, formal verification of sub neural networks, search for counterexamples and retraining. The neural network studied is a pretrained model in which the weight value has been trained.

The purpose of testing-based neural networks pruning is to reduce the scale of neural networks. The test data set here can be generated based on formal specification or using existing training data and testing data. By running the test data, the execution path of the data in the given interval in the pre training neural network can be obtained. Then, the path that the pre training neural network does not execute in the specified interval is cut off to reduce the scale of the neural network. In the second stage, symbolic interval analysis on the specified interval is carried out for the sub neural network. If the verification result is satisfied, the stability of the sub neural network on the interval is guaranteed. If it is unsatisfied, in the final stage, we will look for the counterexample of the sub neural network and retrain the sub neural network on the specified interval. In the following chapters, the technical details of each step will be described in detail.

## 4.2  Testing-based Neural Networks Pruning

**Space Segmentation.** Here, we need to make an assumption, that is, all the training data sets are consistent with the formal specification. This assumption is reasonable because data that obviously does not conform to the formal specification should not be trained by the neural network. The pre training neural

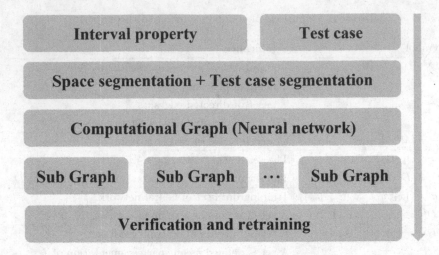

**Fig. 1.** An overview of TBFV-INN

network model ($NN$) obtains the weight from the training data set, and verifies the validity of the weight in the test data set. After that, the execution path of the neural network corresponding to each input is determined. Let's give a training set $Tc = \{(x_1, y_1), (x_2, y_2), ..., (x_m, y_m)\}$, where $x_i \in \mathbb{R}^n$, $y_i \in \mathbb{R}^s$.

**Definition 1.** *Interval segmentation Let's partition an interval $D_i$ into a set of disjoint segmentations $D_i^p = \{D_i^1, D_i^2, ...D_i^s\}$ where each $D_i^j = [\ \underline{d_i^j},\ \overline{d_i^j})$ and $D_i^j$ is a sub interval of $D_i$. In addition, $|D_i^p| = \sum_{j=1}^s |D_i^j|$. The set $D_i^p$ is defined as an interval segmentation of $D_i$.*

In the input layer of $NN$, the input range of each neuron corresponds to the element in $I$. For example, if the number of neurons in the input layer is $w$, then $|I| = w$. According to Definition 1, each interval in $I$ can be divided. We divide each element $D_i$ in $I$ into $s$ sub intervals on average. That is, $\forall D_i \in I$ s.t. $|D_i| = s$.

**Definition 2.** *Space segmentation*

*Let the set $I$ (multidimensional rectangle) be the input space of the $NN$. If the interval segmentation is performed on each element of the set $I$, then the set $I^p = \{D_1^p, D_2^p, ...D_n^p\}$ can be obtained. For all elements in $I^p$, a set $ISS = D_1^p \times D_2^p \cdots \times D_n^p$ can be constructed by Cartesian product. The set $ISS$ is defined as an space segmentation of $I$.*

We perform segmentation using $Definition\ 2$ on the input space of $NN$, denote as $ISS^I$ From the definition of formal specification, we can get:

$$\forall x_i \in TD^I, \exists Is \in ISS^I \quad s.t. \quad xi \in Is$$

That is, there is a function $f : TD^I \rightarrow ISS^I$

Figure 2 is a case study of test case segmentation for input space of neural network. Let the input layer of neural network $NN$ have three neurons and $|D_i^p| = 2$ *where* $i = 1, 2, 3$, then input space segmentation can be represented as a cube $C$ in three dimensional space. The length, width and height of the cube are $|D_1|$, $|D_2|$ and $|D_3|$ respectively. The set composed of all sub cubes is set $ISS^I$. Firstly, the neural network input space is segmented by using the segmentation criteria described in definition 2, as shown in sub Fig. 2(a). The sub cubes in cube $C$ are elements in $ISS^I$. Secondly, each element in $TD^I$ is mapped to different sub cubes, as shown in sub Fig. 2(b).

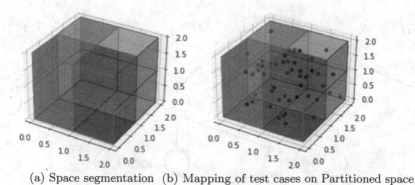

(a) Space segmentation  (b) Mapping of test cases on Partitioned space

**Fig. 2.** Test case segmentation for input space of neural network

The execution path of $IS$ on a neural network must be a sub graph of the whole neural network. However, verifying the stability of large-scale neural networks over the input space $ISS$ is very difficult and almost impossible to accomplish. Therefore, the approximation to find the $ISS$ on the execution path of the neural network is the next step to be solved. When the neural network forward executes a test case in $TD^I$, it can quickly get an accurate path. Therefore, we run the test cases in $IS$, taking the concatenation of all paths to approximate the execution path of the neural network on the $IS$ space. Obviously, approximate paths are a subset of the real paths of $IS$ on $NN$ and do not guarantee the stability of the sub-paths, for which we need to use verification methods, which are described in detail in Sect. 4.3. Next, the algorithm for obtaining the approximate path is described in detail.

First, let's precisely define the execution path of each test case in $IS$ on the neural network computational graph.

**Definition 3.** *Execution path of neural network*

*If the execution path of the neural network is recorded as computational graphs* $G = < V(G), E(G), \varphi_G >$, *then, the execution path of a test case is the sub graph* $g_i = < V(g_i), E(g_i), \varphi_{g_i} >$ *of G. where* $V(g_i) \subset V(G)$, $E(g_i) \subset E(G)$ *and* $\varphi_{g_i} \subset \varphi_G$.

Furthermore, a triplet can be constructed for each Test case and Test oracle. The form is as follows:

$$\{testCase\} \ g_i \ \{testOracle\}$$

In this paper, we take $Argf(x) := \{x| \ \forall x \in TD^I : f(x) \to IS\}$ as test cases. Homologous, we can also get test oracles $Argf(y) := \{y| \ \forall y \in TD^O : f(y) \to IS\}$. Through a group of $Argf(x)$ and $Argf(y)$, we can get a series of execution path $\{g_1, g_2, ...g_t\}$ belonging to $IS$. The execution path of $IS$ in the neural network is the $p^{IS} = \bigcup_1^t g_i$. As shown in Fig. 3,

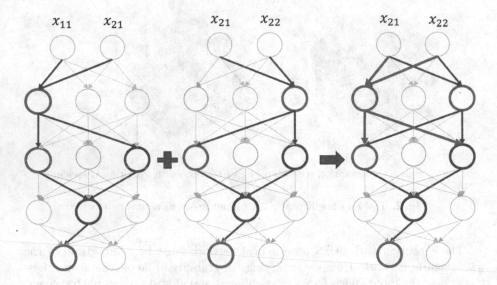

**Fig. 3.** Execution path generation on $IS$

**Criteria for Generating Paths.** The process of neural network executing a test case is equivalent to the forward reasoning stage of neural network. At this time, after receiving the input value, each neuron can output an activation value through the calculation of the activation function. Formally, We can express the process by Formula (1).

$$y_j = f(\sum_{i=0}^{n} w_i x_i - bias) \tag{1}$$

where $x_i$ is the output of all neurons connected to the current neuron in the previous layer. $f$ is the activation function. $y_i$ is the output of the current neuron.

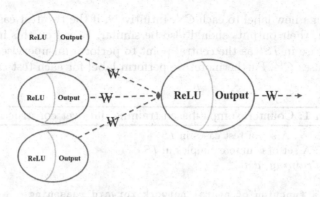

**Fig. 4.** Schematic representation of *ReLU* neurons

It is critical to define threshold and generate test case path of neural network. The absolute value of neuron output affects the input of the next layer of neurons. When the absolute value of the output value of neurons is larger, the influence on the input of neurons in the lower layer is larger, vice versa. Therefore, given the threshold value $\alpha$, When the absolute value of the output value of the neural network is less than or equal to $\alpha$, i.e. $|y_i| \le \alpha$, we consider that the test case has not passed through the neuron. When generating the test case execution path, we will delete the neuron and its associated weights. Figure 4 shows an example, when $\alpha$ is equal to 0, the neuron is in an inactive state. We deleted the neuron and the weights connected to it.

### 4.3   Formal Verification and Retraining of Neural Networks

In $IS$ space, $p^{IS}$ is obtained by pruning the original neural network through the testing-based pruning method. But $p^{IS}$ can only be stable in $IS$ to a certain extent. To understand the actual stability on $p^{IS}$, strict formal verification is required for $p^{IS}$. We propose using symbolic execution to verify the reliability of $p^{IS}$, as the verification results may be satisfied or not satisfied, we further proposed ensemble and retraining to deal with it.

Formally, after the input space $IS^I$ passes through the forward propagation of the neural network $p^{IS}$, its output must belong to $Fo$. We record the output space of the neural network verification algorithm as $Fo^V$. If $\forall e \in Fo^V$, then $e \in Fo$. We claim that $p^{IS}$ is a stable sub neural network of $NN$. If $\exists e \in Fo^V$ s.t. $e \notin Fo$ then $e$ is the counterexample. There are some counter examples to prove that the entire sub neural network is unreliable in the formal specification. For this reason, we propose $VBRC$, a verification based retraining algorithm using counterexample data, which is also one of the core contributions of our article. Firstly, we denote the counterexample data generated by the neural network verification as $C = \{(x_1^c, y_1^c), ..., (x_m^c, y_m^c)\}$. Then, we denote all test cases in $C$ as the set $C^I$, and all test oracles in $C$ as the set $C^O$. Since in the set $C$, the input data $C^I$ belongs to $IS^I$. However, $C^O$ is not part of $Fo$. Therefore, we need to assign a new label to each $C^O$. Intuitively, if the two test cases are close to each other, their outputs should also be similar. Based on this intuition, we use the test case in $IS^I$ as the central point to perform unsupervised clustering on the test cases $C^O$. Furthermore, we perform label for each test case in $C^O$.

---

**Algorithm 1:** Counterexample-based training data set construction

---

**Input:** $TC^{IS}$ : A set of test cases in $IS$
       $C^I$ : A set of counterexamples in $IS$
**Output:** $Training\_data$

1   $y = NN(x)$
   // NN is a function of neural network forward reasoning
2   $distance = L(x, y)$
   // Calculate the Euclidean distance between x and y
3   $setofdis = setofdis(x, Y)$
   // The set of distances between point c and all points in set Y
4   $Lable(x)$
   // The process of labeling some inputs.
5   $Min(setofdis)$
   // Find the element closest to x in set Y.
6   **for** $each\ c\ in\ C^I$ **do**
7      **for** $each\ t\ in\ TC^{IS}$ **do**
8        $distance(c, t) = L(NN(c), NN(t))$
9      **end**
10     $setofdis(c, TC^{IS})$
11 **end**
12 **for** $each\ c\ in\ C^I$ **do**
13     $w = Min(setofdis(c, TC^{IS}))$
14     $Lable(c) = NN(w) + \delta$
15 **end**
16 **return** $Training\_data = (C^I, Lable(C^I));$

---

Algorithm 1 describes the process of constructing a dataset based on the counterexamples generated by verification. We calculate the distance from each counterexample to the test case in is. Here, we choose Euclidean distance to calculate the distance. Find the test case closest to the counterexample in the test case, and then record the output of the counterexample as a, Here $\delta$ is a random error. After adding the random error, the output of the counter example should still belong to $Fo$. Follow the above steps to traverse all the counterexamples in C, and construct the training data set training $dataR$ that can be retraining.

## 5   Case Study

We use a three-layer fully connected neural network to explain the work flow of the algorithm and deduce its effectiveness. It is a pre trained neural network,

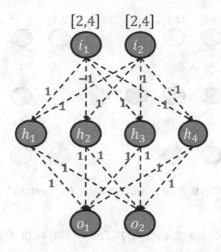

**Fig. 5.** Network structure of $FN$

named $FN$. In $FN$, the weight tensor from the input layer to the hidden layer is denoted as $A$, and the weight tensor from the hidden layer to the output layer is denoted as $B$.

$$A = [first - row, last - col]h_1 h_2 h_3 h_4 1 - 11 - 1i_1 - 11 - 11i_2$$
$$B = [first - row, last - col]h_1 h_2 h_3 h_4 11 11 o_1 1111 o_2$$

where $i_{1,2}$, $h_{1,2,3,4}$ and $o_{1,2}$ represents the marker of neurons in the input layer, hidden layer and output layer, respectively. The network structure of $FN$ can be graphically represented as Fig. 5.

We formally specify the interval property of neural network using SOFL. It is given in the listing 1.1.

```
1  process FN(i₁:real,i₂:real) o₁,o₂:real
2  pre 2 ≤ i₁ ≤ 4 and 2 ≤ i₂ ≤ 4
3  post 6 ≤ o₁ ≤ 8 and 6 ≤ o₂ ≤ 8
4  end_process
```

**Listing 1.1.** The interval property of FN using SOFL

For the preconditions of the $FN$, $D_1$ and $D_2$ are divided into $D_1^p = \{D_1^1, D_1^2\}$ and $D_2^p = \{D_2^1, D_2^2\}$ by definition 1, where $D_1^1 = [2,3)$, $D_1^2 = [3,4]$ and $D_2^1 = [2,3)$, $D_2^2 = [3,4]$. The set $ISS^I$ is the Cartesian product of $D_1^p$ and $D_2^p$. According to definition 2, we can get:

$$ISS^I = \{IS^1 = \{D_1^1, D_2^1\}, IS^2 = \{D_1^1, D_2^2\}, IS^3 = \{D_1^2, D_2^1\}, IS^4 = \{D_1^2, D_2^2\}\}$$

The value interval is substituted into $ISS$, which can be expressed as:

$$IS^1 = \{[2,3), [2,3)\} \quad IS^2 = \{[2,3), [3,4]\}$$

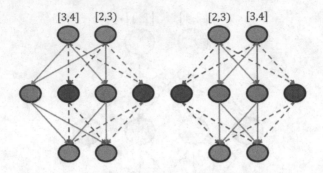

**Fig. 6.** Execution paths on $IS^2$ and $IS^3$

$$IS^3 = \{[3,4],[2,3]\} \quad IS^4 = \{[3,4],[3,4]\}$$

Next, we assign two test cases to each $IS$. See Table 2 for details. If a neuron in $FN$ is activated during the forward propagation of both test cases, the neuron is marked with green. Red indicates that the neuron is not activated in both test cases. If one test case activates the neuron and the other test case does not activate the neuron, it is indicated in yellow.

**Table 2.** Test case corresponding to each $IS^I$

| $ISS^I$ | Test case |
|---|---|
| $IS^1 = \{[2,3],[2,3]\}$ | $i_1 = 2.0 \; i_2 = 2.5$ |
| | $i_1 = 2.5 \; i_2 = 2.0$ |
| $IS^2 = \{[2,3],[3,4]\}$ | $i_1 = 2.0 \; i_2 = 3.0$ |
| | $i_1 = 2.5 \; i_2 = 4.0$ |
| $IS^3 = \{[3,4],[2,3]\}$ | $i_1 = 3.0 \; i_2 = 2.0$ |
| | $i_1 = 4.0 \; i_2 = 2.5$ |
| $IS^4 = \{[3,4],[3,4]\}$ | $i_1 = 3.0 \; i_2 = 4.0$ |
| | $i_1 = 4.0 \; i_2 = 3.0$ |

Figure 6 is the execution path of test cases in $IS^2$ and $IS^3$, where the red neurons are inactive neurons. When the neural network pruning is performed, the neuron and its connected edges will be deleted. Since the test case execution paths in $IS^2$ and $IS^3$ are the same, no neurons marked as yellow appear.

The difference is that in $IS^1$ and $IS^4$, as shown in Fig. 7, the execution paths of the two test cases are different, and the neurons activate in different states when different test cases are executed, and we mark this class of neurons as yellow. Unlike the inactive neurons, such neurons will be retained in the pruning of $FN$.

Finally, we will verify each sub neural network. This step is usually given to the neural network verification tool. If there is a counterexample, the Algorithm 1 can be used to construct a retraining data set for the counterexample returned

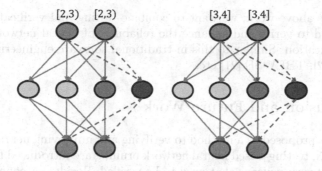

**Fig. 7.** Execution paths on $IS^1$ and $IS^4$

by the verifier. Specifically, we perform symbolic execution on $FN$, and then on $IS^2$, $o_1 = 2x, o_2 = 2x$, on $IS^3$, the output is $o_1 = 2y, o_2 = 2y$. $FN$ is reliable on $IS^2$ and $IS^3$. However, when $i_1 = 2, i_2 = 2$ is executed on $FN$, the result is $o_1 = 4 \leq 6$ and $o_2 = 4 \leq 6$. Therefore, we consider $o_1 = 4 \leq 6$ and $o_2 = 4 \leq 6$ as a counterexample. Using Algorithm 1, the counterexample is made into a training set and the sub network is retrained.

# 6    Related Work

The application of traditional testing techniques and traditional verification techniques to enhance the reliability of neural networks are two separate directions. Since TBFV-INN is derived from traditional TBFV and combines both techniques, we briefly review the existing work on testing and verification in deep learning, as well as recent advances in TBFV.

Currently, the research of neural network testing mainly focuses on how to attack and defend, that is, how to generate adversarial example and how to prevent being attacked by it. Search-based methods such as FGSM, IGSM [4,10] attack neural networks by searching for adversarial examples. Subsequently, deepfool, JSMA [14,15] etc., have made different degrees of improvement in search efficiency and approach. In the area of neural network defense testing, the field is inspired by traditional software testing methods and proposes the criterion of *neuroncoverage* [16]. Other works that use neuron coverage in different dimensions to improve the robustness of neural networks include DeepGauge [18], DeepConcolic [18] etc.

In terms of neural network verification, many scholars have proposed different algorithms for neural network verification. Each algorithm tries to reduce the output range of neural network as much as possible from the perspectives of reachability, optimization and search. Optimization-based neural network verification usually transforms the neural network into a constraint solving problem, such as NSVerify [13], MIPVerify [19]. Reluplex [9] and Planet [3] et al. studied in combining search and optimization like to improve the accuracy and efficiency of verification. In addition, methods that combine search with Reachability include Neurify [22] etc.

Unlike the above work, we want to combine testing and verification to provide a method to verify and enhance the reliability of neural networks under a formal specification. Similar to this in traditional software engineering research are TBFV [12], TBFV-SE [21] etc.

## 7   Conclusion and Future Work

TBFV-INN is proposed as a method to verifying and improving neural networks. In TBFV-INN, testing-based neural network pruning are introduced for reducing the neural network neurons that need to be verified. Besides, A counterexample based retraining data set construction method is proposed to improve the reliability of neural networks. Our case study confirms the feasibility of TBFV-INN to some extent.

In the further work, we will focus on the implementation of TBFV-INN related tools and study the effectiveness of this method on large-scale neural networks. Furthermore, to obtain a better space segmentation algorithm, we will also focus on the relationship between space segmentation and the weights of neural networks.

**Acknowledgements.** This work was supported by JST SPRING, Grant Number JPMJSP2132.

## References

1. Blalock, D., Gonzalez Ortiz, J.J., Frankle, J., Guttag, J.: What is the state of neural network pruning? Proceed. Mach. Learn. Syst. **2**, 129–146 (2020)
2. Bunel, R.R., Turkaslan, I., Torr, P., Kohli, P., Mudigonda, P.K.: A unified view of piecewise linear neural network verification. In: Advances in Neural Information Processing Systems 31 (2018)
3. Ehlers, R.: Formal verification of piece-wise linear feed-forward neural networks. In: D'Souza, D., Narayan Kumar, K. (eds.) ATVA 2017. LNCS, vol. 10482, pp. 269–286. Springer, Cham (2017). https://doi.org/10.1007/978-3-319-68167-2_19
4. Goodfellow, I.J., Shlens, J., Szegedy, C.: Explaining and harnessing adversarial examples. stat **1050**, 20 (2015)
5. Grigorescu, S., Trasnea, B., Cocias, T., Macesanu, G.: A survey of deep learning techniques for autonomous driving. J. Field Robot. **37**(3), 362–386 (2020)
6. Gui, G., Liu, F., Sun, J., Yang, J., Zhou, Z., Zhao, D.: Flight delay prediction based on aviation big data and machine learning. IEEE Trans. Veh. Technol. **69**(1), 140–150 (2019)
7. Hu, H., Peng, R., Tai, Y.W., Tang, C.K.: Network trimming: a data-driven neuron pruning approach towards efficient deep architectures. arXiv preprint arXiv:1607.03250 (2016)
8. Huang, A., Qiu, L., Li, Z.: Applying deep learning method in TVP-VAR model under systematic financial risk monitoring and early warning. J. Comput. Appl. Math. **382**, 113065 (2021)

9. Katz, G., Barrett, C., Dill, D.L., Julian, K., Kochenderfer, M.J.: Reluplex: an efficient SMT solver for verifying deep neural networks. In: Majumdar, R., Kunčak, V. (eds.) CAV 2017. LNCS, vol. 10426, pp. 97–117. Springer, Cham (2017). https://doi.org/10.1007/978-3-319-63387-9_5

10. Kurakin, A., Goodfellow, I., Bengio, S.: Adversarial machine learning at scale. arXiv preprint arXiv:1611.01236 (2016)

11. Liu, A., Liu, S.: Enhancing the capability of testing-based formal verification by handling operations in software packages. IEEE Trans. Softw. Eng. **48**, 304–324 (2022)

12. Liu, S.: Testing-based formal verification for theorems and its application in software specification verification. In: Aichernig, B.K.K., Furia, C.A.A. (eds.) TAP 2016. LNCS, vol. 9762, pp. 112–129. Springer, Cham (2016). https://doi.org/10.1007/978-3-319-41135-4_7

13. Lomuscio, A., Maganti, L.: An approach to reachability analysis for feed-forward relu neural networks. arXiv preprint arXiv:1706.07351 (2017)

14. Moosavi-Dezfooli, S.M., Fawzi, A., Frossard, P.: DeepFool: a simple and accurate method to fool deep neural networks. In: Proceedings of the IEEE Conference on Computer Vision and Pattern Recognition, pp. 2574–2582 (2016)

15. Papernot, N., McDaniel, P., Jha, S., Fredrikson, M., Celik, Z.B., Swami, A.: The limitations of deep learning in adversarial settings. In: 2016 IEEE European symposium on security and privacy (EuroS&P), pp. 372–387. IEEE (2016)

16. Pei, K., Cao, Y., Yang, J., Jana, S.: DeepXplore: automated whitebox testing of deep learning systems. In: proceedings of the 26th Symposium on Operating Systems Principles, pp. 1–18 (2017)

17. Pratt, V.R.: Semantical considerations on Floyd-Hoare logic. In: 17th Annual Symposium on Foundations of Computer Science (SFCS 1976), pp. 109–121. IEEE (1976)

18. Sun, Y., Huang, X., Kroening, D., Sharp, J., Hill, M., Ashmore, R.: DeepConcolic: testing and debugging deep neural networks. In: 2019 IEEE/ACM 41st International Conference on Software Engineering: Companion Proceedings (ICSE-Companion), pp. 111–114. IEEE (2019)

19. Tjeng, V., Xiao, K., Tedrake, R.: Evaluating robustness of neural networks with mixed integer programming. arXiv preprint arXiv:1711.07356 (2017)

20. Tramer, F., Kurakin, A., Papernot, N., Goodfellow, I., Boneh, D., McDaniel, P.: Ensemble adversarial training: attacks and defenses. stat **1050**, 22 (2018)

21. Wang, R., Liu, S.: TBFV-SE: testing-based formal verification with symbolic execution. In: 2018 IEEE International Conference on Software Quality, Reliability and Security (QRS), pp. 59–66. IEEE (2018)

22. Wang, S., Pei, K., Whitehouse, J., Yang, J., Jana, S.: Efficient formal safety analysis of neural networks. In: Advances in Neural Information Processing Systems 31 (2018)

23. Wang, S., et al.: Beta-crown: efficient bound propagation with per-neuron split constraints for neural network robustness verification. Adv. Neural. Inf. Process. Syst. **34**, 29909–29921 (2021)

24. Xu, K., et al.: Fast and complete: enabling complete neural network verification with rapid and massively parallel incomplete verifiers. In: International Conference on Learning Representation (ICLR) (2021)

25. Yuan, X., He, P., Zhu, Q., Li, X.: Adversarial examples: attacks and defenses for deep learning. IEEE Trans. Neural Netw. Learn. Syst. **30**(9), 2805–2824 (2019)

# Alternating Projection Temporal Epistemic Logic

Haiyang Wang(⊠), Jin Liu, and Jing Liu

Xi'an University of Technology, Xi'an, China
hywang@xaut.edu.cn

**Abstract.** Model checking is an automatic technique used to verify the properties of software and hardware systems. In the verification process,the key problem is how to describe the properties of systems using logical formulas accurately. The existing model checking methods based on single logic can no longer meet the increasingly complex verification requirements of Multi-agent systems (MASs) in the current intelligent era. In the MASs, logics of knowledge (epistemic logics) have been advocated for expressing properties. Temporal logic is used for reasoning the correctness of systems and epistemic logic is used for reasoning the information of systems. In order to reason the correctness and information of systems simultaneously, the hybrid logic APTEL that integrating temporal logic APTL and epistemic logic is proposed in this paper.

**Keywords:** Alternating Projection Temporal Logic · Epistemic Logic · Multi-agent System · Alternating Projection Temporal Epistemic Logic

## 1 Introduction

Since the mid 1980s, epistemic logics [1,2] have been increasingly advocated in the formal specification of MASs [3], where they are used for reasoning the information of systems. Model checking as an approach for verifying the properties of finite state systems has focussed predominantly on system specifications expressed in temporal logic. The cases in point are linear temporal logic in the case of SPIN and FORSPEC, branching temporal logic in the case of SMV. However, the model checking for epistemic logics has received comparatively little attention.

In 1977, Pnueli introduced Linear Temporal Logic (LTL) [4] which is a linear logic to specify and verify reactive systems. The universal quantification over all computations is implicit in the LTL semantics. In 1980, Clarke and Emerson introduced Computation Tree Logic (CTL) [4], which is a branching temporal logic and allows the expression of properties of some or all computations of a system. Interval Temporal Logic is also a useful formalism for specifying and

This research is supported by the NSFC Grant No. 61902312,62002290,62202371 and by the Natural Science Basic Research Plan in Shaanxi Province of China No. 2022JZ-40.

S. Liu et al. (Eds.): SOFL+MSVL 2022, LNCS 13854, pp. 142–149, 2023.
https://doi.org/10.1007/978-3-031-29476-1_12

verifying concurrent systems. Projection Temporal Logic (PTL) is an extension of ITL. Alternative approaches have been involved and extended to logics such as MAS logics which make them possible to verify a range of MAS against temporal logics and modalities. For example, Alur et al. introduces Alternating-time Temporal Logic (ATL) [5], which offers selective quantification over those paths that are possible out-comes of games. Alternating Interval Temporal Logic (AITL) and Alternating Projection Temporal Logic (APTL) [6,7] are the extensions of Propositional ITL and PPTL [8–10], respectively. AITL and APTL are also logics indispensable for the specification and verification of MAS. APTL is able to not only express properties specified in classical temporal logic LTL, but also express interval related sequential and periodical properties, as well as express game related properties of open systems and MASs.

MAS is a novel distributed system, which is composed of multiple agents interacting in a specific environment. MAS can describe a large and complex system as a number of small and easy to manage systems that coordinate and communication with each other to achieve their own goals or global goals. Thanks to the strong adaptability and flexibility of MASs, they are widely used in intelligent robots, traffic control, distributed prediction, monitoring and diagnosis, distributed intelligent decision-making and virtual reality. Verifying the properties of MASs is one of the key problems in artificial intelligence research. At present, the verification of MASs mostly uses temporal logic to formally describe the properties of the system, and temporal logic does not have the ability to describe the epistemic properties of MASs. Therefore, the existing model checking methods based on single logic can no longer meet the requirements of MAS verification, so it is urgent to research on hybrid logic based verification methods. Temporal logic is used for reasoning the correctness of systems and epistemic logic is used for reasoning the information of systems. In order to reason the correctness and information of MASs at the same time, some scholars have fused temporal logic and epistemic logic to obtain a hybrid logic that can simultaneously present the temporal and epistemic properties of the system. The existing research on the integration of temporal logic and epistemic logic, the expression ability of temporal logic LTL and CTL has limitations. In view of the strong expressive ability of APTL, APTEL is obtained by combing APTL with epistemic logic in this paper.

The next section presents preparatory knowledge. The hybrid logic APTEL and some applications of APTEL are proposed in Sect. 3. Finally, conclusions are drawn in Sect. 4.

## 2    Preparation

This section briefly introduces the alternating temporal logic APTL, the temporal logic of knowledge –Epistemic logic and the hybrid logic APTEL. For more details on the semantics of Epistemic logic and APTL, refer to [6].

## 2.1    Concurrent Game Structure and AETS

The semantics of APTL formulas are given in terms of Concurrent Game Structures (CGSs) [5]. A CGS is a tuple $C = (\mathcal{P}, \mathcal{A}, S, S_0, l, \Delta, \tau)$ where

- $\mathcal{P}$ is a finite nonempty set of atomic propositions;
- $\mathcal{A}$ is a finite set of agents;
- $S$ is a finite nonempty set of states;
- $S_0$ is a finite nonempty set of initial states;
- $l : S \rightarrow 2^{\mathcal{P}}$ is a labeling function that decorates each state with a subset of the atomic propositions;
- $\Delta^a(s)$ is a nonempty set of possible decisions for an agent $a \in \mathcal{A}$ at state $s$; $\Delta^A(s) = \Delta^{a_1}(s) \times \ldots \times \Delta^{a_k}(s)$ is a nonempty set of decision vectors for the set of agents $A = \{a_1, \ldots, a_k\} \in 2^{\mathcal{A}}$ at state $s$; accordingly, $\Delta^{\mathcal{A}}(s)$ is simplified as $\Delta(s)$ and denotes the decisions of all agents in $\mathcal{A}$; and for a decision $d \in \Delta(s)$, $d_a$ denotes the decision of agent $a$ within the decision $d$, and $d_A$ denotes the decision of the set of agents $A \subseteq \mathcal{A}$ within $d$;
- For each state $s \in S$, $d \in \Delta(s)$, $\tau(s, d)$ maps $s$ and a decision $d$ of the agents in $\mathcal{A}$ to a new state in $S$. Note that in a CGS, for a state $s$ , each transition is made by a decision $d \in \Delta(s)$ of all agents in $\mathcal{A}$. In some cases, if we just concern with the decisions of $A \subseteq \mathcal{A}$ without caring about the ones of other agents, notation $d_A$ is used. Particularly, if $A$ is a singleton, $d_a$ is adopted.

The alternating transition relationship of a CGS is actually can be represented as $T : S \times \mathcal{P} \times 2^{\mathcal{A}} \rightarrow \mathbb{B}^+(S)$, where $\mathbb{B}^+(S)$ is a positive boolean formula. For a given set $S$ of states, the positive boolean formula $\mathbb{B}^+(S)$ is boolean formula built from elements in $S$ using $\wedge$ and $\vee$. We say that $S_1 \subseteq S$ satisfies a formula $\theta \in \mathbb{B}^+(S)$ if the truth assignment that assigns $true$ to the members of $S_1$ and $false$ to the members of $S/S_1$ satisfies $\theta$. For example, suppose $S = \{s_0, s_1, s_2\}$, the set $\{s_0\}$ and $\{s_1, s_2\}$ both satisfy the formula $s_0 \vee s_1 \wedge s_2$, where the set $\{s_1\}$ does not.

A path $\lambda = s_0, s_1, \ldots$ is a nonempty sequence of states, which can be finite or infinite. Let $r_1, \ldots, r_k$ be integers ($h \geq 1$) such that $0 = r_1 \leq \ldots \leq r_h \preceq |\lambda|$. The projection of $\lambda$ onto $r_1, \ldots, r_h$ is the path, $\lambda \downarrow (r_1, \ldots, r_h) = s_{t_1}, s_{t_2}, \ldots, s_{t_l}$ where $t_1, \ldots, t_l$ are obtained from $r_1, \ldots, r_h$ by deleting all duplicates. $t_1, \ldots, t_l$ is the longest strictly increasing subsequence of $r_1, \ldots, r_h$. For example, $s_0, s_1, s_2, s_3, s_4 \downarrow (0, 0, 2, 2, 2, 3) = s_0, s_2, s_3$.

Following the definition of CGS, we define a state $s$ over $\mathcal{P}$ to be a mapping from $\mathcal{P}$ to $B = \{true, false\}$, $s : \mathcal{P} \rightarrow B$. A path $\lambda(s)$ starting from a state $s$ in a CGS satisfies the Epistemic logic formula or APTL formula $P$, denoted by $\lambda(s) \models P$. A CGS $C$ satisfies a formula $P$ iff all of the paths starting from initial states of the CGS satisfy the formula $P$, denoted by $C \models P$.

Alternating epistemic transition systems (AETS)-add epistemic accessibility relations $\sim_1, \ldots, \sim_k \subseteq S \times S$ for expressing agents' beliefs:

$$AS = (\mathcal{P}, \mathcal{A}, S, S_0, l, \Delta, \sim_1, \ldots, \sim_k, \tau), \text{ where}$$

$\sim_a \subseteq S \times S$ an epistemic accessibility relation for each agent $a \in \mathcal{A}$. We require that each $\sim_a$ is an equivalence relation.

**Epistemic Relations.** If $A \subseteq \mathcal{A}$, we denote the union of $A$'s accessibility relations by $\sim_A^E$, so $\sim_A^E = (\bigcup_{a \in A} \sim_a)$. Also, $\sim_A^C$ denote the transitive closure of $\sim_A^E$. We will later use $\sim_A^C$ and $\sim_A^E$ to give a semantics to the common knowledge and "everyone knows" modalities in our logic.

## 2.2  Epistemic Logic

Epistemic logic is a modal logic of knowledge [3,11,12]. Epistemic modal logics are widely recognised as having originated in the work of Jaakko Hintikka, a philosopher who in the early 1960s showed how certain modal logics could be used to formally capture some intuitions about the nature of knowledge. In the 1980s, it was recognised that epistemic logics have an important role to play in the theory of distributed systems. In particular, it was demonstrated that epistemic logics can be used to formally express the desired behaviour of protocols. For example, when specifying a communication protocol, it is quite natural to wish to represent requirements such as "if process $i$ knows that process $j$ has received packed $m$, then $i$ should send packet $m+1$". Using epistemic logic, such requirements can be expressed both formally and naturally.

In addition to interest in the use of epistemic logics in the specification of communicating systems, there has recently been interest in the use of knowledge logics for directly programming systems. A knowledge-based program has the general form:

$$\text{case of}$$
$$\text{if } K_{\langle i \rangle} \psi_1 \text{ do } act_1$$
$$...$$
$$\text{if } K_{\langle i \rangle} \psi_n \text{ do } act_n$$
$$\text{end case}$$

The intuitive interpretation of such a program is that of a collection of rules; the left-hand side of each rule represents a condition, expressed in epistemic logic, of what an agent knows. If the condition is satisfied, then the corresponding action is executed.

# 3  Alternating Projection Temporal Epistemic Logic

This subsection introduces the syntax, semantics and logic laws of APTEL.which is a hybrid logic that integrating temporal logic APTL and epistemic logic.

## 3.1  APTEL Syntax

Let $\mathcal{P}$ be a finite set of atomic propositions and $\mathcal{A}$ a finite set of agents. The formulas of APTEL are defined by the following grammar:

$$P::= p \mid \neg P \mid P \vee Q \mid \bigcirc_{\langle A \rangle} P \mid (P_1, \cdots, P_m) prj_{\langle A \rangle} Q \mid K_{\langle a \rangle} P \mid E_{\langle A \rangle} P \mid C_{\langle A \rangle} P$$

where $p \in \mathcal{P}$, $A \subseteq \mathcal{A}$, $P_1, \cdots, P_m$, $P$ and $Q$ are well-formed APTEL formulas. $\bigcirc_{\langle A \rangle}$ (next) and $prj_{\langle A \rangle}$ (projection) are basic temporal operators with a set of agents. $K_{\langle a \rangle}P$, where $a \in \mathcal{A}$ is an agent, and $P$ is a formula of APTEL. $E_{\langle A \rangle}P$ and $C_{\langle A \rangle}P$, where $A \subseteq \mathcal{A}$ is a set of agents, and $P$ is a formula of APTEL. $D_{\langle A \rangle}$ (distributed knowledge) and $C_{\langle A \rangle}$ (common knowledge) are epistemic operators. The epistemic logic $D_{\langle A \rangle}P$ means the knowledge held by any agent in agent set $A$ makes $P$ true. The epistemic logic $C_{\langle A \rangle}P$ means the knowledge shared by agents in agent set $A$ makes $P$ true.

An APTEL formula is called a state formula if it contains no temporal operators, otherwise a temporal formula. The abbreviations $true$, $false$, $\vee$, $\rightarrow$ and $\leftrightarrow$ are defined as that in the classical propositional logic.

## 3.2   APTEL Semantics

The semantics of APTEL formulas is given in terms of AETS. An AETS is a tuple $AS = (\mathcal{P}, \mathcal{A}, S, S_0, l, \Delta, \sim_1, \ldots, \sim_k, \tau)$.

Following the definition of AETS, we define a state $s$ over $\mathcal{P}$ to be a mapping from $\mathcal{P}$ to $B = \{true, false\}$, $s : \mathcal{P} \rightarrow B$. A computation $\lambda(s)$ starting from a state $s$ in an AETS satisfies the APTEL formula $P$, denoted by $\lambda(s) \models P$. An AETS $AS$ satisfies an APTEL formula $P$ iff all of the computations starting from initial states of the AETS satisfy the APTEL formula $P$, denoted by $AS \models P$.

The relation $\models$ is inductively defined as follows:

- $\lambda(s) \models p$ for propositions $p \in \mathcal{P}$, iff $p \in l(s)$
- $\lambda(s) \models \neg P$, iff $\lambda(s) \nvDash P$
- $\lambda(s) \models P \vee Q$, iff $\lambda(s) \models P$ or $\lambda(s) \models Q$
- $\lambda(s) \models \bigcirc_{\langle A \rangle}P$ iff $|\lambda(s)| \geq 2$, and there exists a strategy $f_A$ for the agents in $A$, such that $\lambda(s) \in out(s, f_A)$, and $\lambda(s)[1, |\lambda|] \models P$
- $\lambda(s) \models (P_1, \ldots, P_m)prj_{\langle A \rangle}Q$ iff there exists a strategy $f_A$ for the agents in $A$, and $\lambda(s) \in out(s, f_A)$, and integers $0 = r_0 \leq r_1 \leq \ldots \leq r_m \leq |\lambda(s)|$ such that $\lambda(s)[r_{i-1}, r_i] \models P_i$, $0 < i \leq m$ and $\lambda \models Q$ for one of the following $\lambda$:
   (a) $r_m < |\lambda(s)|$ and $\lambda = \lambda(s) \downarrow (r_0, \ldots, r_m) \cdot \lambda(s)[r_m + 1, \ldots, |\lambda(s)|]$ or
   (b) $r_m = |\lambda(s)|$ and $\lambda = \lambda(s) \downarrow (r_0, \ldots, r_m)$ for some $0 \leq h \leq m$
- $\lambda(s) \models K_{\langle a \rangle}P$ iff for all $s'$ such that $s \sim_a s' : \lambda(s') \models P$;
- $\lambda(s) \models E_{\langle A \rangle}P$ iff for all $s'$ such that $s \sim_A^E s' : \lambda(s') \models P$;
- $\lambda(s) \models C_{\langle A \rangle}P$ iff for all $s'$ such that $s \sim_A^C s' : \lambda(s') \models P$.

For every $s$, $s'$ such that $s \sim_a s'$, it is required that $d_a(s) = d_a(s')$. $d_a$ denotes the decision of agent $a$ within the decision $d$.

## 3.3   Applications of APTEL

We hope it is clear that APTEL is a succinct and expressive language for expressing complex properties of MAS.

Since APTEL is a suitable language to represent the properties of epistemics, it is also convenient to analyse communication protocols. First, consider a system containing a sender $S$, a receiver $R$, and an environment *env* through which message are sent. Under certain fairness conditions (the environment does not get rid of messages forever), we can express the fact that the environment cannot prevent the sender from sending a message until it is received. Where $Sm$ means the sender $S$ send a message.

$$\Box_{\langle S \rangle} Sm;_{\langle R,S \rangle} K_{\langle R \rangle} m \tag{1}$$

The formula (2) expresses the cooperative property that the environment *env* can guarantee that the message $Sm$ sent by the sender $S$ eventually becomes explicitly known by everyone in the receiver group $R$.

$$Sm \rightarrow \Diamond_{\langle R \rangle} E_{\langle R \rangle} Sm \tag{2}$$

Both as a pre- and as a post- condition, ignorance may be important. In security protocols, where agents $a_1$ and $a_2$ share some common secret (a key for instance), what we typically want as formula (3), expressing that $a_1$ can send private information to $a_2$, without revealing the message to another agent *agt*:

$$(K_{\langle a_1 \rangle} \psi \wedge \neg K_{\langle a_2 \rangle} \psi \wedge \neg K_{\langle agt \rangle} \psi);_{\langle \rangle} \Diamond_{\langle a_1, a_2 \rangle} (K_{\langle a_1 \rangle} \psi \wedge K_{\langle a_2 \rangle} \psi \wedge \neg K_{\langle agt \rangle} \psi) \tag{3}$$

Common knowledge $C_{\langle A \rangle}$ of a group $A$ is also important. In particular, one is interested in conditions that ensure that

$$C_{\langle A \rangle} \mathcal{X}_{\langle A \rangle} \psi \quad (\mathcal{X} \text{ a temporal operator}) \tag{4}$$

Formula (4) expresses that common knowledge in the group $A$ that it can bring about $\mathcal{X}_{\langle A \rangle} \psi$ (*next*, or *sometime*, or *prj*, etc.). It is not clear at forehand that we have a negative result about obtaining common knowledge, since it seems we can model actions stronger than communication. For instance, we may have knowledge-producing actions, and also common-knowledge producing actions, like making an announcement. If $a$ can make an announcement $p$, he can choose a set of worlds in which the transitive closure of all the accessibility relations only leads to $p$-worlds.

For a multi-agent system which contains agents $a_1$, $a_2$ and $a_3$, agent $a_1$ is supposed to know whether $\psi$ is satisfied or not, which is a common knowledge and specified as $K_{\langle a_1 \rangle} \psi \vee K_{\langle a_1 \rangle} \neg \psi$. It is also a common knowledge that $a_1$ always tells the truth. If $a_1$ knows $\psi$, we can model that $a_1$ can tell the truth only to $a_2$, or to $a_2$ and $a_3$ separately, or he can announce $\psi$ in public:

$$K_{\langle a_1 \rangle} \psi \rightarrow \bigcirc_{\langle a_1 \rangle} (K_{\langle a_2 \rangle} \psi \wedge \neg K_{\langle a_3 \rangle} \psi) \vee \bigcirc_{\langle a_1 \rangle} (K_{\langle a_2 \rangle} \psi \wedge K_{\langle a_3 \rangle} \psi \wedge \neg C_{\langle a_2, a_3 \rangle} \psi)$$
$$\vee \bigcirc_{\langle a_1 \rangle} (C_{\langle a_2, a_3 \rangle} \psi) \tag{5}$$

Knowledge games can investigated as a particular way of learning in multi-agent systems. Epistemic updates are interpreted in a simple card game, where the aim of player $a_1$ is to find out the decision $d$ of cards. Then having a winning strategy can be specified as

$$d \rightarrow \Diamond_{\langle a_1 \rangle} (K_{\langle a_1 \rangle} d \wedge \bigwedge_{a_1 \neq a_2} \neg K_{\langle a_2 \rangle} d) \tag{6}$$

The applicability of APTEL goes beyond epistemic updates (where epistemic post-conditions are the rule): knowledge also plays an important role in pre-conditions, expressing knowledge-dependent abilities, as in $(K_{\langle a_1 \rangle} \varphi_1 \wedge K_{\langle a_2 \rangle} \varphi_2) \rightarrow \Diamond_{\langle a_1, a_2 \rangle} \psi$. Formula (7) expressing that if $b$ knows that the combination of the safe is $s$, then he is able to open it, i.e. $O$, as long as the combination remains unchanged.

$$K_{\langle b \rangle}(c = s) \rightarrow (\Diamond_{\langle b \rangle} O);_{\langle b \rangle} \neg (c = s) \tag{7}$$

Typically, when an agent makes strategic choices, both epistemic pre- and post-conditions should be considered: a rational agent bases his choices upon his knowledge, and will typically try to maximize his own knowledge, at the same time minimize that of his competitors. Epistemic conditions are also needed in security communication protocols, where an agent needs to know a secret key in order to read a message, to obtain new knowledge.

## 4   Conclusion

This paper proposes a novel hybrid logic APTEL, that integrating temporal logic APTL and epistemic logic. The syntax and semantics of APTEL are presented and some applications of APTEL are also specified. In the future, the model checking method of APTEL will be investigated.

## References

1. Lomuscio, A, Raimondi, F.: Model checking knowledge, strategies, and games in multi-agent systems. In: Proceedings of the Fifth International Joint Conference on Autonomous Agents and Multiagent Systems, ACM, 161–168 (2006)
2. Halpern, J.Y., Moses, Y., Vardi, M.Y.: Reasoning about Knowledge. MIT press, Cambridge (1995)
3. Jamroga, W.: Some Remarks on Alternating Temporal Epistemic Logic. In: Proceedings of Formal Approaches to Multi-Agent Systems, FAMAS 2003, pp. 133–140 (2003)
4. Baier, C., Katoen, J.P.: Principles of Model Checking. MIT press, Cambridge (2008)
5. Alur, R., Henzinger, T.A., Kupferman, O.: Alternating-time temporal logic. J. ACM **49**(5), 672–713 (2002)
6. Wang, H., Duan, Z., Tian, C.: Symbolic model checking for alternating projection temporal logic. In: Combinatorial Optimization and Applications - 9th International Conference, COCOA 2015, 18–20 December 2015, pp. 481–495. Proceedings. Houston, TX, USA (2015)
7. Tian, C., Duan, Z.: Alternating interval based temporal logics. In: Dong, J.S., Zhu, H. (eds.)Proceedings of Formal Methods and Software Engineering (ICFEM 2010), LNCS6447, pp. 694–709. Springer, Cham 2010. https://doi.org/10.1007/978-3-642-16901-4_45
8. Duan, Z., Tian, C., Zhang, L.: A decision procedure for propositional projection temporal logic with infinite models. Acta Inform. **45**, 43–78 (2008)

9. Duan, Z., Tian, C.: A practical decision procedure for propositional projection temporal logic with infinite models. Theoretical Comput. Sci. **554**, 169–190 (2014)

10. Duan, Z.: Temporal Logic and Temporal Logic Programming. Science Press, Beijing (2005)

11. Hoek, W., Wooldridge, M.: Model checking knowledge and time. In: Proceedings of the 9th International SPIN Workshop on Model Checking of Software (2002)

12. Novak, N.: Practical extraction of evidence terms from common-knowledge reasoning. Electron. Notes Theoretical Comput. Sci. **312**, 143–160 (2015)

# Author Index

S. Liu et al. (Eds.): SOFL+MSVL 2022, LNCS 13854, p. 151, 2023.
https://doi.org/10.1007/978-3-031-29476-1

Printed in the United States
by Baker & Taylor Publisher Services